PHOTOGRAPHIC SPECIAL EFFECTS

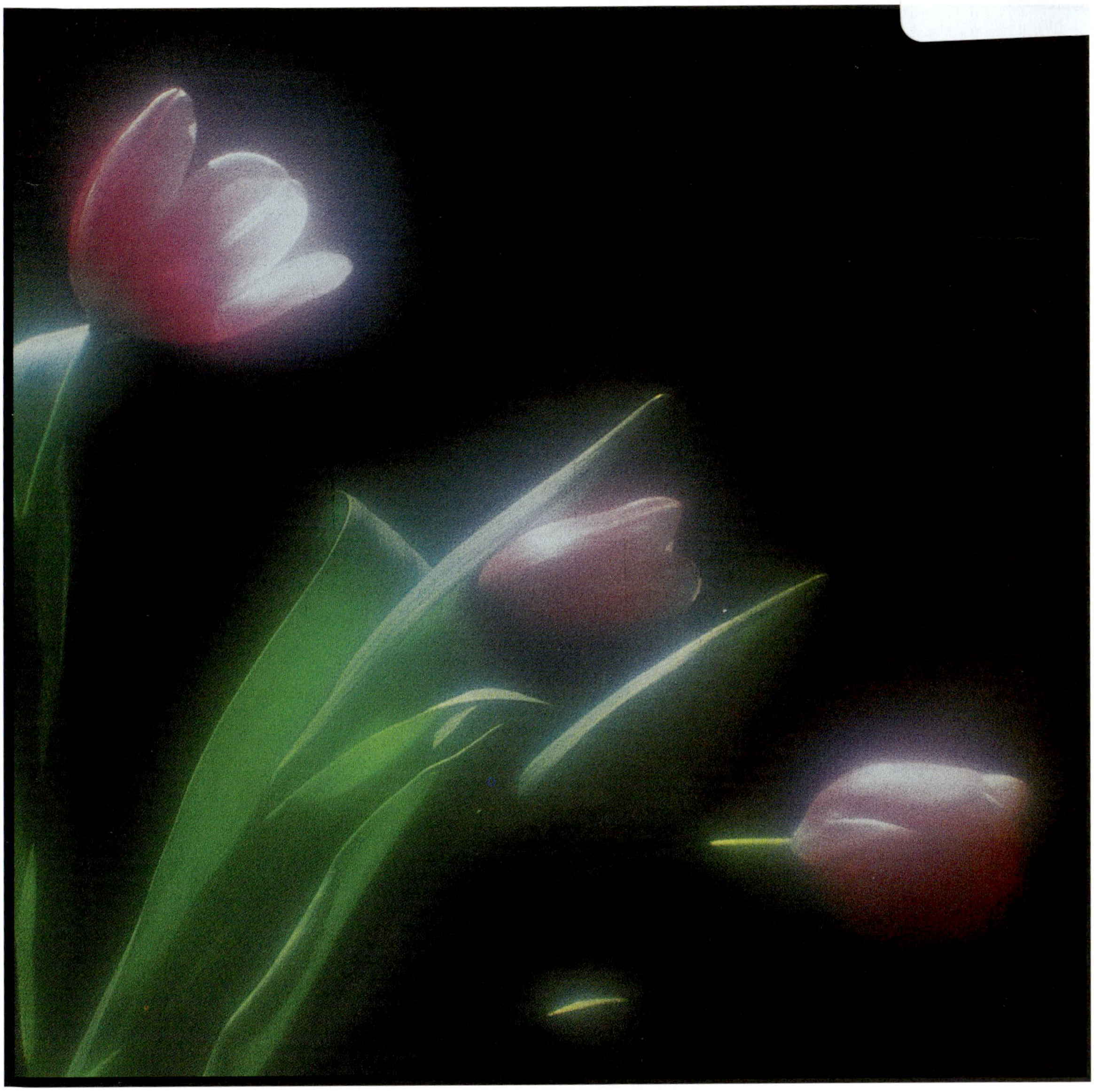

Making memorable pictures

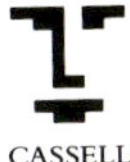

CASSELL

ACKNOWLEDGEMENTS
Front cover (main) Roger Howard, front cover(t) David Fairman,
front cover(c) Trevor Melton/EP, front cover(b) John Heseltine, 1-5
ICL, 6 TSI, 7 Roger Howard, 8 Frank Coppi/EP, 9 Frank
Coppi/EP, 10 Frank Coppi/EP, 11(t) Ilford Photos, 11(b) TSI, 12(t)
TSI, 12(b) David Fairman, 13 TSI, 14(t) Shona Wood/EP, 14(b)
Stuart Windsor/EP, 15(t) TIB, 15(b) Sue Atkinson, 16(t) The
Picture House (Annabel Williams), 15-16(b) Mike Busselle, 16(t)
Zefa, 16(b) Seamus Ryan/EP, 18 Richard Platt/EP, 19-22 Michael
St Maur Sheil, 23 Mike King, 24 Ace Photo Library, 25(t) Zefa,
25(b) Carl Lyttle, 26(tl) Arcaid, 26(tr) Steve Tanner/EP, 26(b)
Arcaid, 27 Ed Buziak, 28 Simon Page-Ritchie/EP, 29(t) John
Heseltine, 29(b) Ed Buziak, 30 Ed Buziak, 31 Vincent Oliver, 32
RHPL, 33 TSI, 34 Steve Tanner/EP, 35-38 Kevin Westenberg, 39
TSI, 40(t) Action Plus, 40(b) TSI, 41 Robin Bath, 42(t) Roger
Howard, 42(b) TIB, 43-45 Trevor Melton/EP, 46 TIB, 47 Michael
Freeman, 48 Richard Platt, 49 TIB, 50 Richard Platt, 51 Telegraph
Colour Library, 52(t) The Photographers Library, 52(b) Zefa, 53
Alastair Scott, 54(t) Sandie (Struan Wallace), 54(b) RHPL, 55-58
Michael Fong, 59-62 Simon Donnelly, 63(main) John Suett/EP, 63
(inset) TSI, 64(t) Collections, 64(b) John Suett/EP, 65(tl) TSI, 65(tr)
Jennifer Rigby, 65(cr) Collections, 65(b) Jennifer Rigby, 67(t)
Jennifer Rigby, 67(b) Zefa, 68(t) Vincent Oliver, 68(b) Roger
Howard, 69(t) Vincent Oliver, 69(b) Robert Eames, 70 Robert
Eames, 71-74 Trevor Melton/EP, 75-78 Peter Stone, 79(main)
Simon Page-Ritchie/EP, 79 (inset) Sarah Jackson, 80 Tim
Woodcock, 81 Steve Tanner/EP, 82 Simon Page-Ritchie/EP, 83-
86 Trevor Melton/EP, 87 Trevor Melton/EP, 88(tl) John Heseltine,
88(tr) John Heseltine, 88(c) TIB, 89(tl) TIB, 89(tr) TSI, 90(l) Trevor
Melton/EP, 90(ct) TSI, 90(cb) TIB, 90(r) TSI/TIB, 91-94 James
Elliot, 95 Nigel Robertson, 96 TIB.

Key: EP - Eaglemoss Publications; ICL - Images Colour Library;
      RHPL - Robert Harding Picture Library; TIB - The Image Bank;
      TSI - Tony Stone Images

Consultant editor: Roger Hicks

First published 1994 by Cassell
Villiers House, 41/47 Strand, London WC2N 5JE

Distributed in Australia
by Capricorn Link (Australia) Pty Ltd
2/13 Carrington Road, Castle Hill, NSW 2154

British Library Cataloguing-in-Publication Data
A catalogue record for this book is available from the
British Library

ISBN 0-304-34399-4

Printed in Spain by Cayfosa Industria Grafica

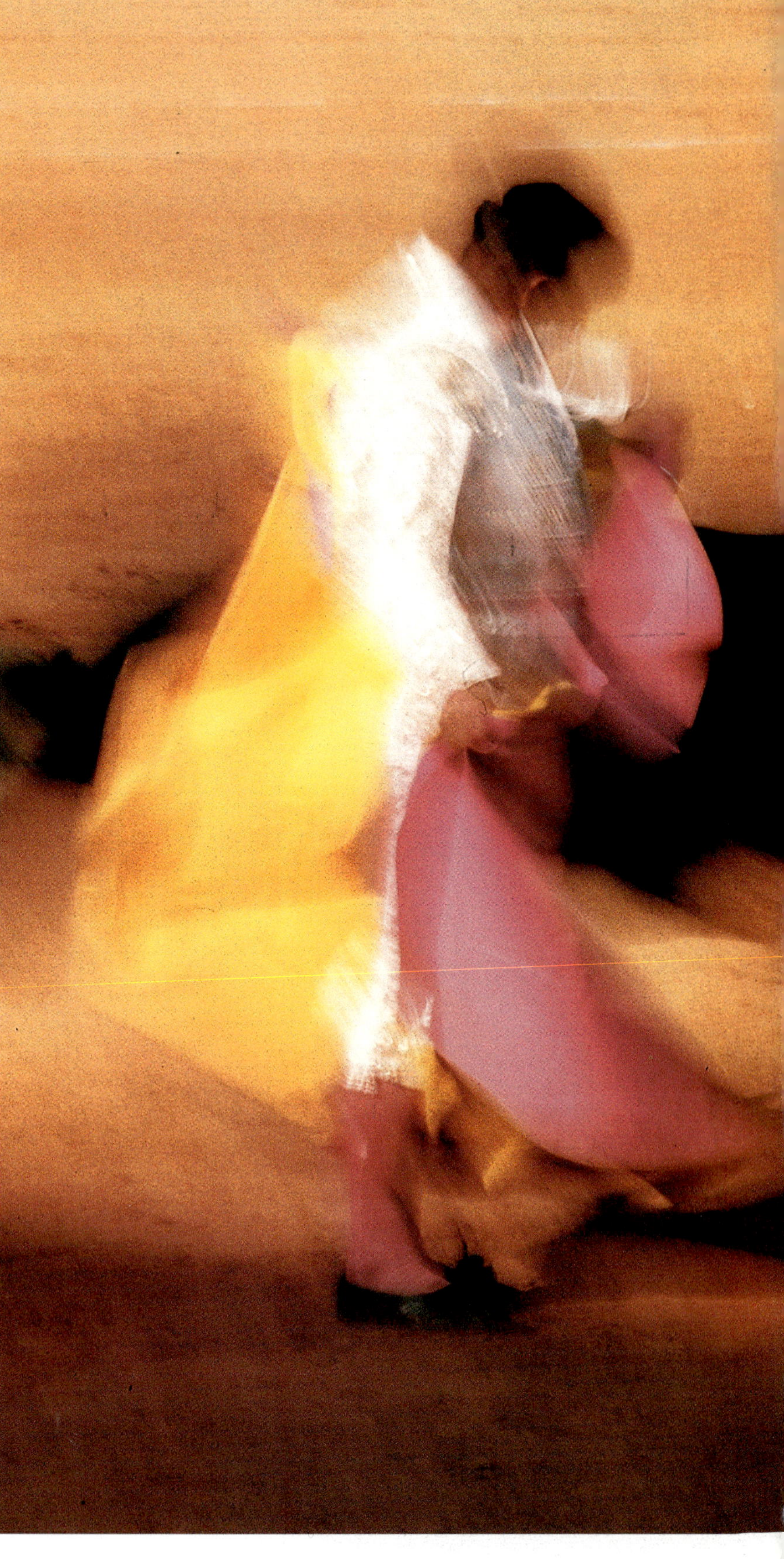

CONTENTS

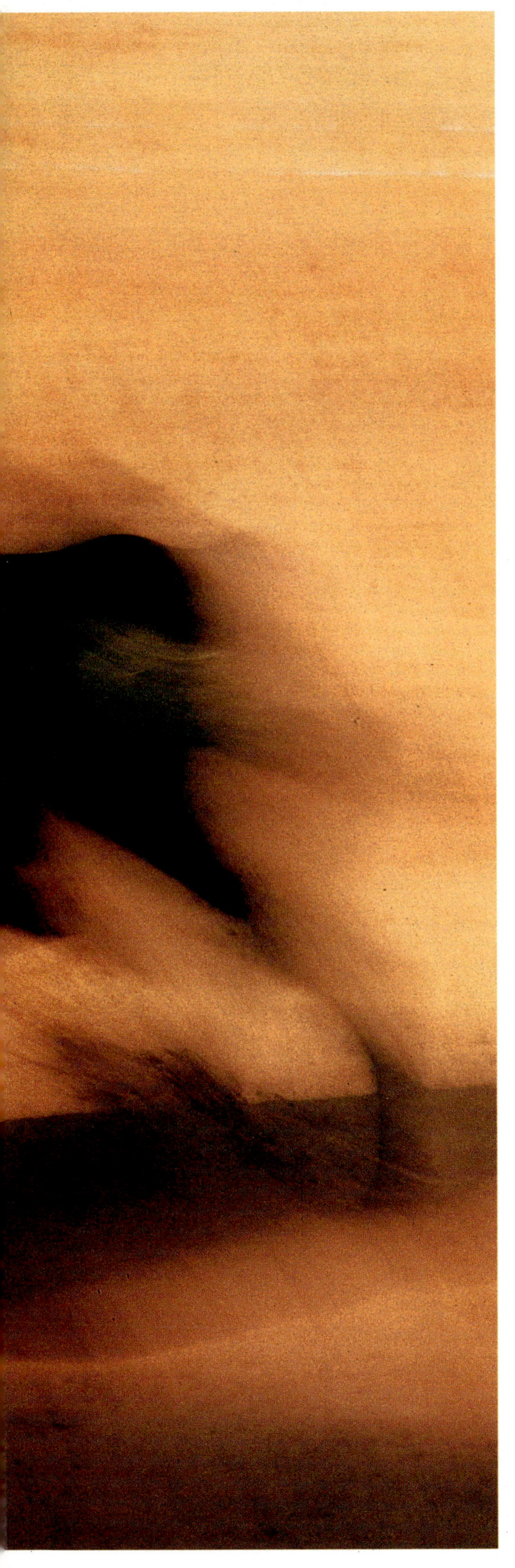

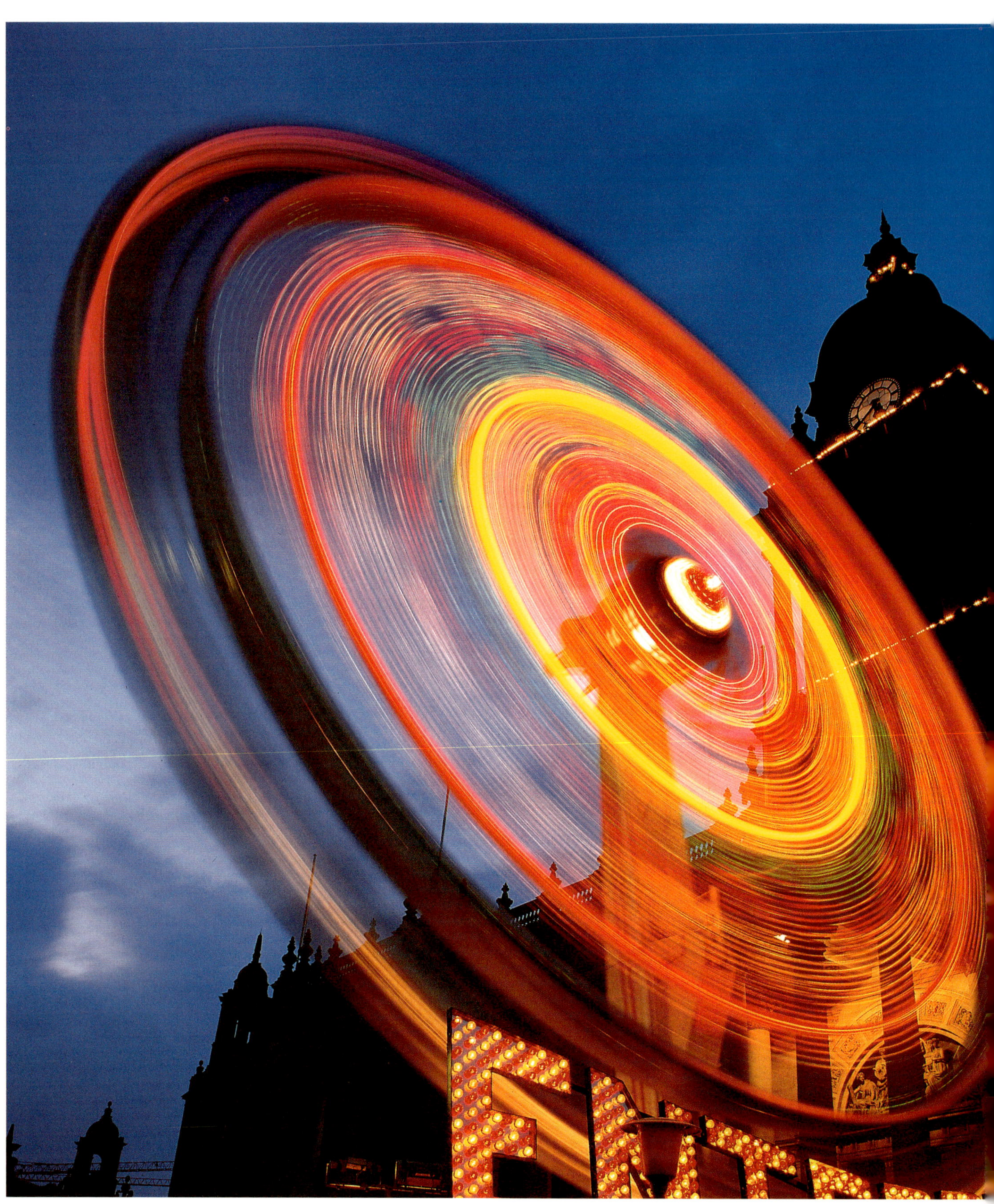

INTRODUCTION

HOW do you create great pictures – and how do you present them attractively, so that they will be seen and enjoyed? With step-by-step illustrations of a wide range of techniques, and with stunning examples of the work of many leading photographers, this book is about developing and realising your creative vision and presenting that vision, whether as pictures on the wall or as slide shows that people will really enjoy.

Some of the techniques described are so simple that you may be surprised that they work so well. They are the sort of thing where you ask yourself, 'Why didn't I think of that?' You can use a mirror to create a 'lake' for example (page 50), or a projector to superimpose one image onto another. You can put a perfume bottle on a flower, or even turn a dog tartan (page 44).

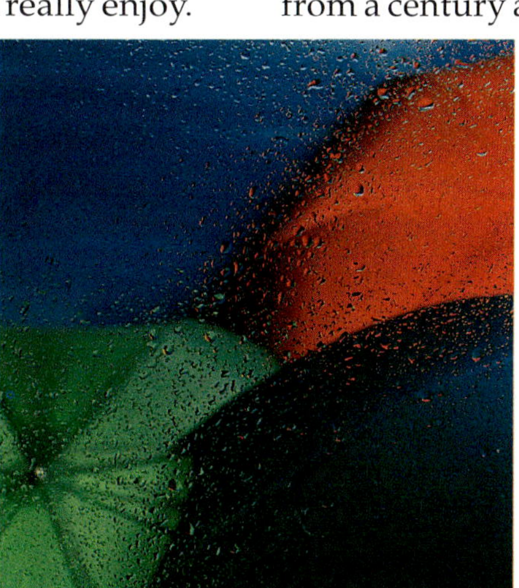

Other ideas give rise to a very different question:'How on earth did anyone think of that?' Kevin Westenburg's rock-star portraits are a good example; you can follow the trail he has blazed, or possibly think up equally unusual ideas for yourself. Many of the most effective pictures in this book are the result of deliberately doing things 'incorrectly' or of finding ways of turning the limitations of the photographic process into advantages.

Then again, there is plenty we can learn from the past. It's not so very long ago that black and white was the everyday medium, while colour commanded attention because of its novelty value. Today, when even newspaper pictures are often printed in colour, it is black and white which has the novelty value. There is a good deal about how to use black and white in this book, and even a little about how to use sepia, a technique which dates from a century and more ago.

Choosing which special effects techniques to use is very much a matter of personal taste, and some of the images in this book will undoubtedly appeal to you more than others. But you will also find pictures which knock you out with their inventiveness, originality, or technical execution. Some, such as Michael St. Maur Sheil's industrial images, achieve their impact by total mastery of conventional techniques. Others, such as Michael Fong's painterly Polaroid nudes, are achieved with materials which most photographers would not think of using for the purpose to which they have been put.

Some of the ideas in this book may already be familiar to you. But, familiar or unfamiliar, the techniques shown are guaranteed to stimulate your creativity, perhaps by giving you a new twist or angle on an idea you may have had for some time.

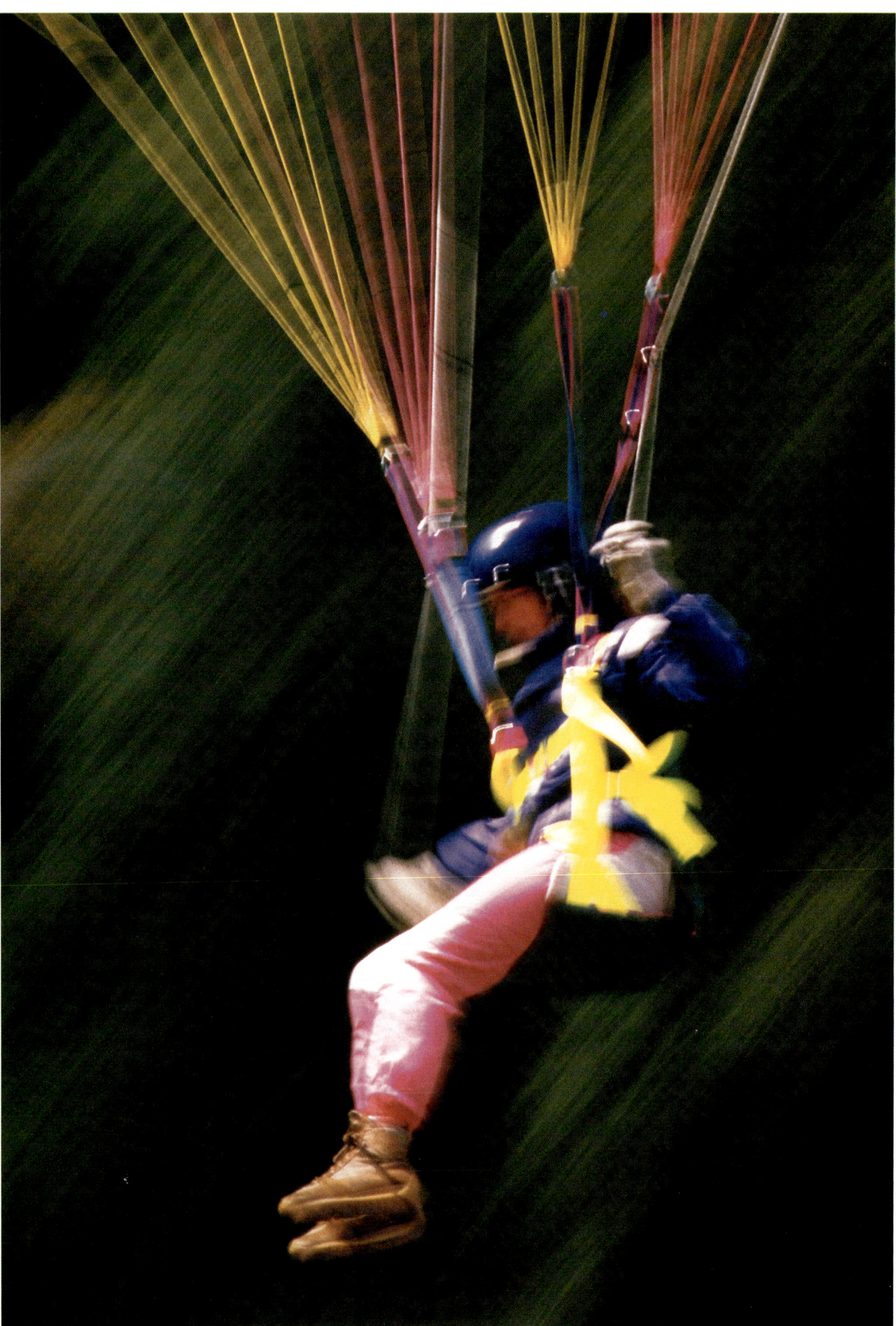

Panning and zooming

With almost any SLR, and some compact cameras, you can introduce creative blur into your shots and add dynamism to otherwise dull images.

If you want to inject a sense of excitement and energy into your pictures, try panning and zooming. With both techniques you must be prepared to lose some detail in your photograph. However, the gain is action filled images.

Panning is always done on moving subjects. It involves making the exposure while following the subject with the camera. The standard pan will turn the background into a series of streaks while keeping the subject relatively sharp.

Zooming, on the other hand, can be just as successfully done on stationary subjects. It involves changing the focal length of a zoom lens during an exposure. The standard zoom shot gives a kaleidoscopic effect with streaks radiating outwards from the subject.

Shutter speed control

The basic requirement for good results with panning and zooming is control over the shutter speed. If you have an SLR, set the exposure mode to manual or shutter speed priority.

The problem with auto-only cameras is that they usually give you a shutter speed no slower than 1/60th sec to prevent camera shake. For panning and zooming, though, you

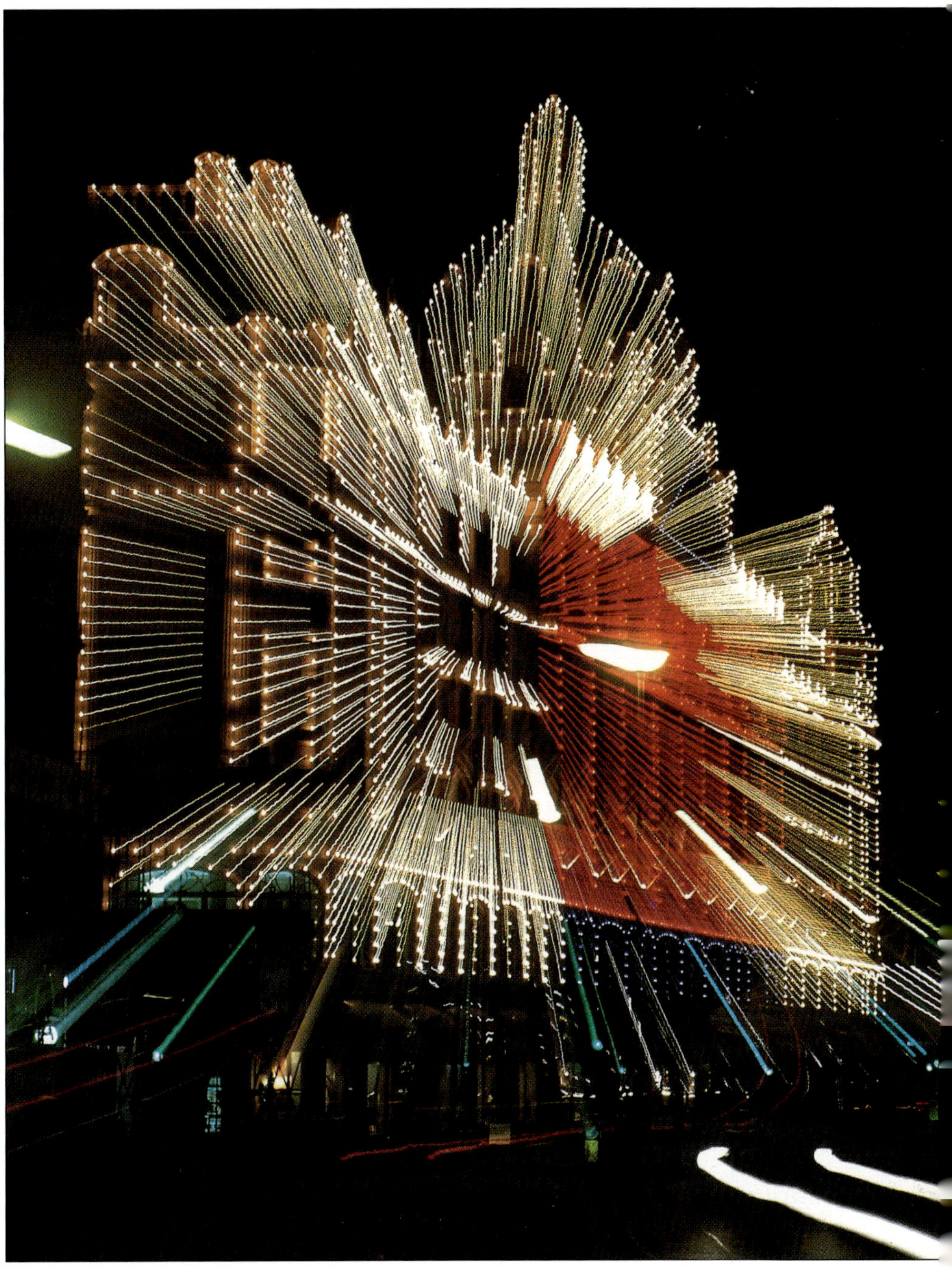

▲ Step zooming while photographing Harrods at night produced this spectacular image. Mounting the camera on a tripod meant that camera shake during the necessary long exposure was not a problem.

generally need shutter speeds of no *faster* than 1/60th sec to obtain the blurred effects. Compact cameras that give you no shutter speed controls aren't really suitable for panning, and zooming is often impossible.

Once you are used to panning and zooming, you will become confident in adjusting the shutter speed to obtain the precise effect you're after.

Slowly does it

For maximum effect in a panning or zoom shot, use very slow shutter speeds. To obtain these long exposures, you often need to close the aperture to its smallest setting – this is usually f16 or f22.

If this still does not give you a long enough shutter speed, you can do one or more of the following:

Use a slow film The slower the film, the more light needed to expose it correctly, and therefore the longer the shutter speed required.

Use a neutral density filter This cuts down the amount of light reaching the film, again making longer exposures necessary.

Shoot in dull light You can obtain some very effective zoom shots of night lights. However, for most conventional subjects, pan and zoom shots often look best when taken on a bright day with a good deal of contrast – so try one of the above options first.

Panning

The panning action

The act of panning is really quite simple. First, follow the moving subject in your viewfinder. Just as it approaches your pre-focus point, release the shutter. Continue following the subject after the shutter has been closed.

Make sure that the subject is in the centre of your viewfinder throughout this panning motion. So that you can do this smoothly, keep your feet still while letting your upper body and head twist to follow the subject.

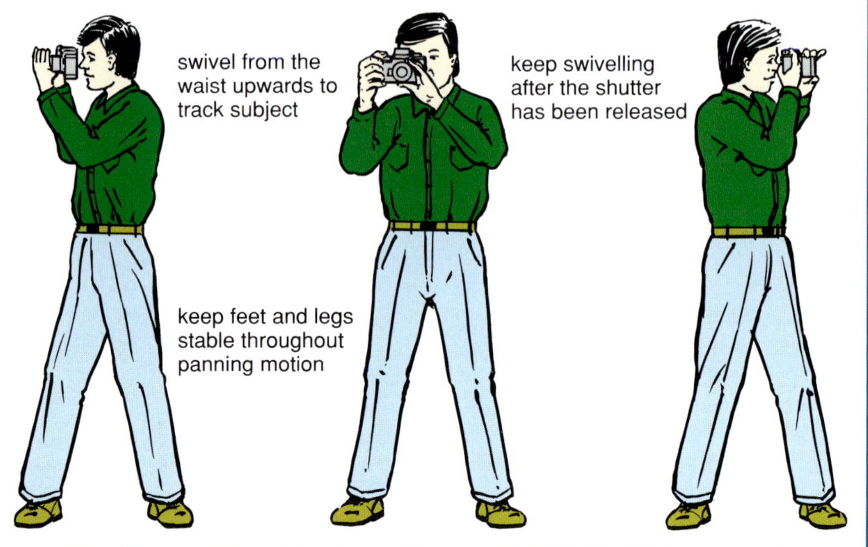

Some photographers emphasize movement by freezing it in sharp focus. Others emphasize movement by allowing the subject to blur with a slow shutter speed. Panning lets you have the best of both worlds.

With a perfect pan, the moving subject is pin sharp while the background is reduced to streaks of blur. To record the subject in sharp focus, the camera must be panned in unison with the moving subject (see The panning action). Start by practising without any film in your camera to get the feel of the action. Good practice subjects would be a friend running or passing cars.

Pre-focus

Remember, you must be able to pre-focus on your subject when panning. Subjects that move randomly are not suitable – it's next to impossible to pan and focus at the same time.

Ideal subjects for pre-focusing are track athletes, cars travelling along a road and trains moving along a track – anywhere that your subject has to move along a predictable route. Try experimenting with different shutter speeds. The slower the shutter speed, the more dramatic the panning effect will be. However, slower shutter speeds require you to pan for longer, so start by practising with shutter speeds of 1/30th and 1/15th sec rather than half a second.

Also, panning produces more startling shots with fast moving subjects that move close by. To begin with, though, practise on subjects that are a good distance away from you and moving relatively slowly – a pedal cyclist, for instance, rather than a motorcyclist.

Changing shutter speeds

These three shots show the different effects you can achieve by panning with different shutter speeds. The cyclist rode at the same pace in all the shots while the photographer used progressively longer shutter speeds.

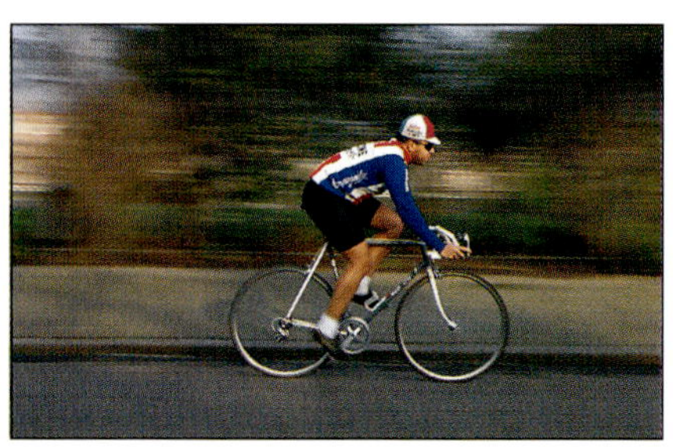

▲ With a shutter speed of 1/30th sec, the cyclist is in relatively sharp focus. You can almost make out the writing on his shirt and his bicycle. Note how the frame of the bike has been frozen against the blurred background.

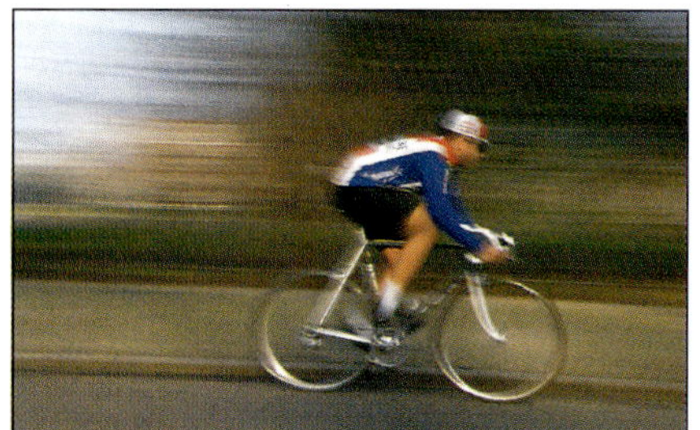

▲ With a shutter speed of 1/8th sec, the cyclist now seems to have a 'ghost' image that helps convey the sense of movement. In addition, the streaks in the background have become much more pronounced.

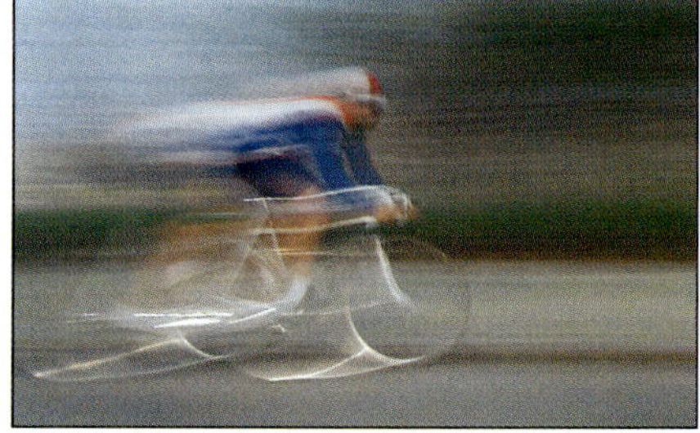

▲ With a shutter speed of half a second, the speed of the cyclist is most graphically illustrated – it's impossible to distinguish the bushes in the background and the cyclist leaves a trail of streaks in his wake.

Zooming

For an effective zoom shot, you generally need to have your subject in the centre of the frame. Choose a subject that's already bold and visually interesting – don't simply rely on the zoom effect to make the picture noteworthy.

The background to the subject is not so important because, to a large extent, it will be 'wiped' by the outward streaks of the zoom action. However, a background that recedes into the distance often looks effective. And the more colourful the background, the better.

A subject with a reasonable amount of contrast usually makes for a good zoom shot. Specific points of highlight will make dramatic outward streaks. However, try not to include large expanses of highlights in your picture – too much white makes the radiating streaks much less prominent.

For a conventional zoom shot, zoom fractionally after you have released the shutter or stop zooming fractionally before the shutter closes. If you zoom before you release the shutter and continue zooming until after the shutter is closed, your image will be completely blurred.

Unless you want complete abstracts, stop the zooming action for part of the exposure so that you have a recognizable, reasonably sharp image as well as the streaky zoom effect.

You need a long shutter speed to get the zooming right. To begin with, try putting your camera on a tripod and setting a one second exposure. As you become better at zooming, you may find that it is more convenient to hand hold or use a monopod, and that you can zoom with shutter speeds as fast as 1/8th or 1/15th sec.

You don't have to zoom for the whole length of the focal length range. You may find that a very bold zoom effect becomes repetitive after a while and that you can achieve much more subtle images by using only part of your zoom range. Also, try experimenting with zooming in and zooming out.

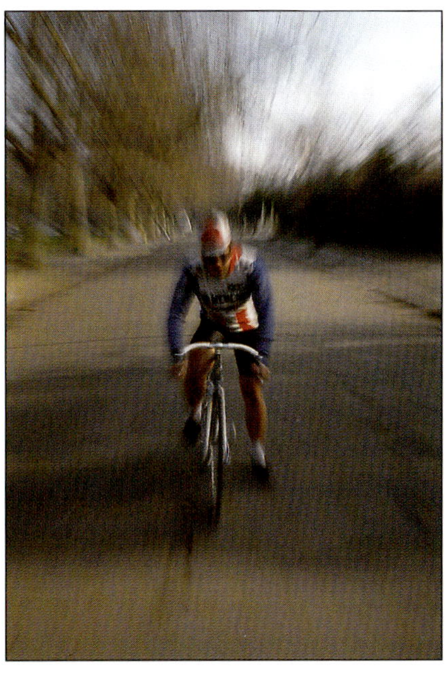

▲ ▼ *In both these photographs the cyclist was stationary, but the photographer created a sense of movement by zooming. The exploding impression of the photo (above) was created by zooming in – that is, from a wide angle to a telephoto. For the imploding effect (below) the photographer zoomed out.*

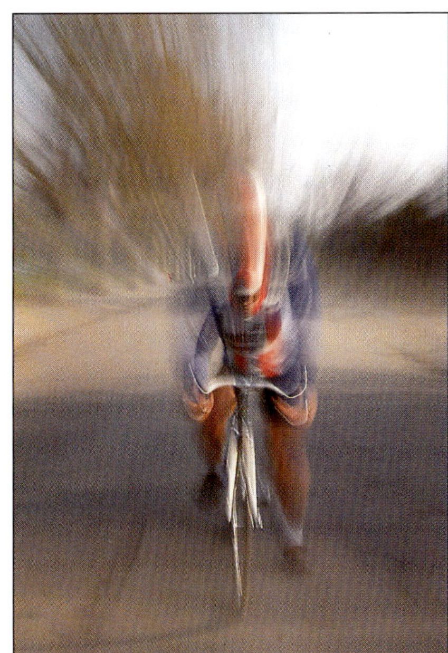

The zooming action

Zoom lenses are available with two types of zooming action. Some zooms have a barrel that you push and pull in order to zoom out and in respectively. Other zoom lenses, however, have a collar which you twist to change the focal length.

One touch zooms – that is, lenses on which you control the focusing and zooming with one barrel – always have a push-pull action.

Two touch zooms – lenses which have two separate rings to control focusing and zooming – often have a twist action collar.

Most photographers find it much easier to operate the push-pull action when trying to obtain zoom shots. With the twist action zoom, you often need to have very supple wrists to zoom from the two extreme settings with one movement. In particular, zooming and panning in one shot is hard with twist action (see overleaf).

One point to check before you buy a push-pull type zoom is the smoothness of the zoom action. If it's very stiff, you'll end up with jerky pictures.

Occasionally, this effect might look quite effective. However, the drawback is that you won't be able to obtain the control and consistency given by a smooth action zoom.

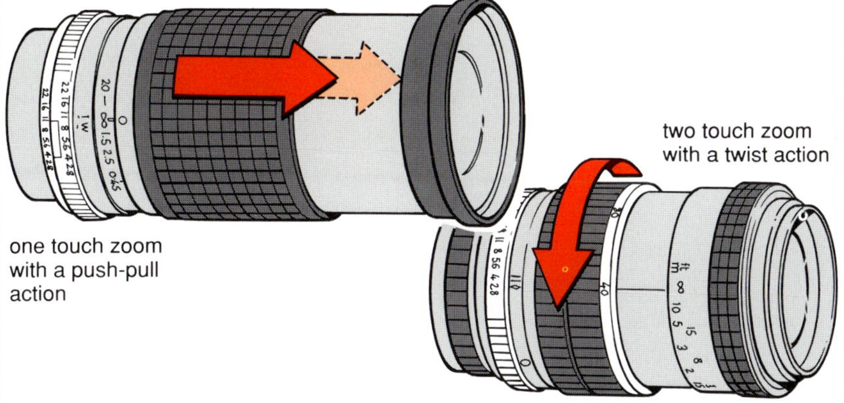

Experimental imagery

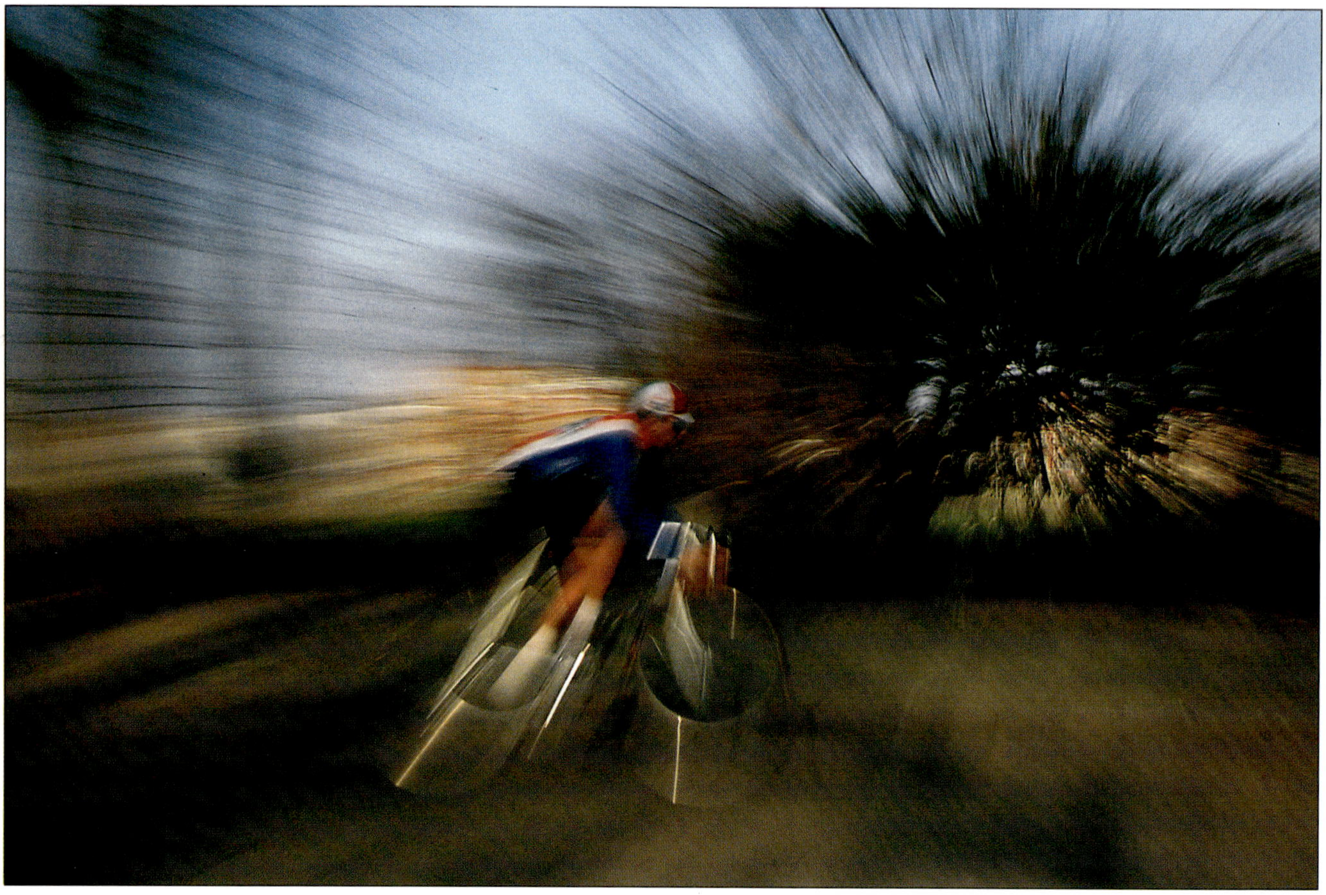

Once you have mastered the arts of panning and zooming, why not try some more adventurous techniques?

For instance, although you usually want to pan as smoothly as possible, you may obtain some surprisingly vibrant results with a vicious, jerky pan. Follow the subject as for a normal pan, but let the camera move vertically as well as horizontally. For the best effects, try doing this with a slow shutter speed and a fast moving subject.

With zooming you may want to experiment with some exposures of several seconds. To do this, mount the camera on a tripod. One interesting effect can be created by stopping the zoom action two or three times during the exposure. You end up with different sized images of the same subject superimposed on one another.

Pan and zoom

You can even attempt to pan and zoom at the same time. This is a difficult camera technique to get con-sistently right – so be prepared to waste film.

To achieve successful zoom pans, one hand must hold the camera body and be responsible for the panning movement, while the other hand must hold the zoom ring and control the zooming movement.

▲ *Panning and zooming during one exposure is a hard technique to master – but it certainly creates outstanding all action images.*

▼ *Using a pan with a slow exposure allows you to obtain extraordinary stylized pictures. Here the jerky movement of the camera has created curved streaks of light from the bright highlights on the bike.*

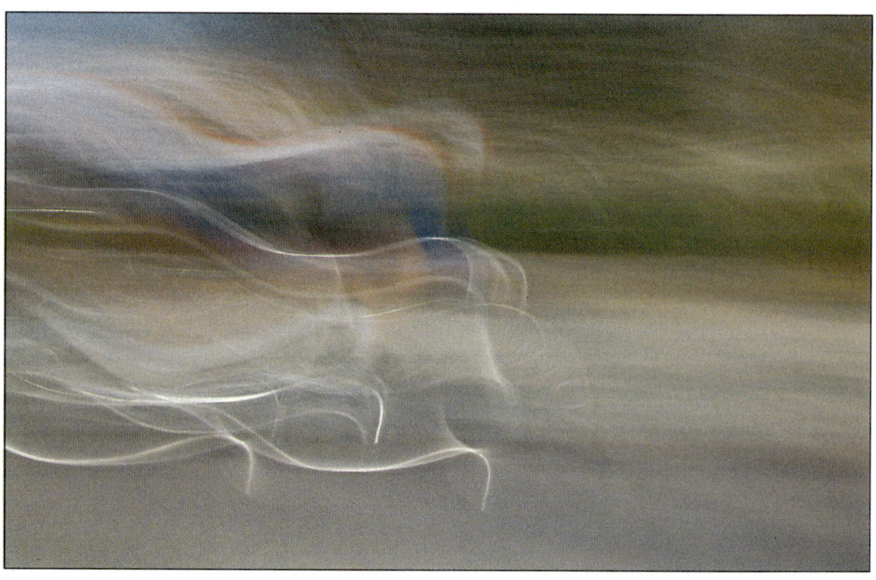

Using grain creatively

Whatever type of camera you own, you can use grain in an imaginative way. You'll find it brings a whole new mood to your pictures.

When you deliberately exaggerate grain for creative effect, the emphasis is not on pin sharp, true to life shots, but on images with a 'painted' feel. Form and shape become more important than detail and texture, and colours are muted.

You'll find that some subjects are more suited to grainy treatment than others. A soft, romantic quality is appropriate for portraits, nature or rural landscapes, for example. Equally, grain can be used to convey a moody, gritty feel on shots of industrial landscapes or architecture.

The technique is also ideal for transforming conventional subjects into eyecatching, abstract images. You can start from scratch or transform existing images. The final effect is entirely up to your own imagination, so why not have a go at experimenting with different techniques and subjects to find out the range of effects possible?

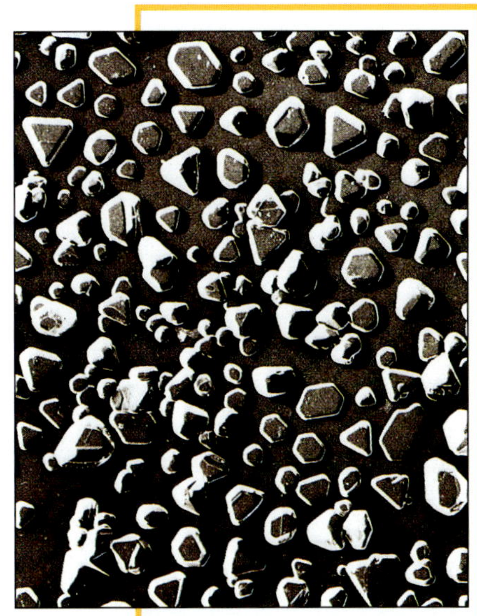

What is grain?

A photographic image is formed by silver halide crystals arranged on the surface of the film or paper. Although they are microscopic, the number and size of these crystals determines how 'grainy' a picture is.

In a fine grained photograph they are very small whereas in a coarse grained picture they are larger and more numerous, and consequently more obvious.

In this greatly magnified picture (above) of ISO 400 black and white film, you can clearly see the irregularly shaped, individual silver halide crystals, which give an impression of grain.

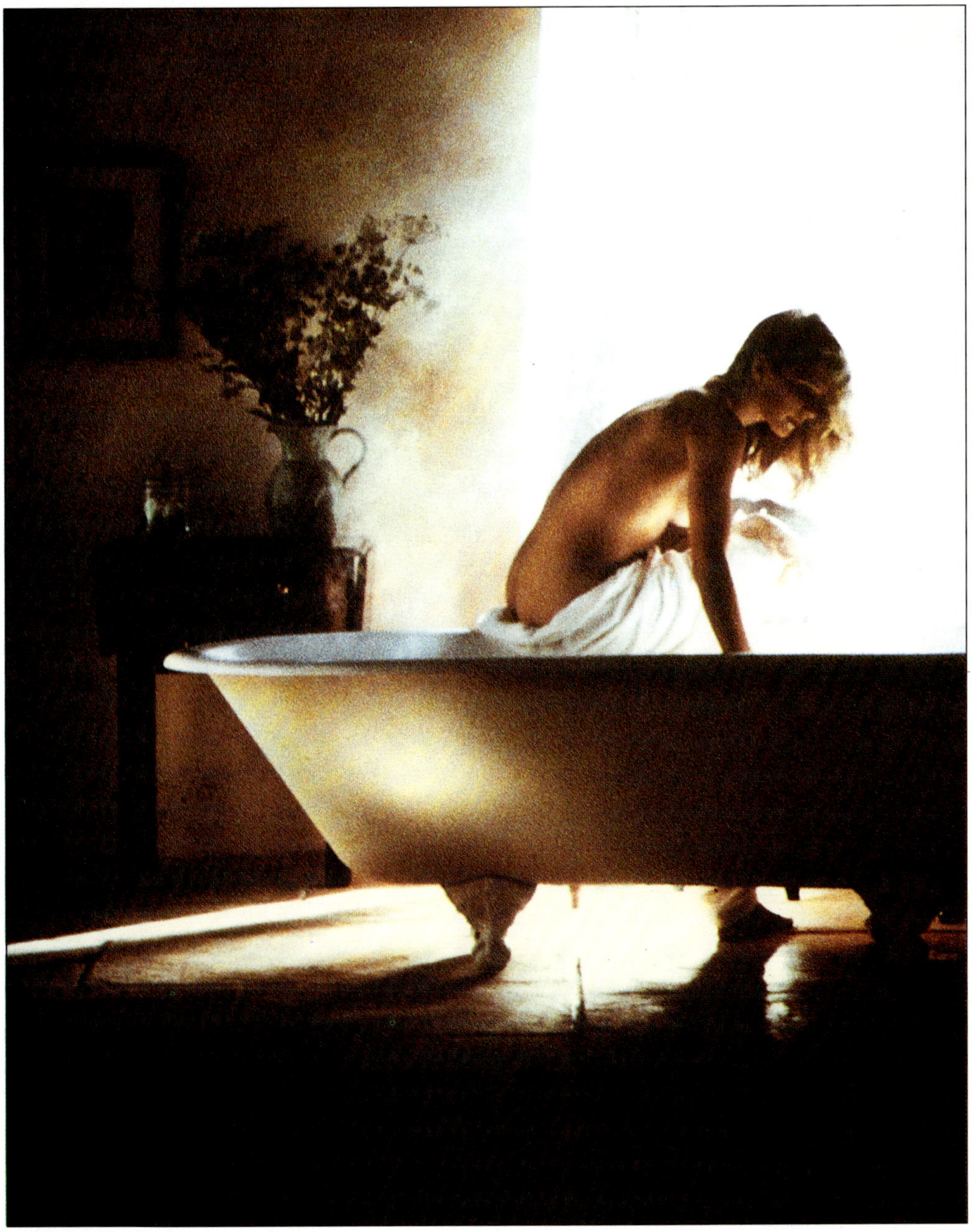

◀ *Here, grain is most obvious in areas of even tone, like the side of the bath. It helps give the shot an attractive, romantic feel. The reduction in tonal range turns the image almost monochromatic.*

How to emphasize grain

There are several ways to make grain more obvious in your shots. Often the most successful photographs use a combination of more than one method.

Fast film

The easiest way to achieve the effect is to load your camera with ultra fast film – ISO 1000 or higher. In general, the faster the film, the more obvious the grain.

This method is suitable for both compacts and SLRs, but if your camera is DX coded (that is, it sets the film speed automatically), read its instruction manual to find out the highest speed film it can accept. Some ultra fast films are not DX coded and so unsuitable for cameras which read DX coding.

Because this type of film is so fast, you may find it difficult to avoid overexposure in bright lighting conditions. This film was originally designed for low light, so you'll find it easiest to use in overcast conditions, at night or in poorly lit interiors.

For the best colour saturation in your pictures, you should aim to correctly expose them, as usual. However, underexposing colour print film (and Ilford XP2 black and white film) exaggerates grain. Overexposing ordinary black and white print film does the same.

Ultra fast film is available for prints (both colour and black and white) and colour slides. It's easier to see grain on black and white film than colour. This is because with black and white you actually see

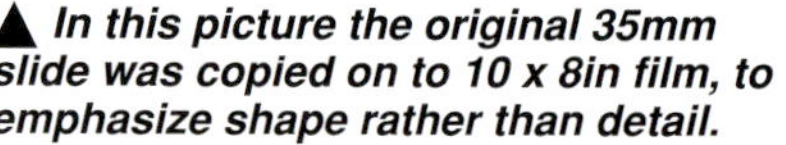

▲ *In this picture the original 35mm slide was copied on to 10 x 8in film, to emphasize shape rather than detail.*

the grains, while with colour and Ilford XP2 film, you see clouds of dye. Larger photographic shops usually stock a limited range of ultra fast film, but you might have to place a special order.

Processing can be done by your usual processor, as long as the film cassette is marked either E6 (for slides) or C41 (for prints). With a few films, however, you need a specialist lab.

Enlargements

If you want to show grain on a print or slide that you've already had processed, this is quite easy to do. Simply have a small area (say, 1/6th) of the picture enlarged. You can do it yourself or order a selective enlargement from your usual lab. What enlargement factor you need depends on the film speed – 20X is a good starting point. If the grain is too subtle, it will look more like a mistake than deliberate.

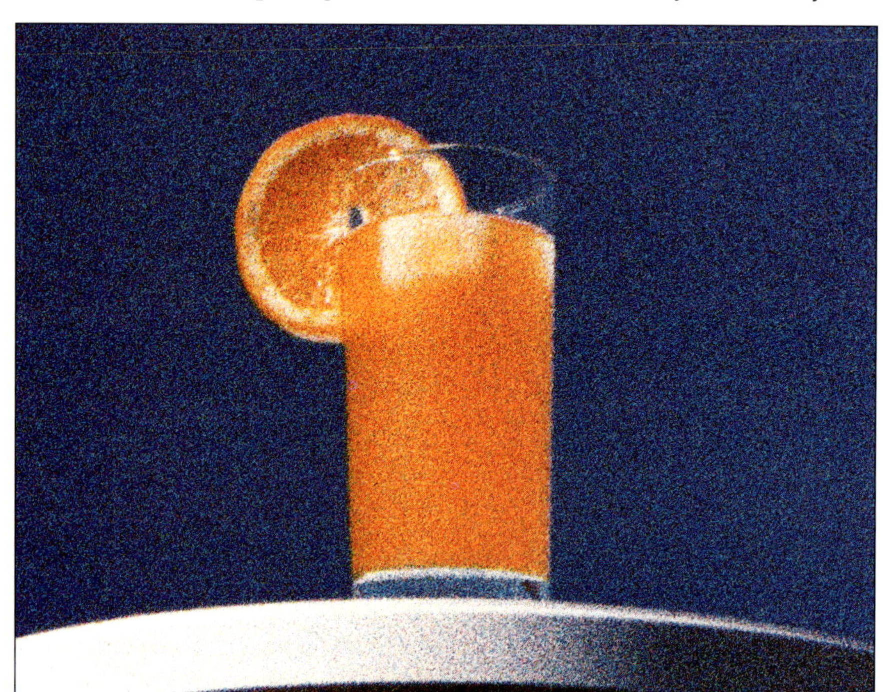

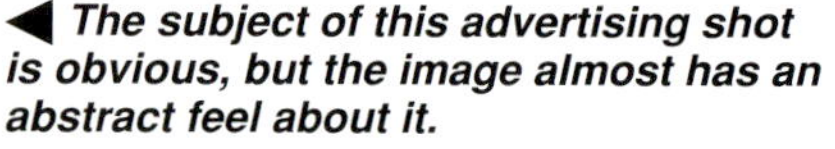

◄ *The subject of this advertising shot is obvious, but the image almost has an abstract feel about it.*

This method of enlarging the image is fine if you're happy seeing just a portion of the original shot, which makes it ideal for abstracts. You can't make the whole image really grainy unless you want a huge enlargement of poster size or more. Selective enlargements are also quite expensive, so don't choose a larger area of the original picture than you need.

Push it

Treating colour slide or black and white print film as if it's a higher speed than stated on the box (pushing or uprating) is a good way of enhancing graininess. Most colour print films are unsuitable for pushing because of the odd colour balance you end up with, but both Kodak Ektapress Gold 400 and 1600 can be pushed. You can only use this method if there's some way of altering film speed on your camera, so it's not suitable for most compacts.

With a camera that sets the film speed manually, adjust the film speed dial to a faster speed – ideally, this should be 2 stops higher than the film is rated at to maximize the grain. ISO 800 film pushed 2 stops, for example, becomes ISO 3200. If you have an exposure compensation dial, set this to -2 or 1/4 to push the film by 2 stops – in other words, underexpose it by 2 stops. It's not worth pushing very slow film because you won't see enough grain.

When you have your film processed, make sure you tell the processor it has been pushed, and by how many stops. To be on the safe side, stick a label on to the cassette as well. Most high street processors don't deal with pushed film, but professional labs are used to it. Few charge extra for the service.

Copying

Another way of emphasizing grain with slides is to copy a fine grained original on to fast film. You can do this yourself if you have a slide copier, or ask a professional lab to do it for you. A lab can do the same for print film. Opt for this technique if you want to reproduce the whole of an existing picture as a grainy version. Stress to the lab that you are after extra grain.

The final picture will not be quite as high quality as the original. You may find it's more contrasty, but this is not necessarily a disadvantage – it may suit the picture very well.

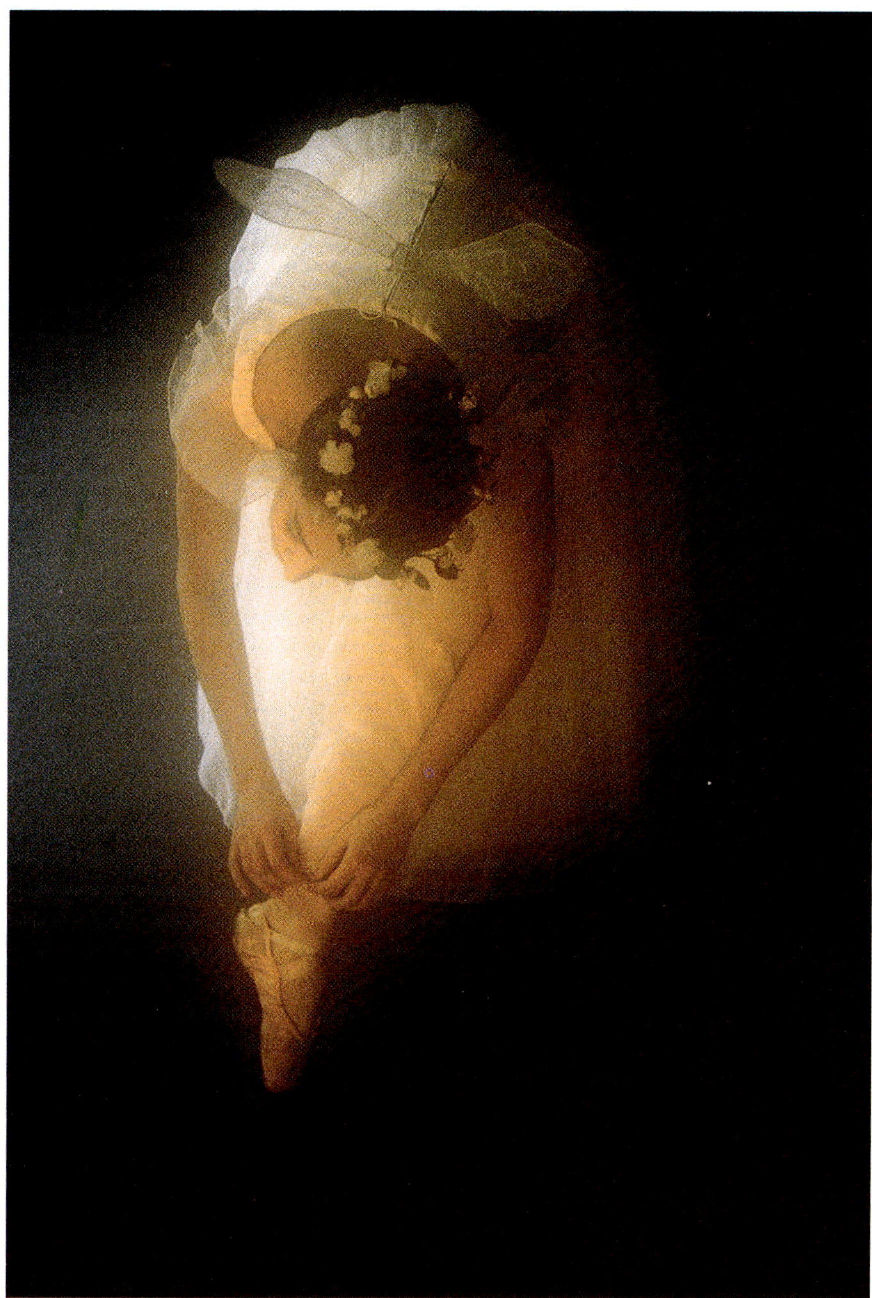

▲ *The low lighting conditions in this situation made it easy to use fast film, plus a soft focus filter.*

Dim the light

Tip

If you want to use ultra fast film in strong lighting conditions, buy a 4X or 8X neutral density filter (*not* the graduated type). When fitted to your lens, this cuts down the light meeting the film by 2 or 3 stops, allowing you to use a more manageable shutter speed.

Choose your level

With practice, you'll find which technique or combination of techniques gives you the result you're after, but it helps to know how noticeable the grain is, depending on which film speed you use. However, remember that different brands of film show grain to differing extents, so experiment with more than one make.

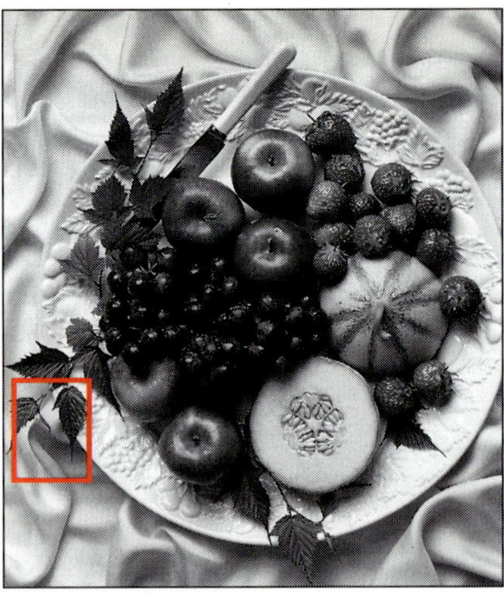

▶ *The original, full frame shot photographed on ISO 400 print film. Grain is barely noticeable.*

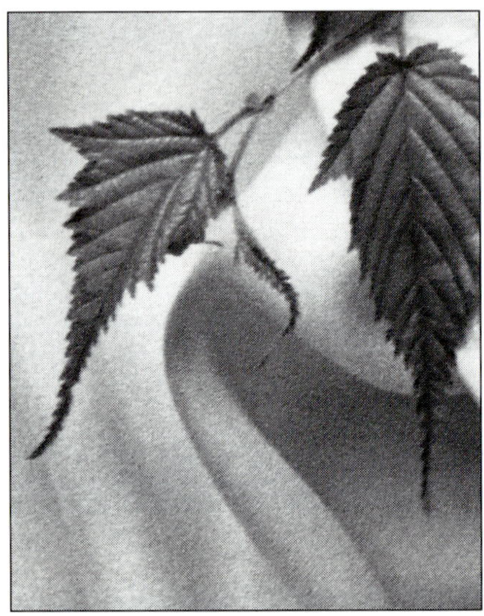

▲ *ISO 400 enlarged 20 times. Grain is obvious in areas of a single tone and smooth texture, but less so elsewhere.*

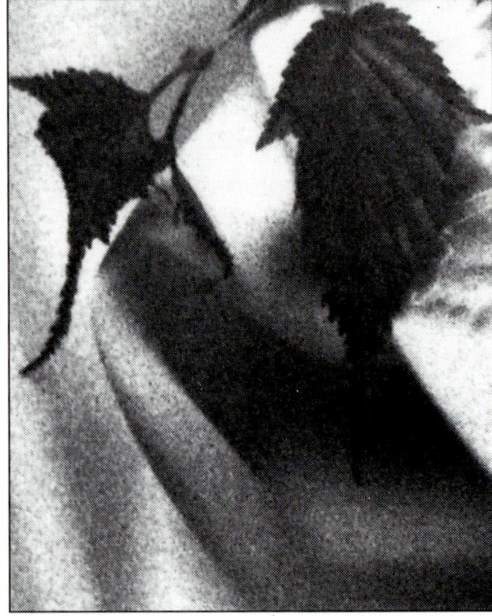

▲ *ISO 1600 film pushed 1 stop to 3200. You can see grain very clearly and a lot of detail is lost.*

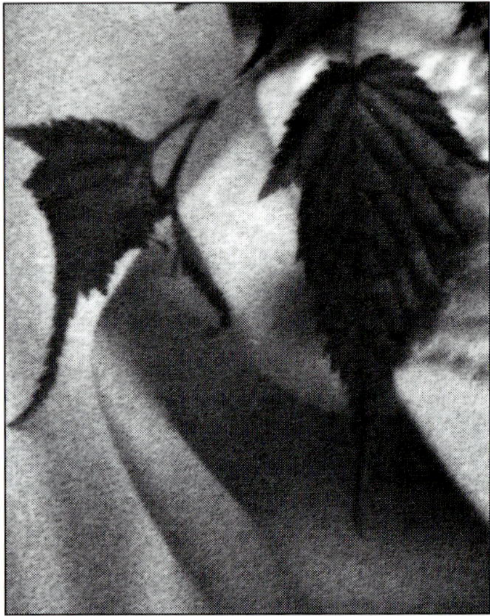

▲ *With ISO 3200, grain is slightly less obvious than with pushed ISO 1600 film. You can see more detail, too.*

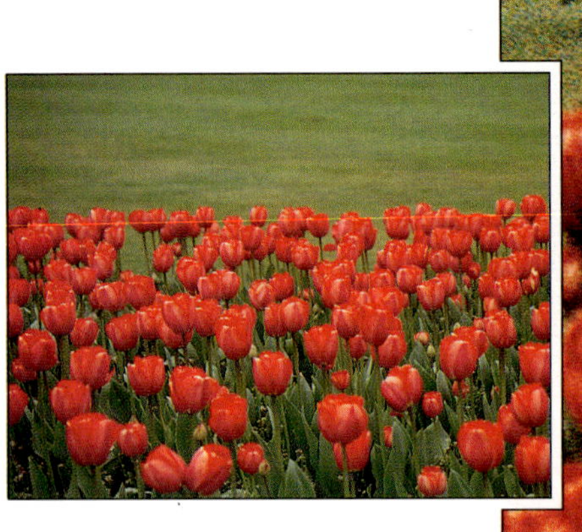

▲▶ *The original subject (above) was shot on ISO 100 slide film. To emphasize the grain, the slide was copied on to ISO 3200 print film by a lab. An enlargement was then made of one section. The result (right) is a picture which shows much coarser grain, with less saturated colours.*

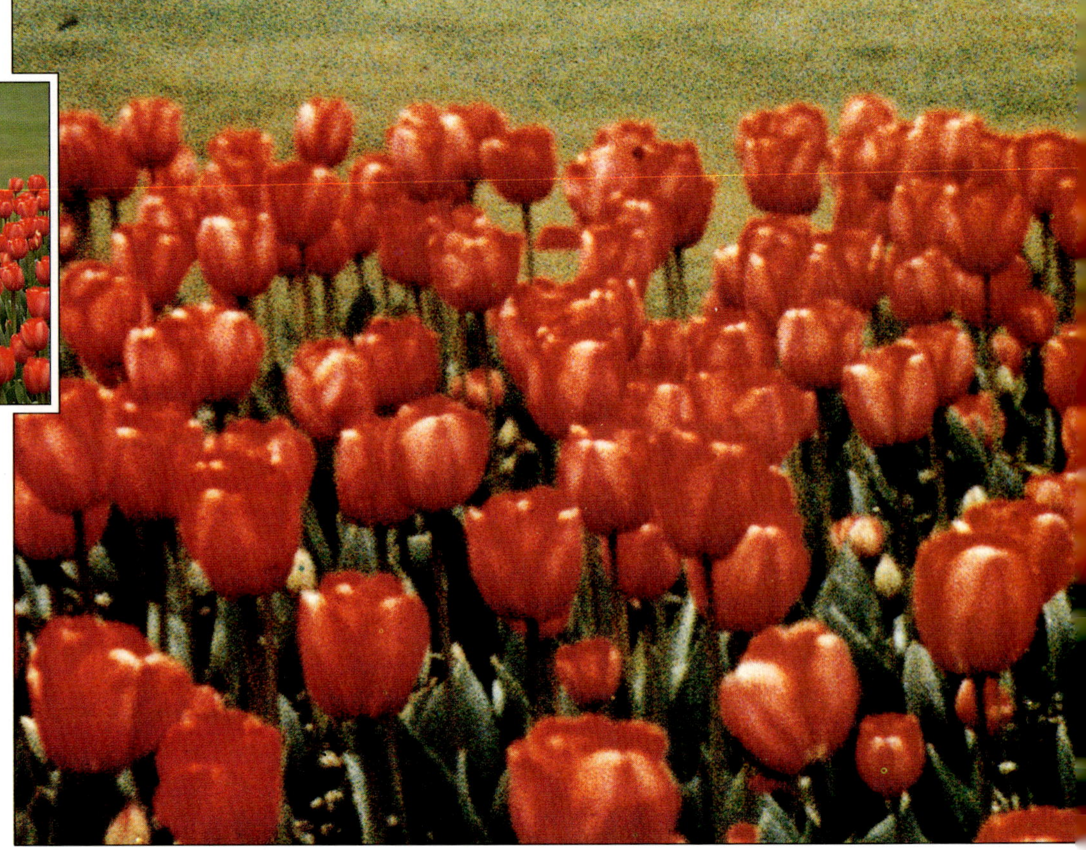

Creating soft focus

Soft focus filters can completely alter the mood of a photo and lift your subject matter into the realms of dreams, nostalgia, or the surreal. You can choose from a range of soft focus filters for SLRs, or improvise DIY effects for compacts.

Soft focus is not the same as out of focus, when the lens itself is unfocused. For a soft focus photo you focus the lens on the subject and place something to act as a filter over the lens, to soften the image and artificially diffuse the light.

Splashing out

Several manufacturers make special soft focus filters, often called diffusion filters, for SLR cameras. Many have a hole in the middle so that the centre of the photo is sharp and unaffected by the filter.

There are also specially made smaller filters for those compacts which accept them. A few compacts have built-in soft focus – but this offers no choice as to the degree of softening.

If you have an SLR, you could buy a soft focus (also called special portrait) lens. Usually around 90 to 120mm, they are intended for people who take a lot of portraits.

They produce a subtly different effect from filters – often giving glowing highlights to photos. The drawback is that they are very expensive, and so may not be worth buying unless you intend to do a lot of soft focus portrait work.

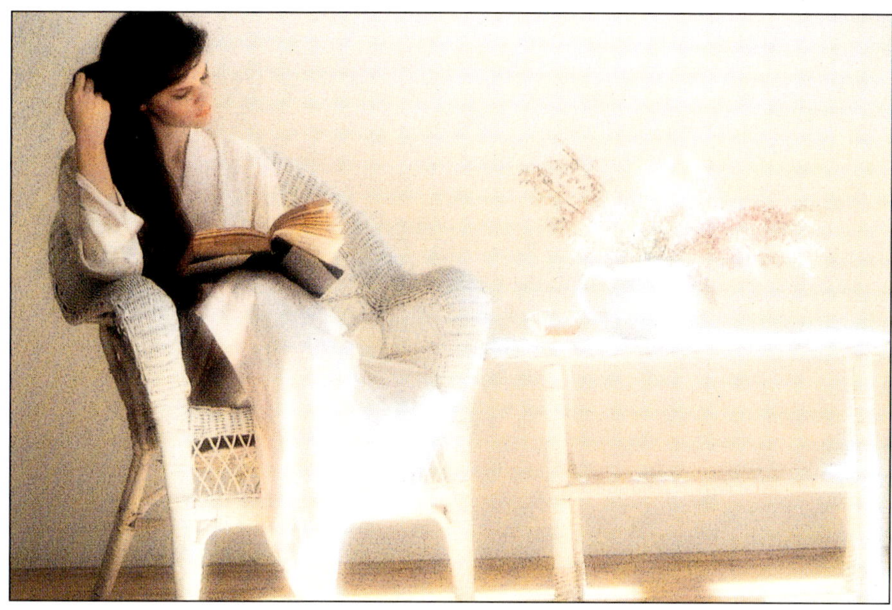

▲ *Soft focus lends this picture a romantic quality. White areas are given a bright halo effect and the dramatic impact of the girl's dark hair is emphasized.*

▼*Still life photographers use soft focus to give their shots a dreamlike finishing touch. A soft focus filter adds a warm glow to the bloom and colour of these peaches.*

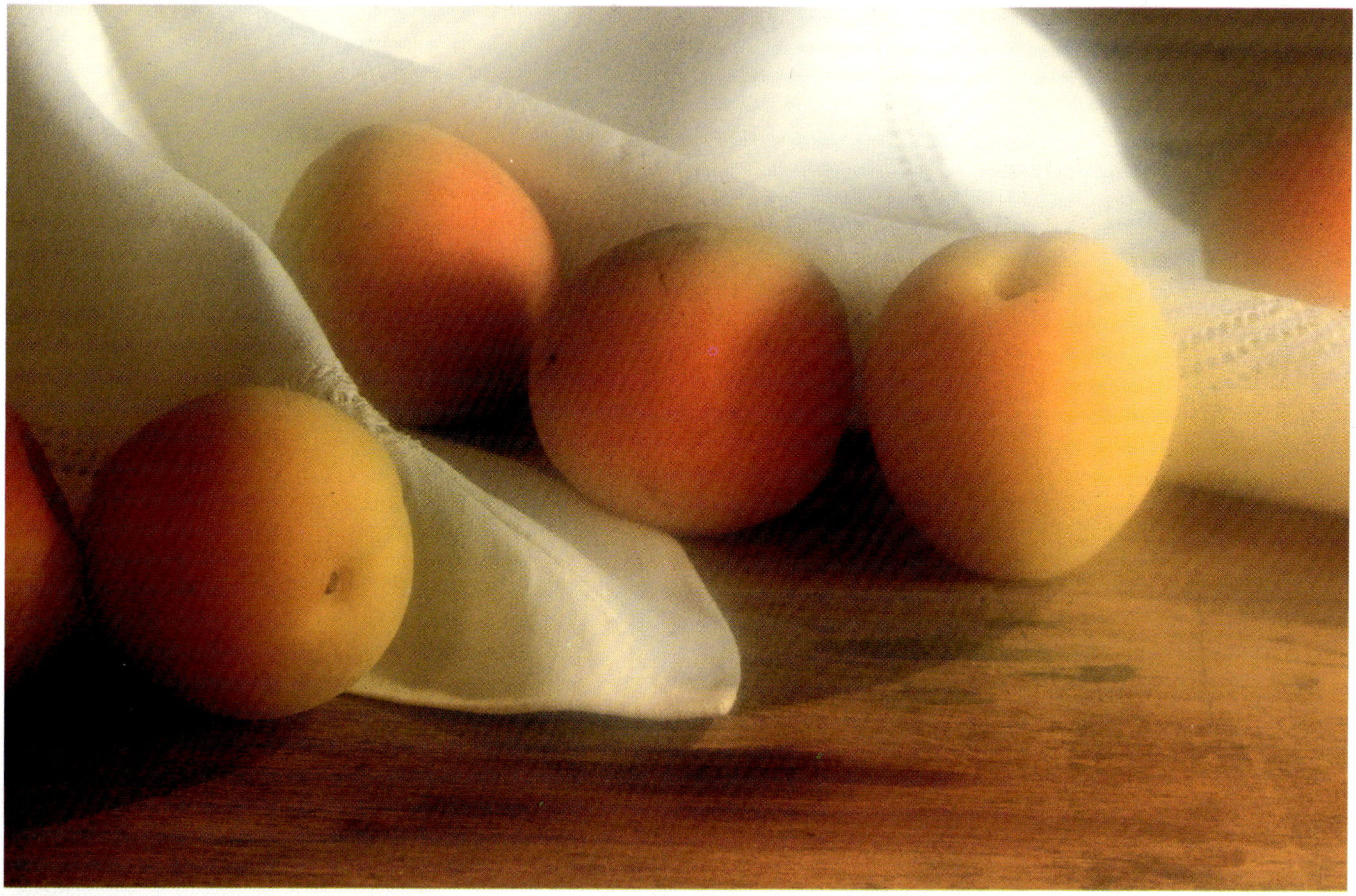

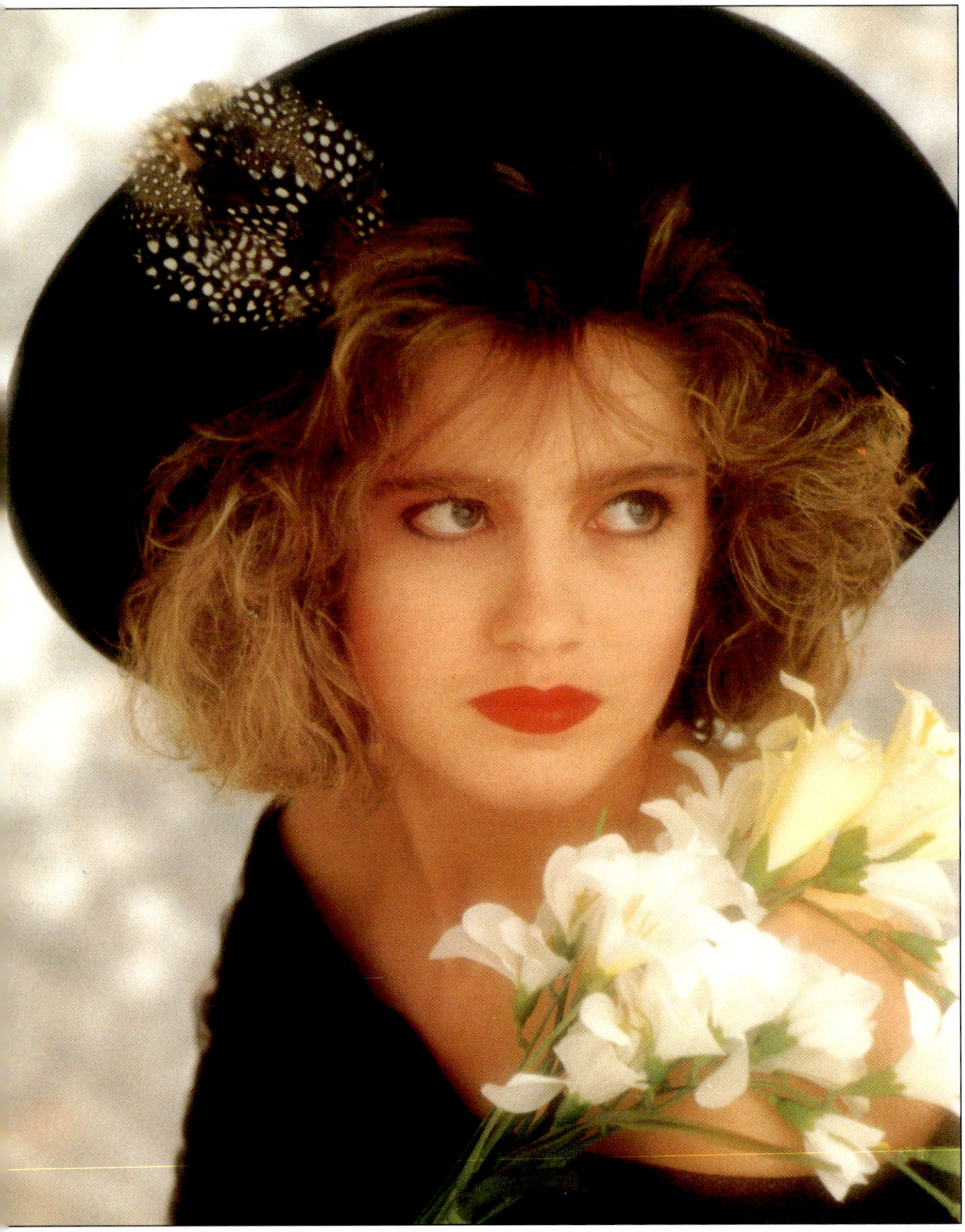

When to use soft focus

As you experiment with soft focus you'll discover when to use it and when not to. It is most effective for subjects, such as back lit portraits, with a contrast range greater than the film can produce. Fun though it is, soft focus is at its best when you don't overdo it – too many abstract blurs tend to overwhelm the subject matter. A mass of soft focus pictures can become a bit boring, so take some pin sharp images too.

A good way to learn when a soft image is appropriate is to compare versions of the same subject matter – ranging from pin sharp shots through improvised soft focus to purpose made filter effects.

▶ *Soft focus sacrifices fine detail. To retain the texture of the fur, the photographer positioned the dog between the camera and the sun. The backlighting created a halo of light which picked out every whisker.*

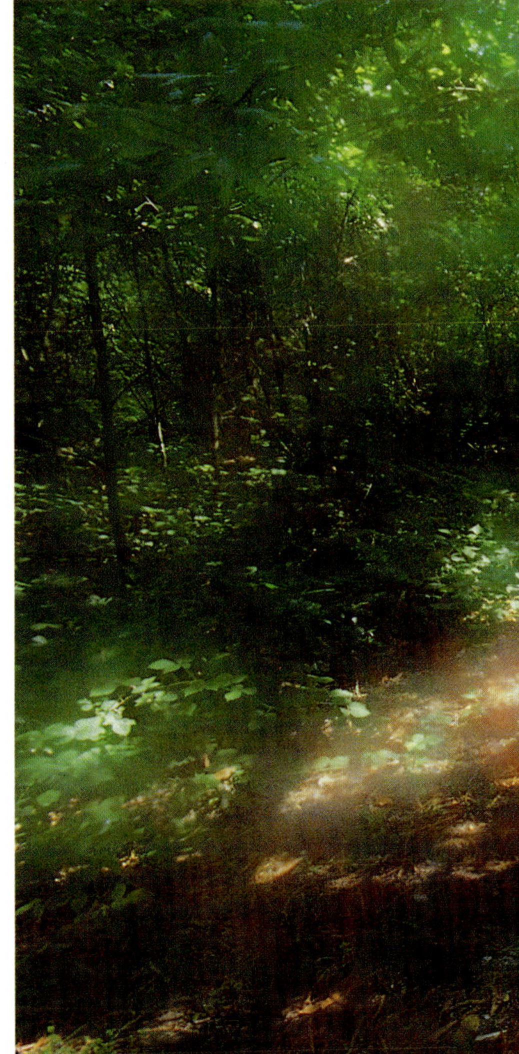

▲ *Soft focus is a favourite technique of professional portrait and wedding photographers because it flatters the subject. The softening effect disguises any tiny imperfections in the person's face.*

Tip

Using grease

Any grease does the job when you want to smear a filter to create soft focus. Photographers have even been known to rub the side of their nose when petroleum jelly is not to hand! Whatever you use, never smear the lens itself – use a filter.

To clean the filter afterwards wash it in warm soapy water, rinse and dry it with a lint free towel. If you're out on a trip, wipe off most of the jelly with a tissue and then rub it with a cloth soaked in alcohol. You can buy such cloths in sachets from camera shops.

▶ *To achieve a dappled effect, the photographer uses a special diffusion filter which, by the way it reflects light, adds a multicoloured sheen to the photograph. As the result is so striking, be especially careful not to overuse this type of filter.*

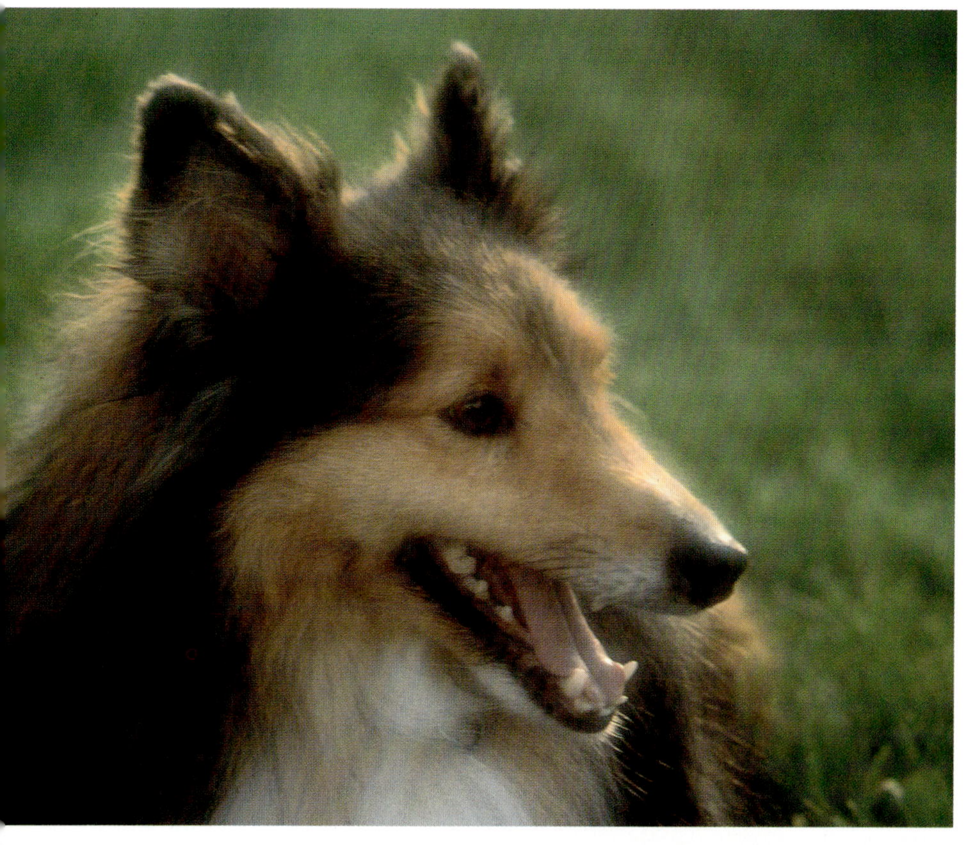

Improvizing

It isn't essential to buy expensive accessories – with a little ingenuity, soft focus effects are available to anyone. The simplest and cheapest way to achieve a softening effect with any camera is to breathe on the lens. Take the picture quickly, before the lens clears. If you have an SLR and you're worried about harming the lens, attach a clear filter and breathe on to that instead.

You could take it a step further by stretching a stocking taut over the lens on a compact or SLR. Notice how the effect varies according to what colour stocking you use – black works best.

If your camera takes filters you can smear some grease, such as petroleum jelly, on to a filter. Try smearing the jelly in all sorts of different directions and see how this affects the soft focus streaks. Whatever you do, *don't* smear it directly on to your camera lens, because you won't be able to remove it all afterwards.

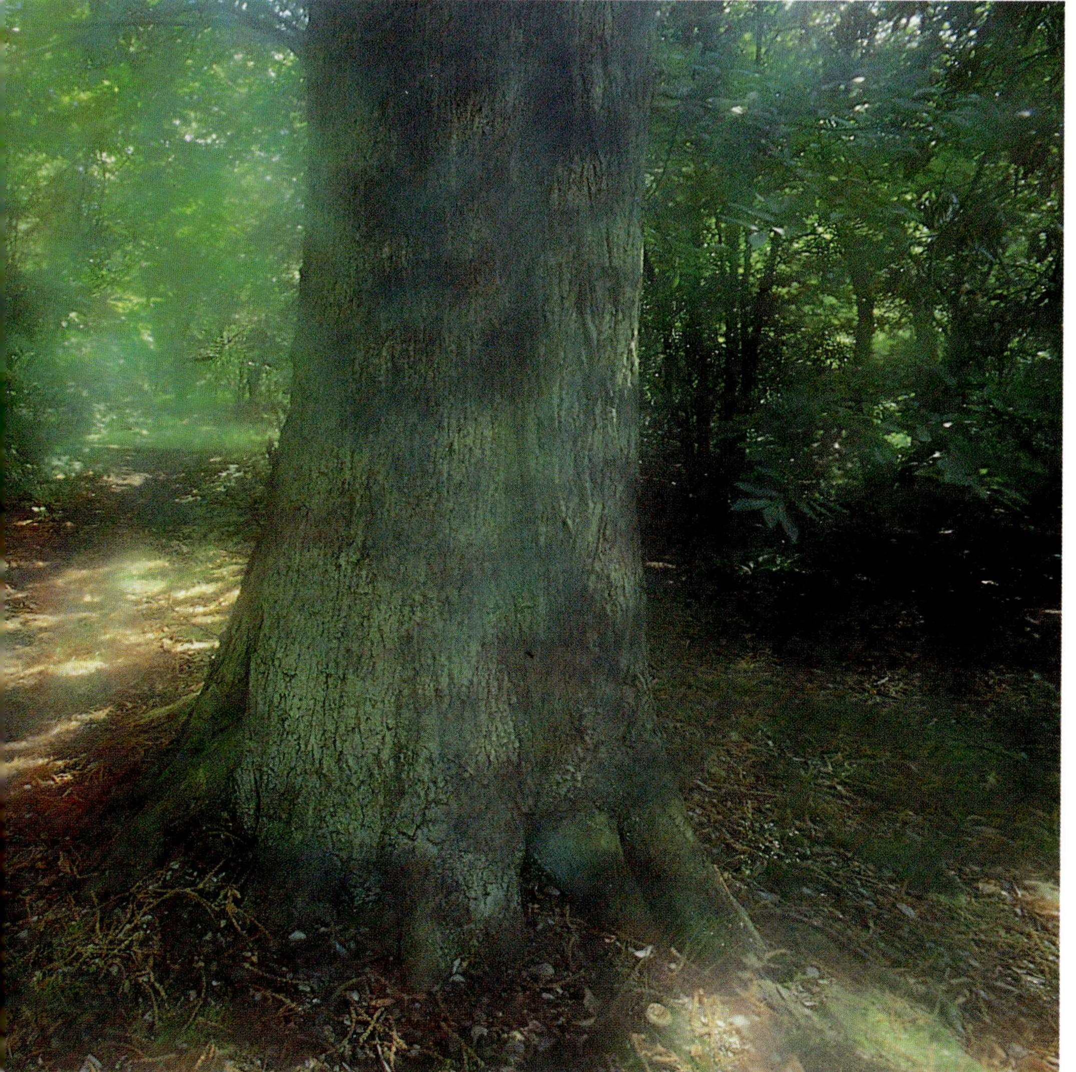

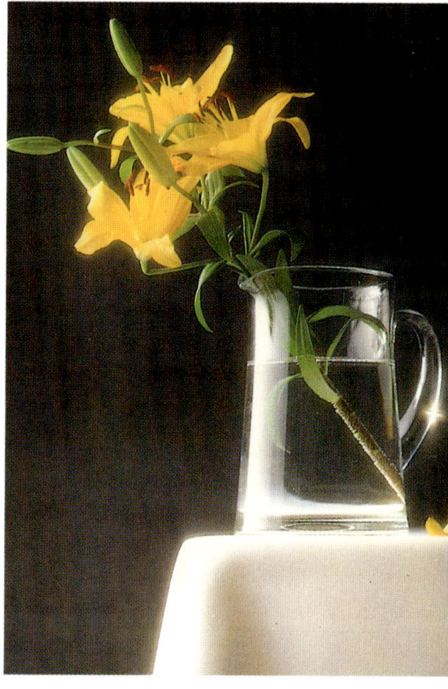

▲ *Flowers are ideal subjects for soft focus, as they suit a delicate treatment. Here the photographer stretched a black stocking over the lens. The thicker the stocking (measured by the number of denier), the more noticeable the effect.*

Trying out soft focus

Choose a suitable soft focus image – daffodils, for example – and start experimenting. These photos were all taken with petroleum jelly on the filter.

Suitable filters to use for soft focus are clear, skylight and UV, and ideally you need either an SLR or a compact that accepts filters.

Otherwise you'll have to tape the filter on or hold the filter in front of the lens with one hand – this can take a little practice.

You'll find the extent of soft focus varies with different apertures. If you have an SLR which allows you to alter the settings, take several photos at different apertures and compare your results.

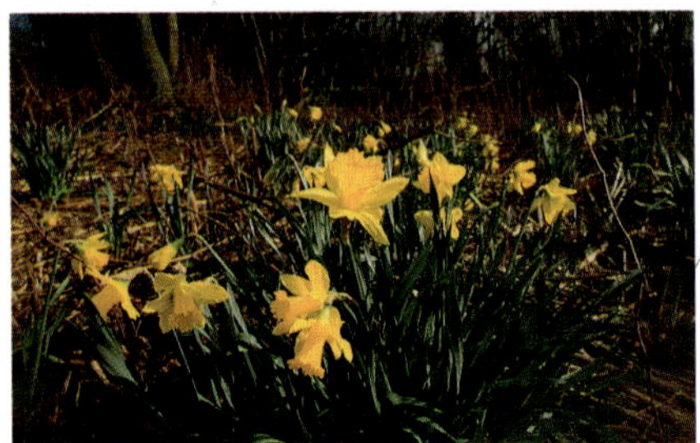

▲ *Smear circles of petroleum jelly around the edge of the filter, leaving the centre clear. With an aperture of f16, the scene still looks sharp.*

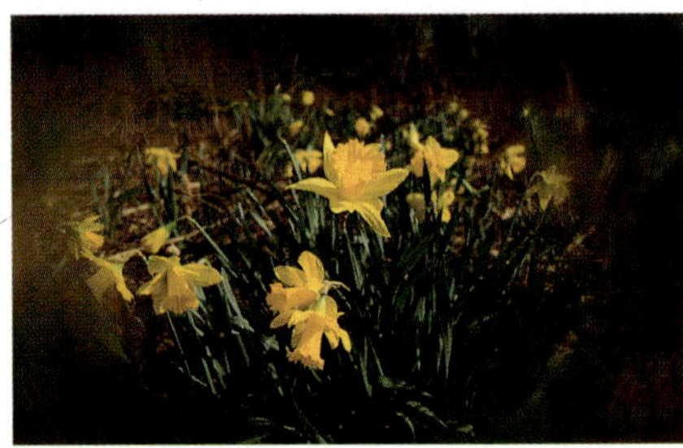

▲ *With a wider aperture of f4, the softening effect is much more noticeable.*

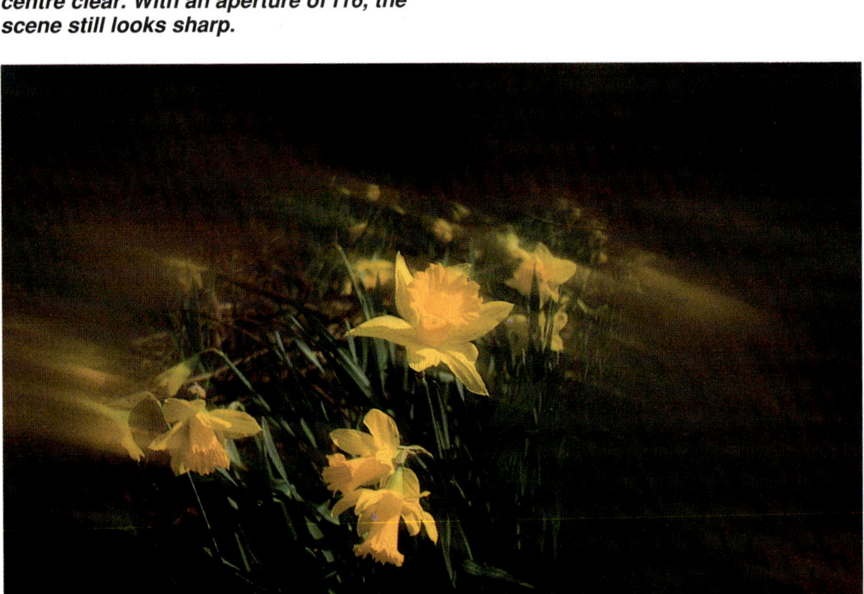

▲ *Smear the gel diagonally to suggest shafts of hazy sunlight. The edges of the photograph are very soft, but the centre remains pin sharp.*

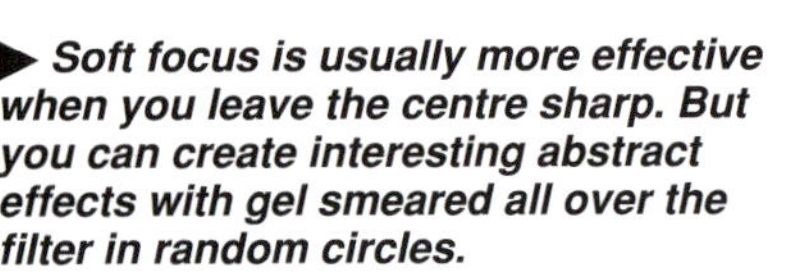

▶ *Soft focus is usually more effective when you leave the centre sharp. But you can create interesting abstract effects with gel smeared all over the filter in random circles.*

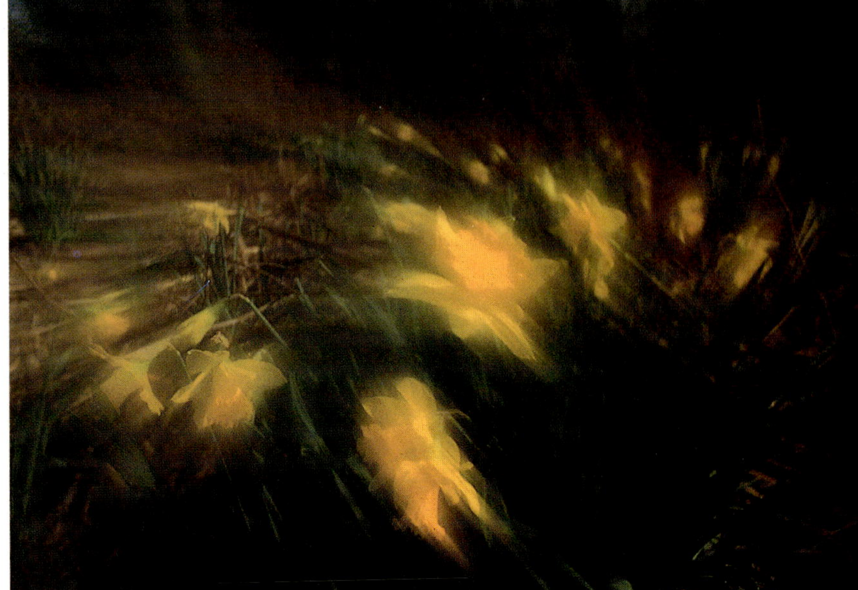

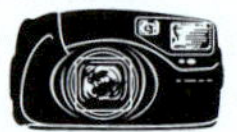

SLR tips

❏ Soft focus is easiest to control with an SLR because you can see exactly what's happening in the viewfinder and you can vary the lens aperture.

❏ With a clear centre filter, a wide aperture softens the image the most, a small aperture the least. A short focal length (as in wide angles) increases the softening extent, while a long focal length (with a telephoto lens) reduces it.

❏ On a sunny day, putting anything in front of the lens can cause problems with flare (where highlights spread into the shadows). Use a lens hood so that a shadow is cast on the lens.

Compact tips

❏ When using filter attachments (available for some advanced compacts), use the wide angle end of your zoom, rather than the telephoto end, as the effect of the filter will be more noticeable.

❏ Take care when you smear petroleum jelly on the filters of compacts because they have a smaller area than SLR filters.

❏ To reduce flare, point the camera away from the sun. You can also shield the camera lens with your hand.

Michael St Maur Sheil – Industrial images

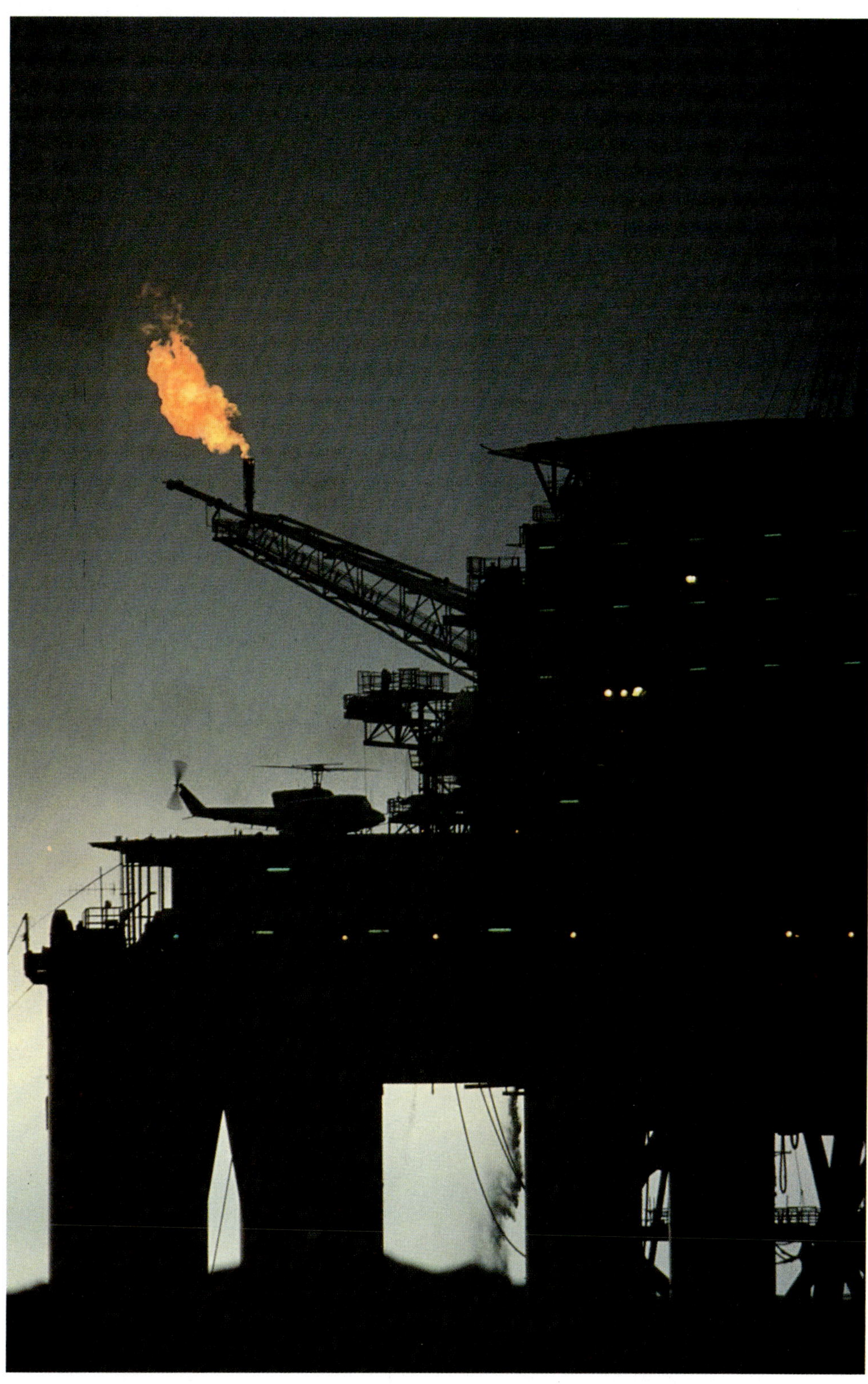

You can do it

The drama of Michael Sheil's photographs doesn't demand special access privileges: many industrial sites look striking even from the fence. Shoot at dusk so that the different light sources pick out the scene in widely different colours. Choose daylight balanced film unless the sky is completely black.

Whenever you see a really striking image, try to work out what techniques the photgrapher used. As Mike Sheil's pictures show, you can use viewpoint, exposure and (especially) time of day to create dramatic images.

While most industrial photographers travel from location to location with a large format camera, a barrage of lighting equipment and several assistants, Mike has a more mobile approach. Using 35mm cameras and only as much equipment as he can carry, he's free to roam around in search of the most dramatic images a subject has to offer.

Mike believes that industrial photography has great potential. 'But you must have the right client – one who gives you enough scope. All too frequently the

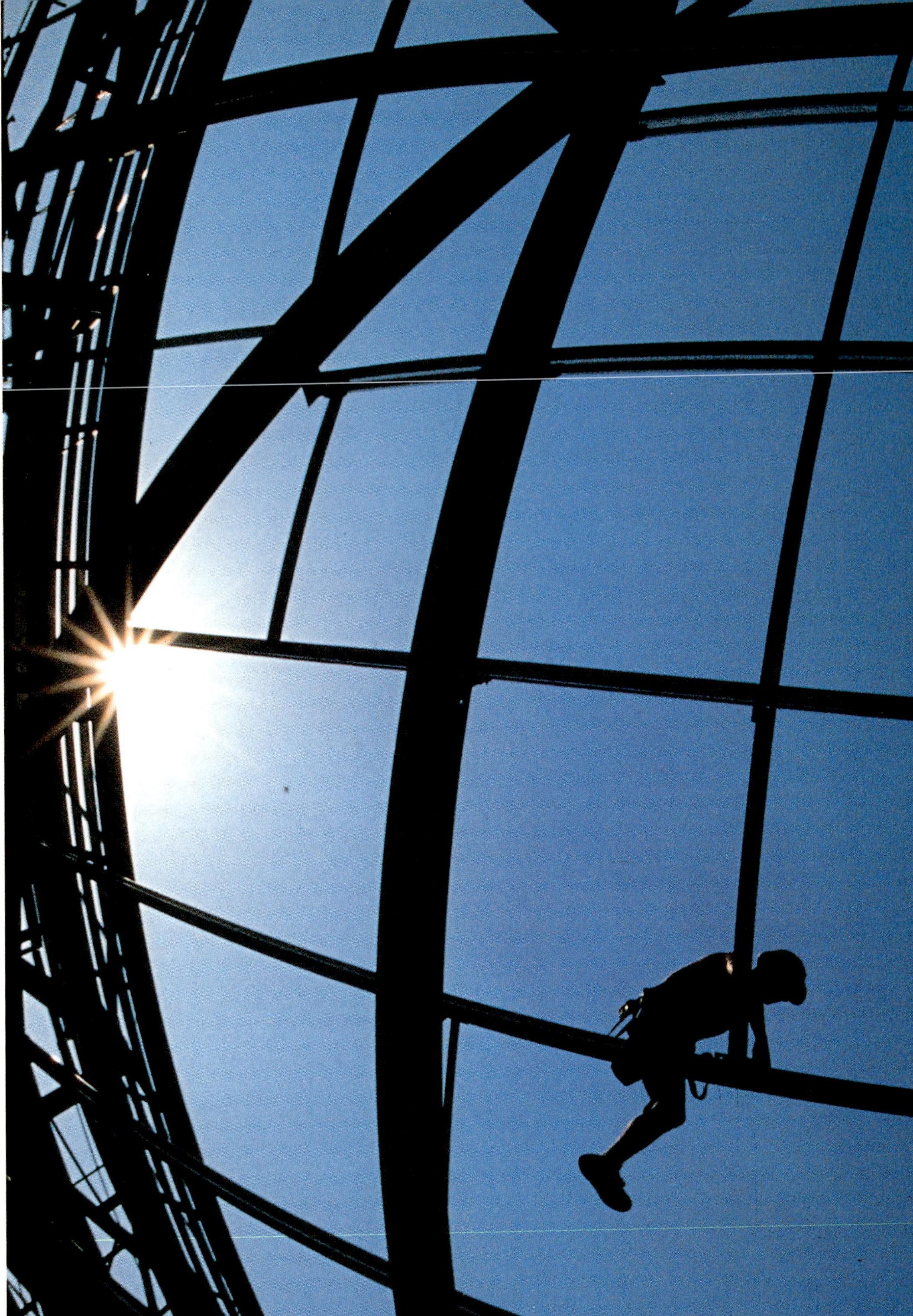

Technical details

Mike is quite a purist –
he strongly disapproves
of retouching and uses
available light when he
can. This was one of the
few occasions when he
used a 'gimmicky' lens –
a fisheye on a Nikon FM.

'I don't use fisheye
lenses that often, but
they can be very
effective – this shot
wouldn't have worked
without one.'

client just wants a straight shot showing the product.
There's a lot of pressure, too. Often you only have two
days to finish a job.'

Industrial beginnings

It was an eye-opening assignment in the North Sea that
inspired Mike to concentrate on industry.

'Shell sent me up there for three days', he remem-
bers, 'and when I saw my first oil rig I flipped – it was
an incredible sight. I decided to do a series on the
North Sea for one of the colour supplements. So I went
back up and spent two weeks hitching lifts off heli-

copters and supply boats. I ended up shooting about
200 rolls of film – the opportunities were endless. But
when Shell saw the results they asked me not to sell
them to a magazine – they wanted to use them all
themselves.'

On assignment

He now works for a number of huge corporations,
including RTZ, the world's largest mining company,
and travels constantly. Last year alone, he worked in
33 countries. So it's hardly surprising that he's also
renowned for his travel photography.

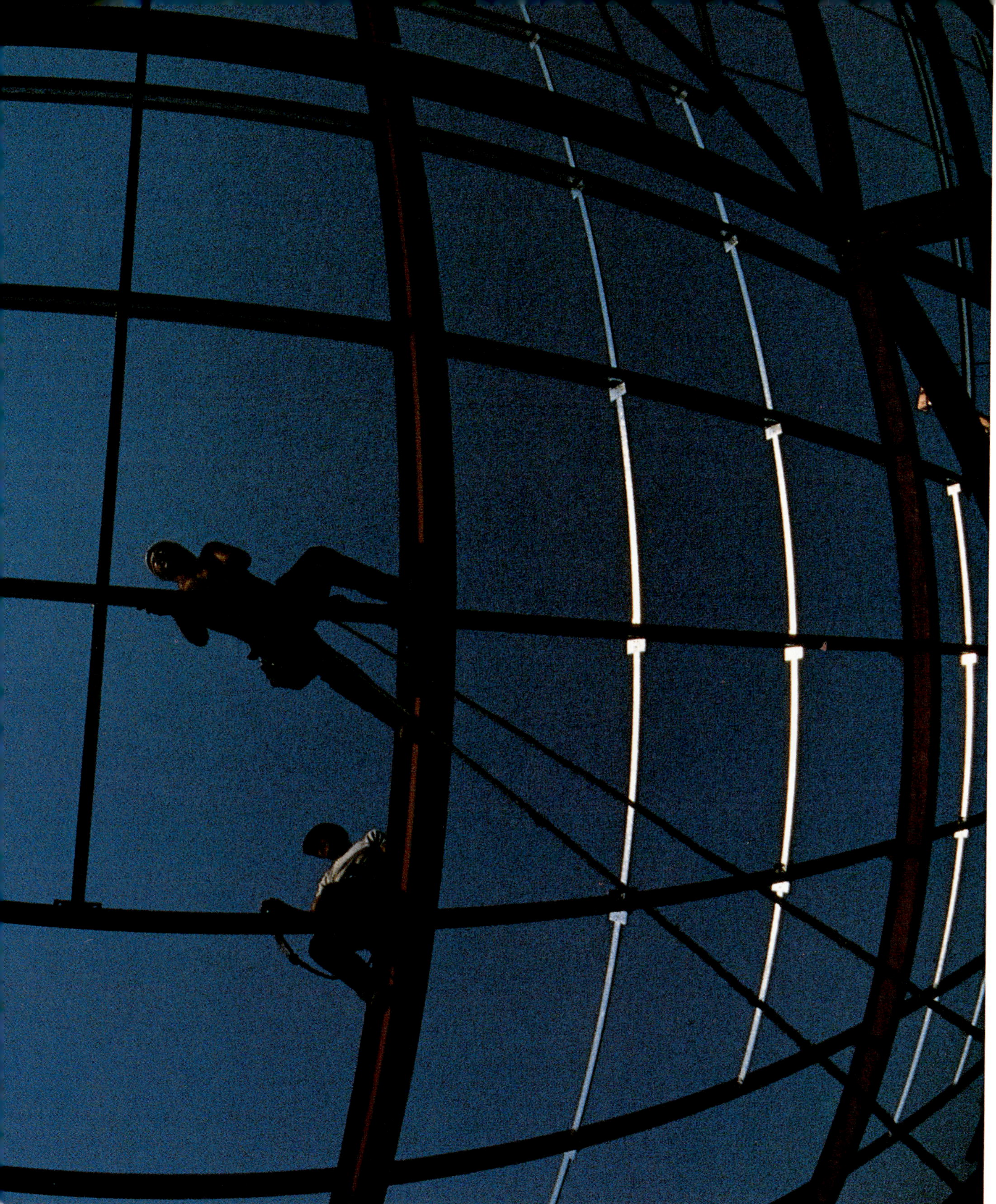

When out on a shoot, Mike generally carries three 35mm Nikon camera bodies, a number of lenses ranging from 24mm to 500mm, a tripod and two stands. He uses an American portable flash system, and on a long trip will carry around 1200 joules of power – the equivalent of some 30 portable flash units. He also takes two small Vivitar hand flashes.

'Most industrial photographers use 5 x 4in cameras and loads of artificial light, but I'm not a technical photographer. I use natural light whenever possible, and with small format cameras I can make use of greater depth of field.' At any given aperture, the smaller the format, the greater the depth of field.

'I don't need that much lighting, and because I use a portable flash system I can move around without having to worry about power points.

'Besides, I'm rarely lucky enough to have an assistant with me on long shoots, so my choice of lighting is dictated by how much I can comfortably carry. The simpler the system I use, the easier it is for me to set up on my own.

'You've got to be quick with industrial photography – you can't stop a production line just because you want to take a picture.'

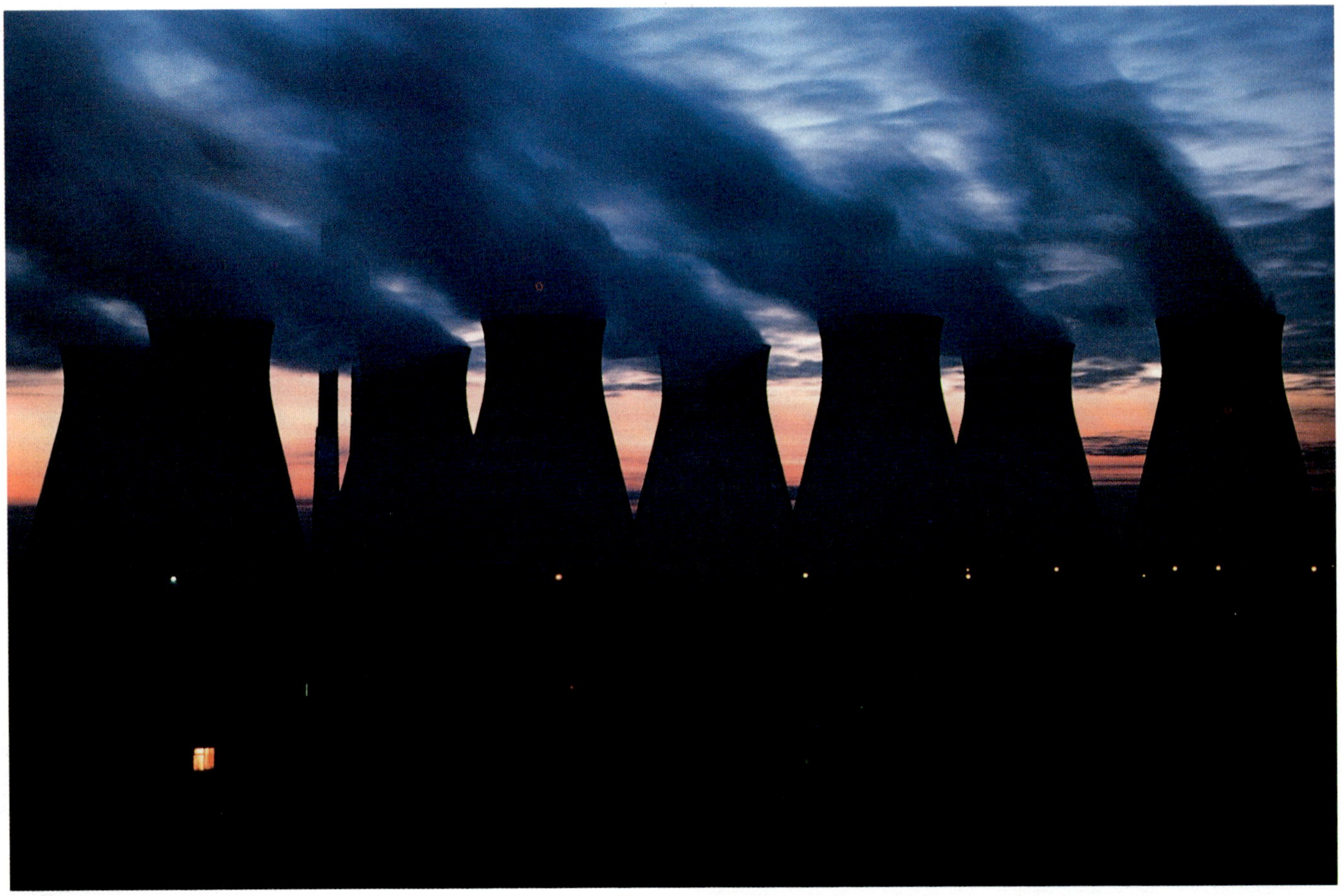

"I took this photograph of Boroughbridge Power Station in northern England from the side of the A1, using a slow exposure and a tripod. It was dusk but what really made the shot special was the house light in the left hand corner. I took a whole roll of photos of the station, but only one has that light in it. Someone must have walked into a room, got something, and walked out again. That's not pollution by the way, it's steam."

Taken on Kodachrome with a Nikon FM.

"This was taken in a Canadian steel plant. I decided to aim the light into those huge coils of rolled steel and see what happened. Because it was so highly polished, the steel acted as a mirror for itself and sent the light bouncing around inside – hence the unusual effect."

Shot on ISO 120 on a Bronica 645 medium format camera.

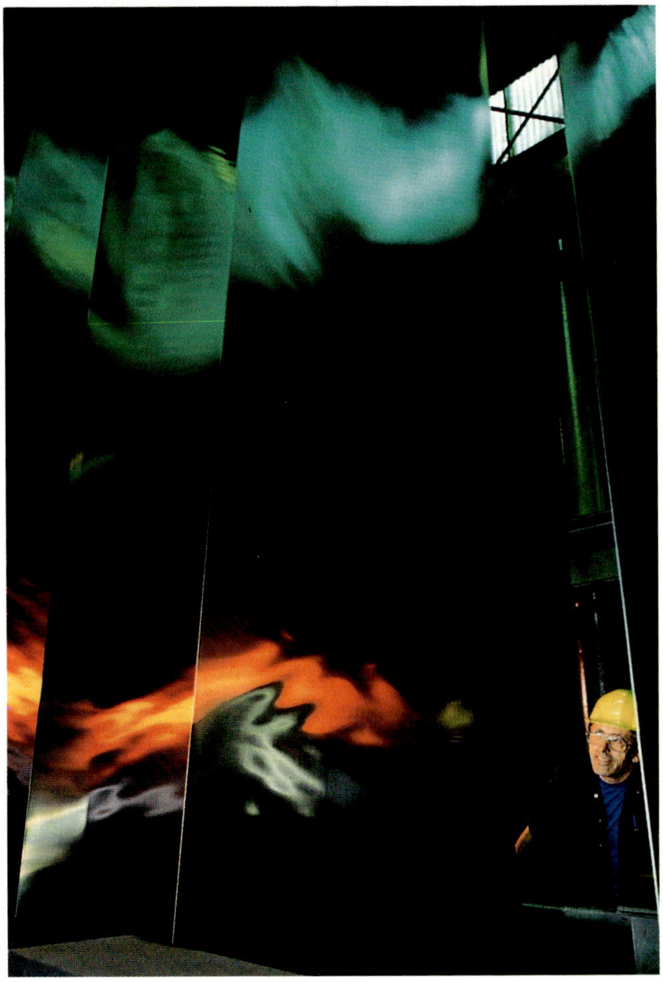

Technical details

When he's shooting indoors, Mike prefers to use his Bronica instead of a standard 35mm SLR. 'The Bronica has a good Polaroid facility so you can swap the film and see an instant print of your intended composition.

'Although most Bronicas take square 6 x 6cm pictures, I use a 645, which takes rectangular shaped 6 x 4.5cm pictures. I don't use square format – I find it too limiting.'

Monochrome for impact

In the past, black and white was the norm, and colour attracted attention because it was unusual. Now, it is the other way round. As you explore the possibilities of working with shades of grey, an exciting new world opens up.

While colour film can give you life-like pictures, black and white photography lets you interpret what you see and put a more personal stamp on it.

If you watch classic black and white movies, you'll notice that they are often more atmospheric than colour ones. That's partly because the directors carefully selected which colours would come out well in black and white. They were also masters at using the interplay between light and shade to create striking, attention grabbing images.

It's exactly the same with black and white (also known as mono or monochrome) prints. Exploring the variations of light and shade to create tonal interest is central.

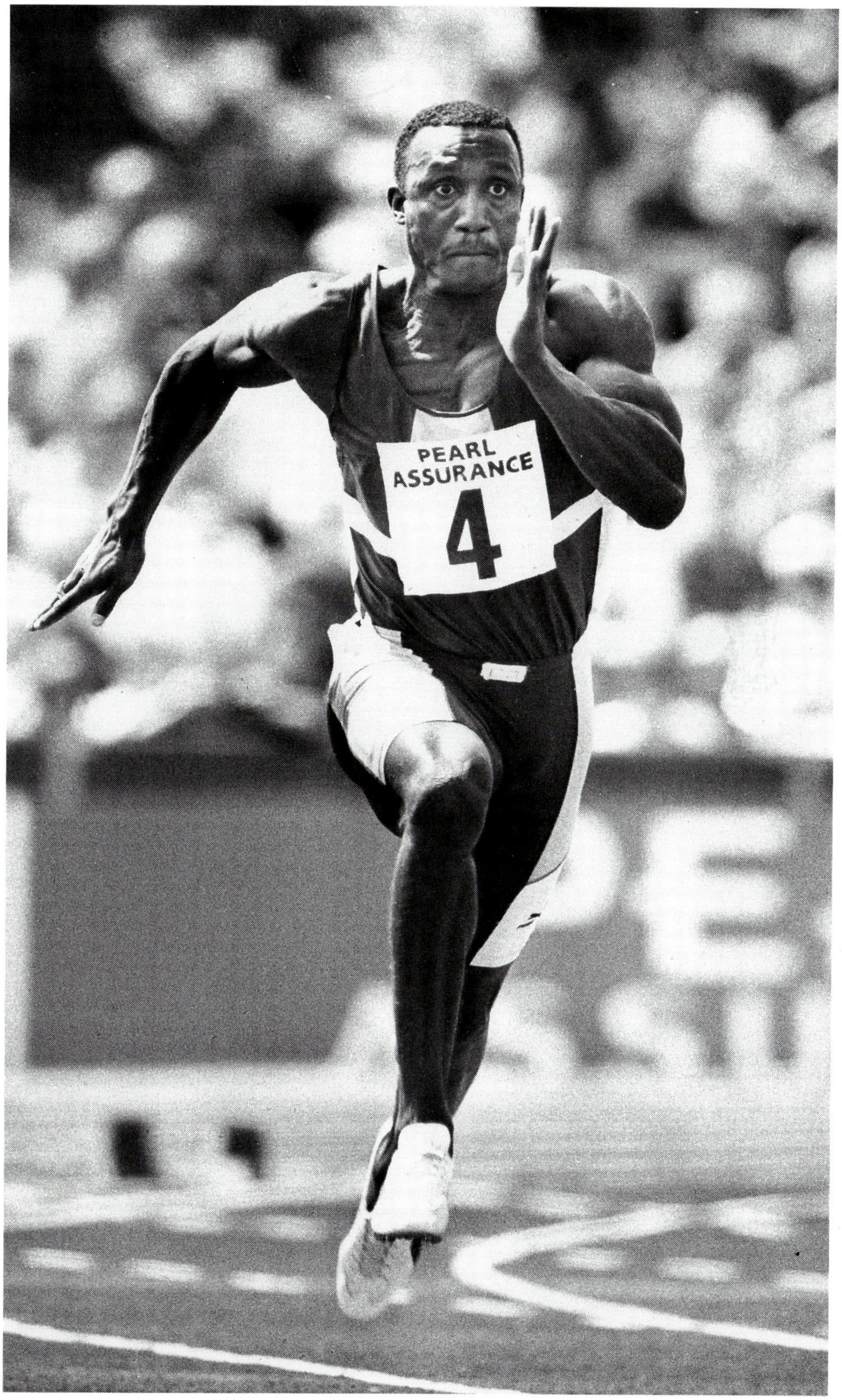

▶ *Black and white strips out clutter and reinforces drama. Undistracted by the colour of the athlete's clothes or the crowd behind him, your eye is immediately drawn to the most powerful elements of the photo – the concentration on his face and the tension in his body.*

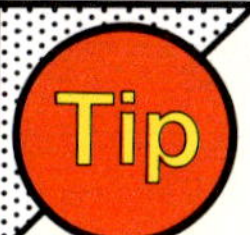

Black and white film facts

Mono film is usually cheaper than colour film. Most black and white films are print, as this gives you greater scope for being creative with tone and contrast in the darkroom. You can buy mono print film from ISO 25 to ISO 3200. Popular speeds – ISO 100, 200 and 400 – are available from chemists and high street shops, but you have to go to a specialist shop or place an order for very slow or fast films.

If you do not have your own darkroom, look in the backs of photo magazines for ads for specialist black and white printers.

A matter of tone

The first step to successful black and white photography is understanding how the tonal range in a finished print relates to the colours you see through the lens.

The second step is to recognize the link between tones and light and shade.

Tone and colour

The only way of learning to see colour as tone is to practise. Shoot a wide range of subjects so that you can then see what happens to the original colours and learn to predict how black and white film responds.

Something that looks dull in colour – greys and browns, for example – may have a really exciting tonal range in monochrome.

On the other hand, a scene full of brilliant reds, blues and greens (like garden flowers, for instance) may turn out to have too many similar tones in monochrome, and not enough contrast to break up the picture.

When experimenting, start with scenes that offer a wide range of strong colours: market stalls stacked with fruit and vegetables, a pile of cushions or brightly coloured clothes make good test subjects.

Then start looking at how muted colours behave. See what effects you can create when pale colours are in shadow, and how they change when brightly lit. Compare the results with your test run using strong colours.

You can distinguish between a surprisingly wide number of tones based on just one colour, and black and white film is almost as sensitive as your eyes. Try looking out of the window on a sunny day and seeing how many tones of a single colour you can see, starting with a deeply shadowed object and moving on to one displaying brilliant highlights.

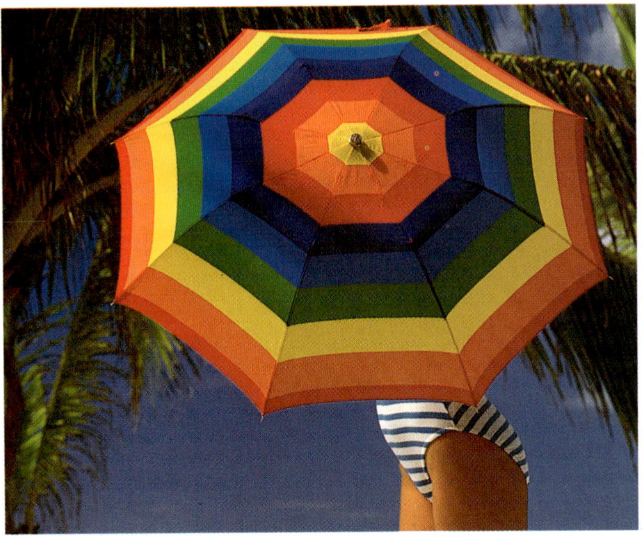

▲ *In colour, the bright stripes of the umbrella and the swimming costume provide a lively focus and separate the subject from the muted backdrop of the palm trees.*

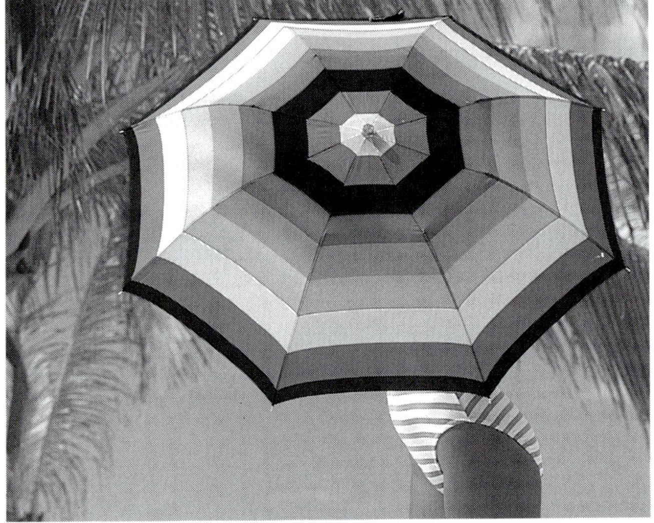

▲ *In monochrome, the picture looks drab because most of the colours in it have such similar tones. There are no interesting textures or shadows to compensate.*

Seeing colours as tones

With practice you'll soon look at a scene and know roughly what tones its colours turn into. There are some surprises: yellow becomes white, and red turns into quite a light tone.

You begin to recognize recurring patterns when you reduce colour to tone. For example, grass and green leaves become mid tone greys, while the sky during the day takes on a light tone.

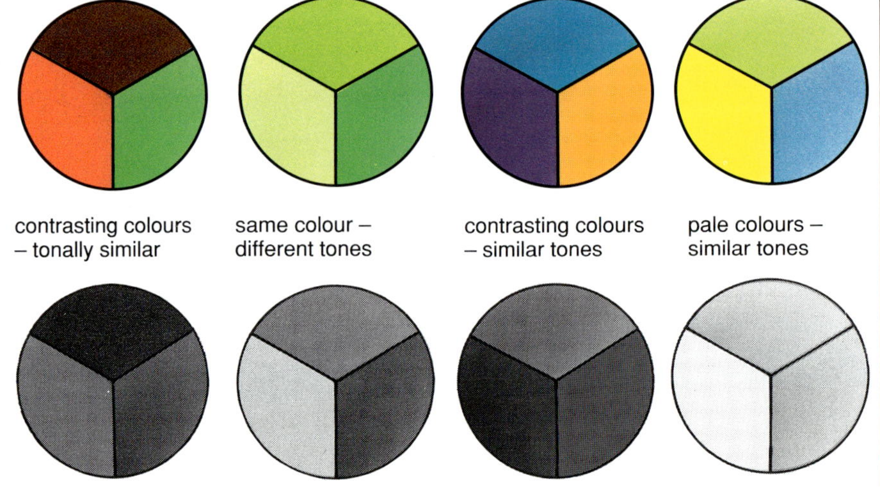

contrasting colours – tonally similar

same colour – different tones

contrasting colours – similar tones

pale colours – similar tones

Quick routes to tone

There are some short cuts to learning how colours translate into tones.
❏ Look at the subject with your eyes half closed. This makes colour less distracting so that you can identify shadow and highlight areas and locate important blocks of tone.

❏ Use the colour control on your television to switch from colour to black and white and back again. Choose a programme with a lot of colour in it, such as children's and gardening programmes. Snooker is also ideal with its clearly defined colours.

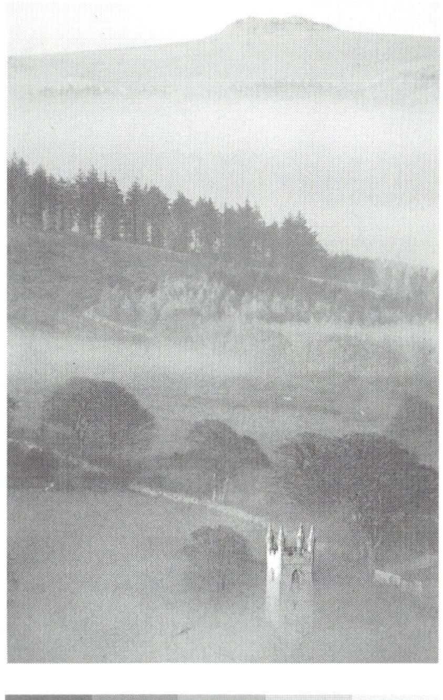

Light and shade

Colour is not the only source of tonal variation in black and white – lighting has an equally important effect. A successful black and white print often has a full range of tones, from dark shadows through mid tones to brilliant highlights.

A photograph that contains a subtle gradation of tones is pleasing to look at and can often work much better than a similar colour picture.

Wide tonal range The colours in a picture compete with light and shade for your attention. In black and white, however, you are freed from the distraction of colour in the image. You can use contrasting tones for maximum impact.

Narrow tonal range You can also achieve appealing results with a reduced number of tones. Mainly sombre or pale pictures – the shadowy interior of a forest or a snow scene, for instance – stand out. Dark and light in stark contrast, with few or no mid tones – like a figure silhouetted against a pale sky – can make striking studies too.

▲ *With a limited tonal range the few dark shades and light tints stand out. A shroud of mist subdues detail and leaves in its place a restfully mid toned country scene.*

▼ *Use the chart below left to see how many variations in tone you can identify in this photo. The range – from deep black under the bridge to a brilliant white highlight in the reflected sky – gives a tonal richness that brings out the detail in the scene.*

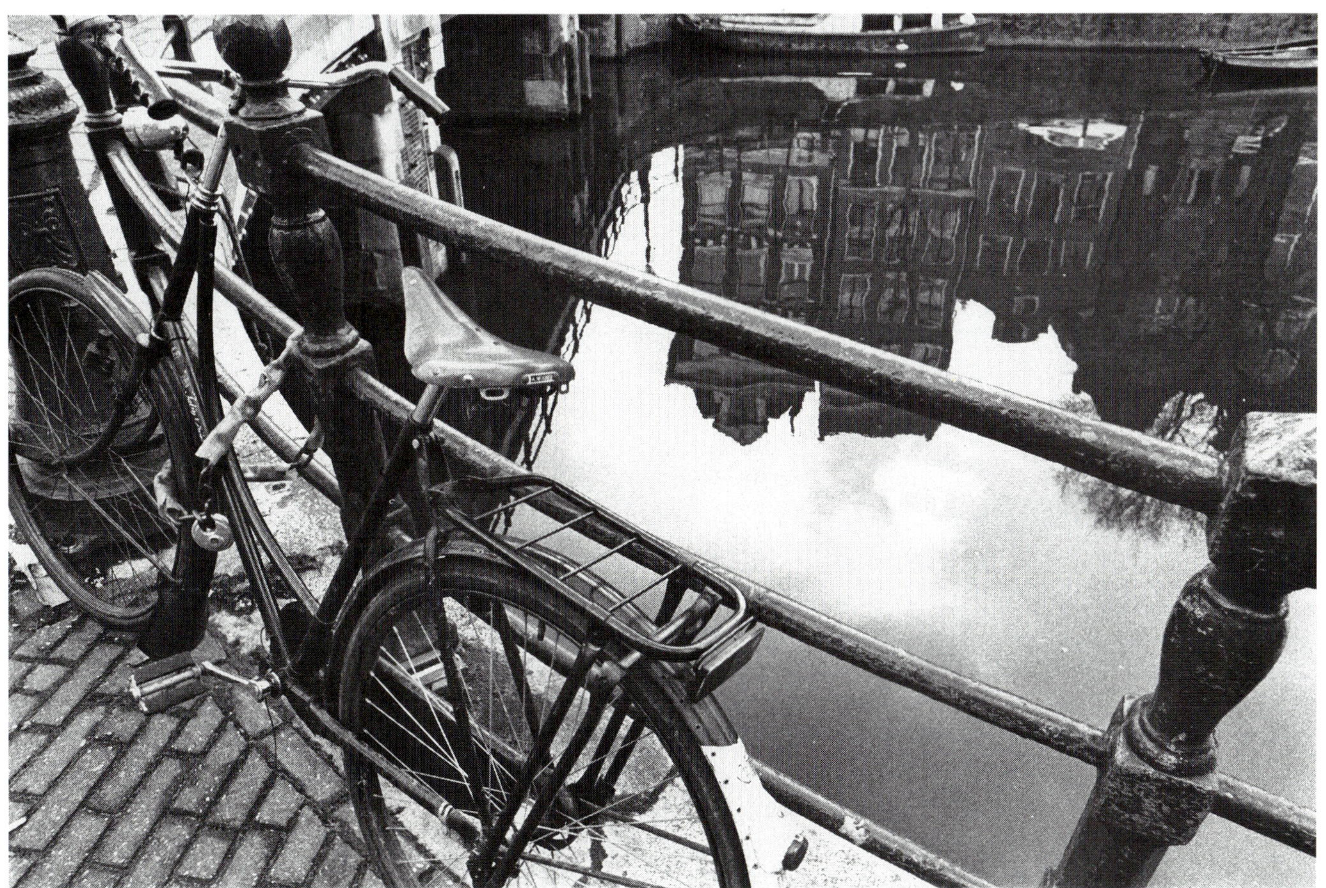

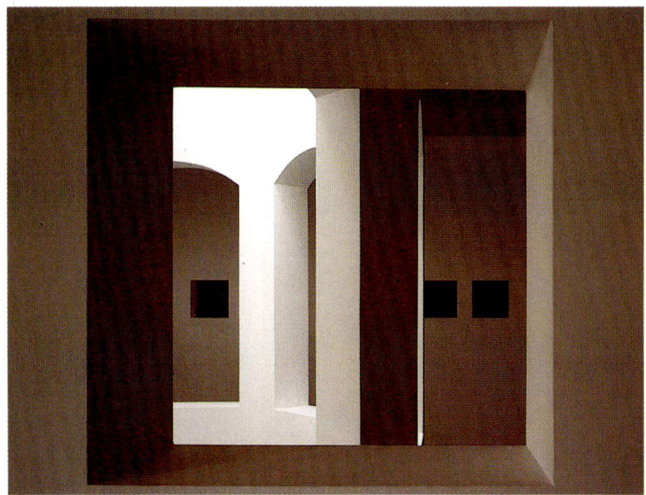

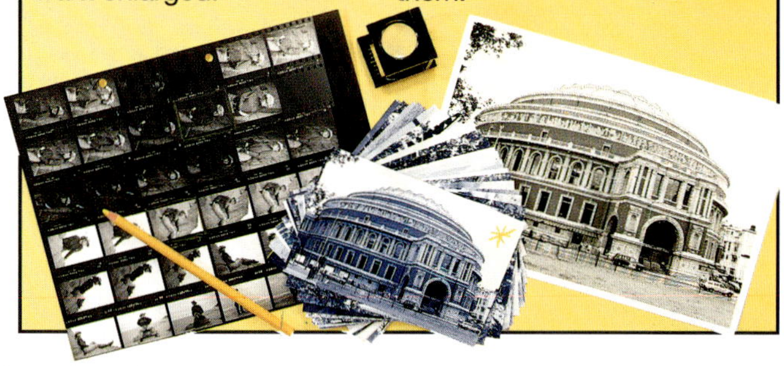

▲ Although the range of colours is narrow, it brings out depth and makes the subject matter recognizable as a building. The cool interior already looks quite abstract, but black and white can take the image a step further.

▼ The monochrome version turns the three dimensional building into a graphic pattern of shapes and contrasting tones. The thin white line stands out less in colour, but now becomes particularly striking because there are dark tones on either side of it.

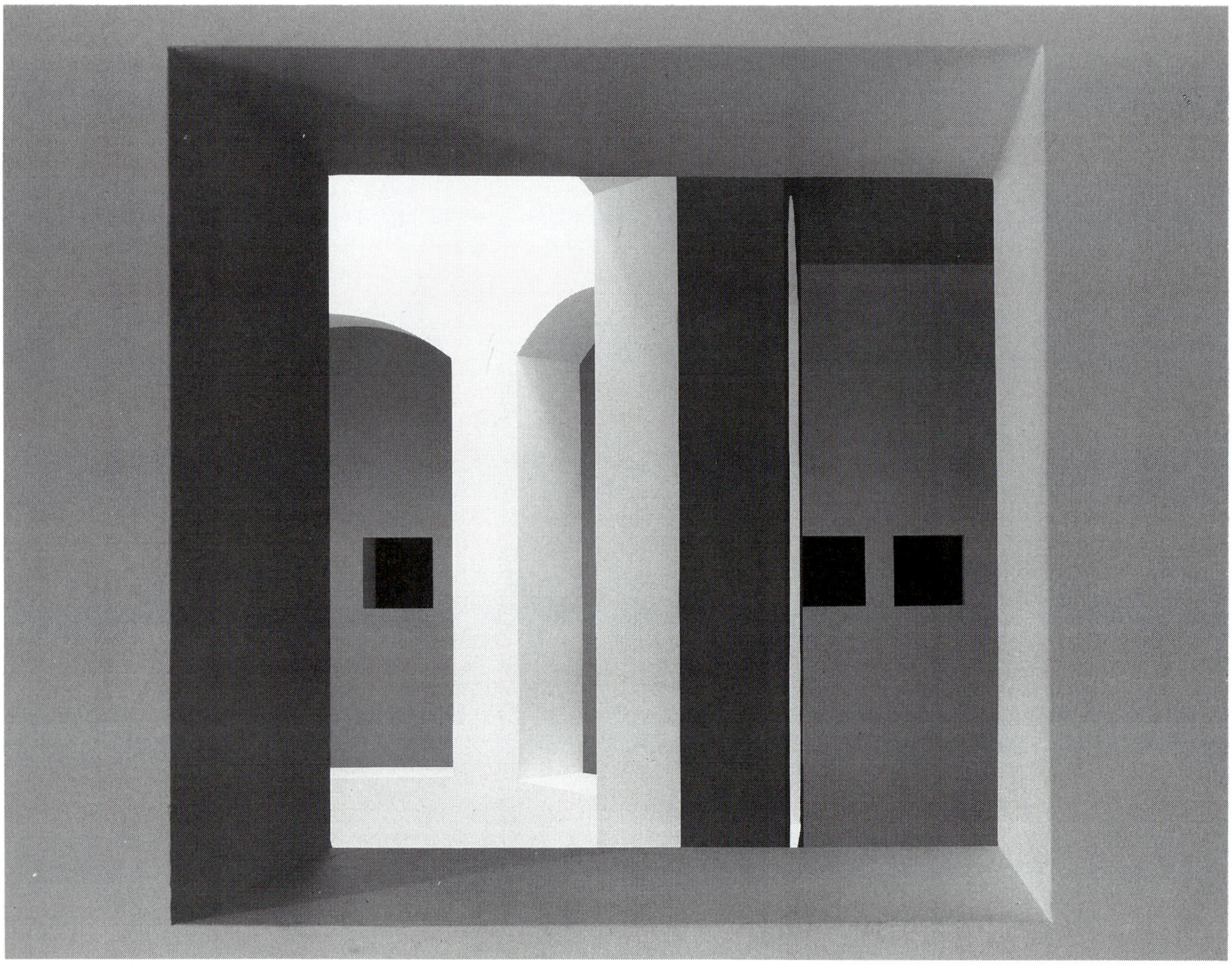

The monochrome process

Most labs take longer to develop monochrome prints than colour ones. When you take mono film to be processed, the shop sends it to a lab, or you can send it direct. Several days later you get a set of prints back, or you can ask for a contact sheet which shows same size (36x24mm) images of each negative. You can then choose which ones you want enlarged.

Speedy prints with XP2
XP2 is a mono film made by Ilford which is processed in the same way as colour prints. It's quick and easy – you can pop it into any one hour processing lab and they supply you with a set of prints. These may have a blue or brown tint because they're printed on to colour paper. If you want enlargements on black and white paper you can order them.

Exposure in black and white

Correct exposure is the key to good black and white photography. It is the single most important factor that governs the accurate reproduction of tones on film.

If you give film too little or too much development, you can save the pictures by printing on a harder or softer grade of paper. But if you expose a film insufficiently, nothing can get rid of the solid black shadows produced because there is no shadow detail recorded.

Generous exposure, on the other hand, provides you with extra creative leeway in the darkroom. A slight degree of overexposure helps record full shadow detail, without sacrificing too much of the highlights.

You can defer the decision about how much detail the picture retains, and where it appears, until the negative is printed. You can then lighten or darken the whole print, or selectively lighten ("dodge") or darken ("burn") specific areas.

Correct exposure

Exposure is the product of the light intensity falling on the film in the camera (controlled by the aperture), and the length of time you allow this light to fall on the film (controlled by the shutter).

Exposure is less critical than for colour negative, but more critical than for colour transparency. Like colour negative, but unlike colour transparency, slight overexposure will often give the best image.

The exception to this rule is Ilford's XP2, which uses the same technology as colour negative film, and should be exposed in a similar way. In general, the best exposure for black and white negative film is the minimum that produces adequate detail in the shadow areas.

You gain two main benefits by keeping exposure to the minimum:
❑ Prints have minimum grain because grain increases with exposure.

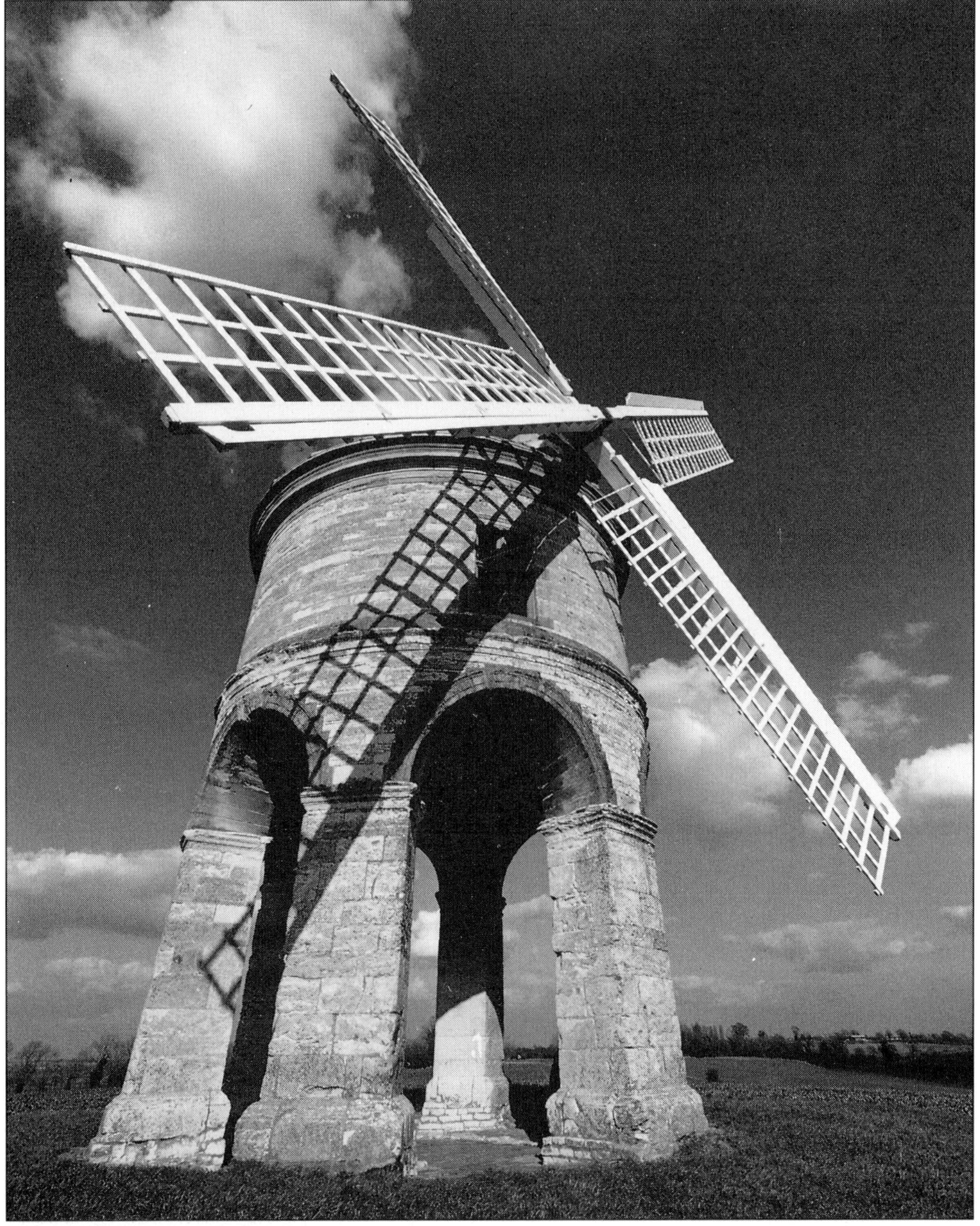

◀ *A correctly exposed negative gives the best print. Here, both the shadow and highlighted areas of the windmill are well defined. Details in the brickwork show up clearly, adding interest in both shape and texture. None of the background detail is lost, either.*

❏ Negatives retain more fine highlight detail because minimum exposure produces maximum image sharpness.

To ensure that your negatives receive just enough exposure, first decide which parts of the subject are most important. Is it the shadow areas, or the middle areas, or the highlights?

In a contrasty subject which contains a wide range of tones, you cannot hope to obtain clear tonal differentiation in all three areas at once, though if you give extra exposure and cut the development time, you can come close.

Alternatively, you may give extra

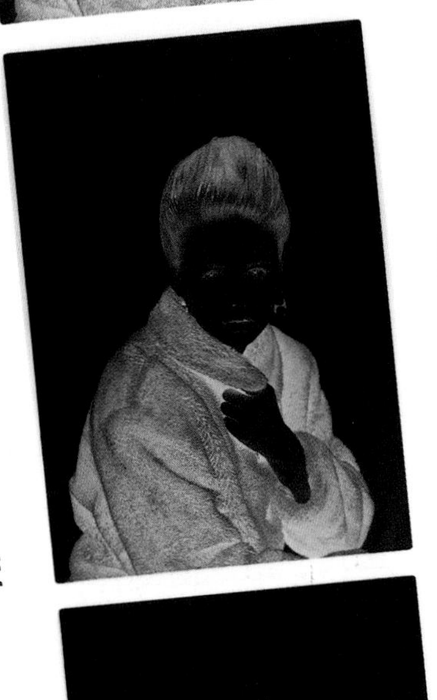

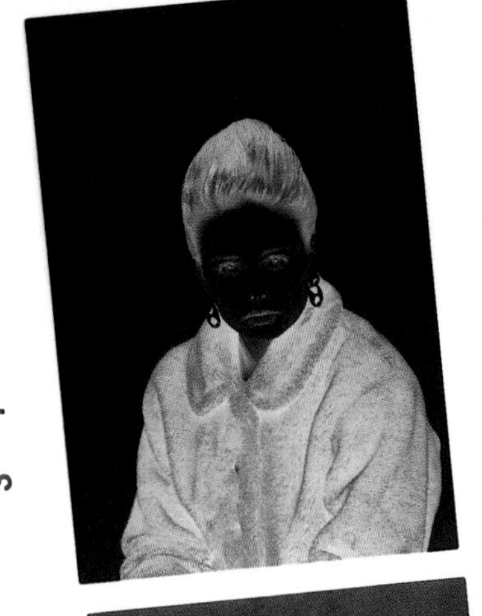

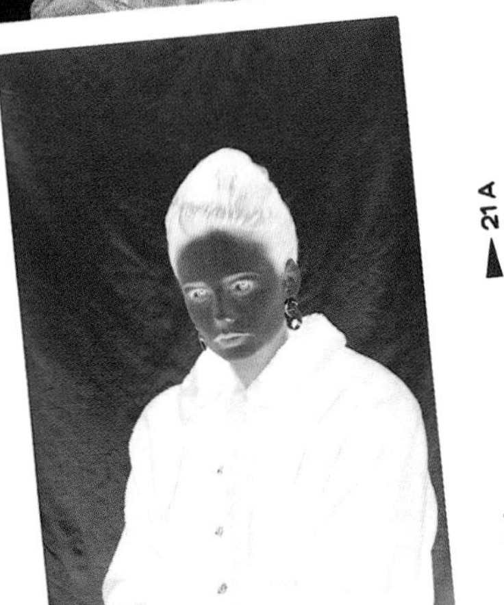

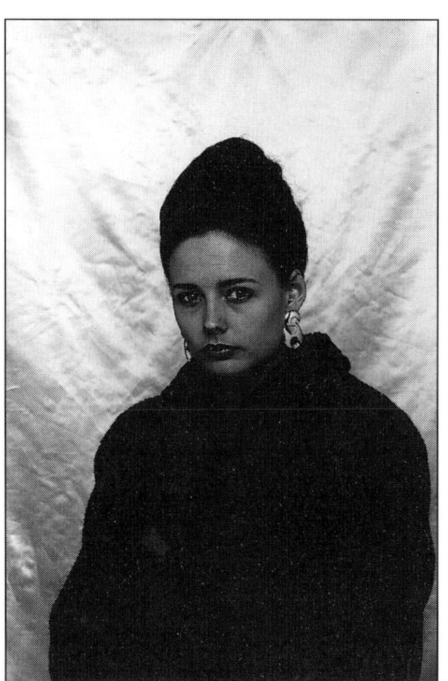

▲ *The underexposed negative produces a flat, dull looking print which lacks detail in the dark tones – especially in the hair and coat. Also, the dark tones are not well separated.*

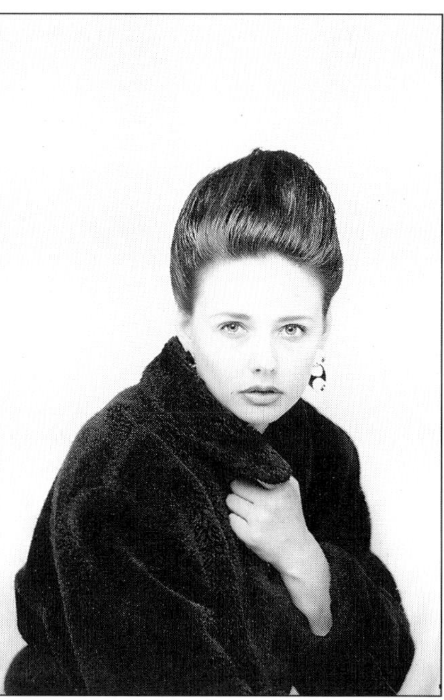

▲ *The print from the overexposed negative brings out detail in the fur coat but the face is burnt out, the features lack modelling and there are too many highlights in the hair.*

◀ *The centre negative is correctly exposed – it makes fullest use of the film's ability to record the range of tones of an average subject, where the important areas are middle grey.*

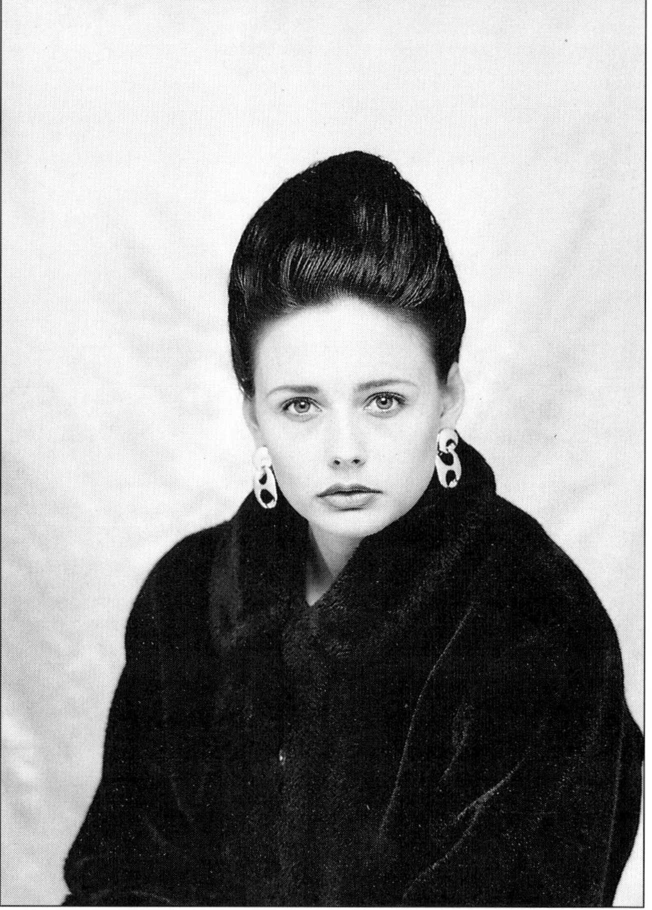

▲ *The print from the correctly exposed negative is the best. While a print can be made from a negative which has been over or underexposed by about four stops, this cannot give the optimum quality of which the film is capable.*

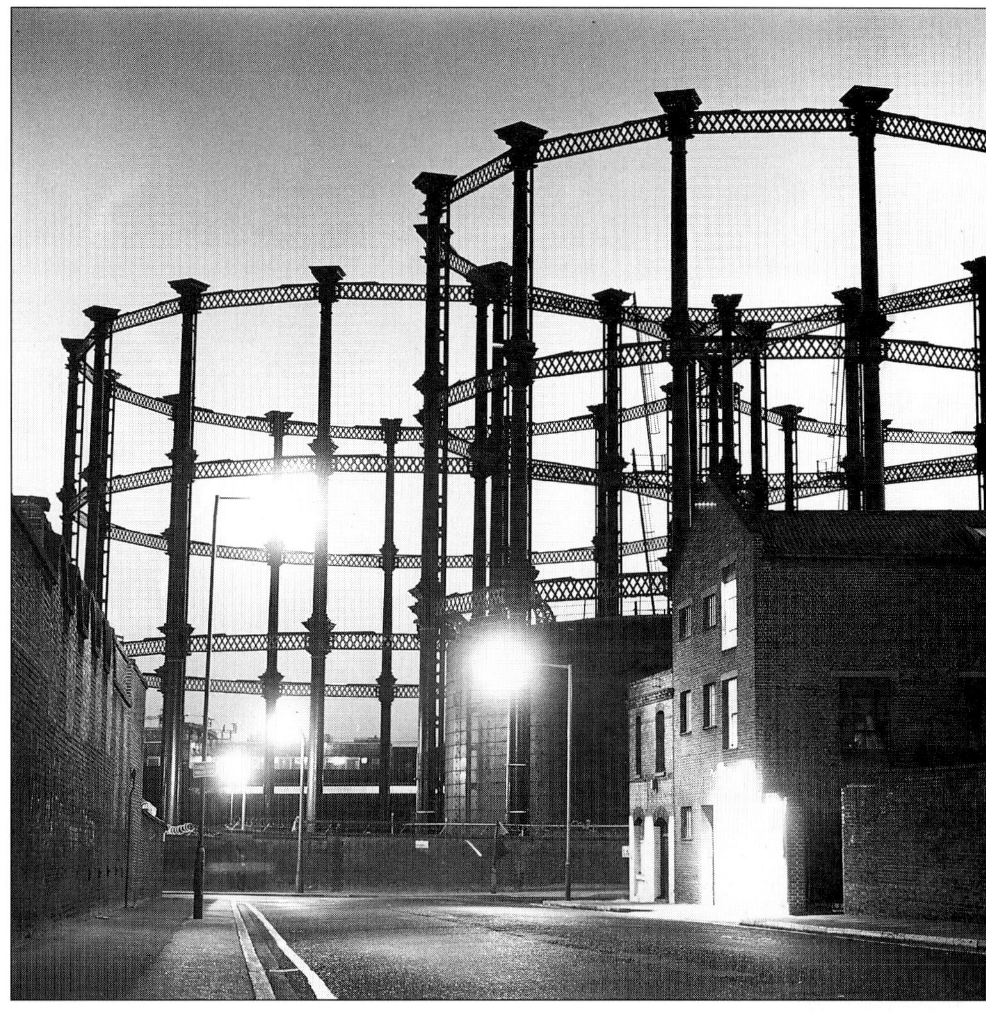

▶ In this shot of a gas works, shadow areas are more important than highlights – so the photographer exposed for the shadows. Contrast was high, with the result that brilliantly lit areas are overexposed, and have burned out to a featureless white.

▼ Here the photographer exposed for the highlighted areas, because the shadow details were irrelevant or even undesirable. The appeal of the picture springs from its graphic silhouette, which would have been ruined if the boat's details had been clearer.

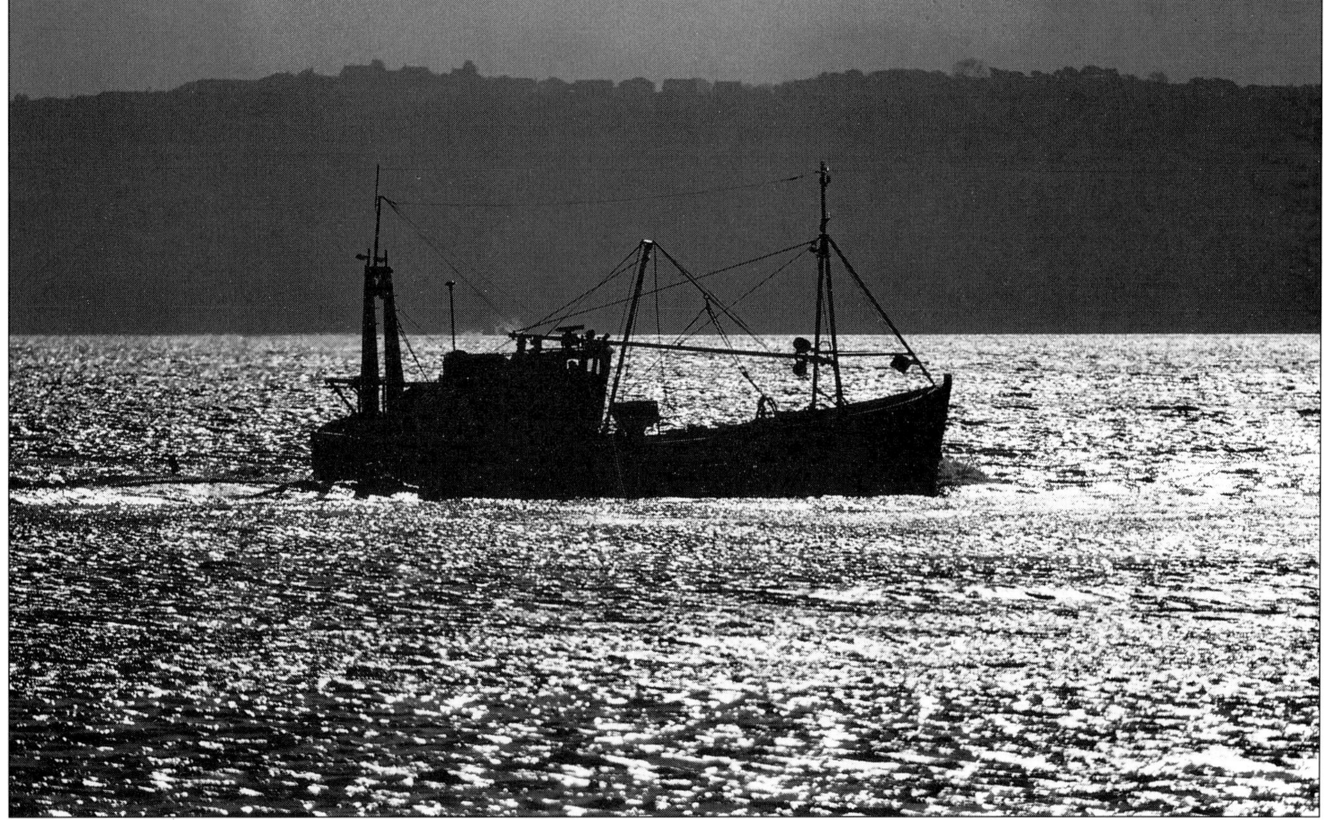

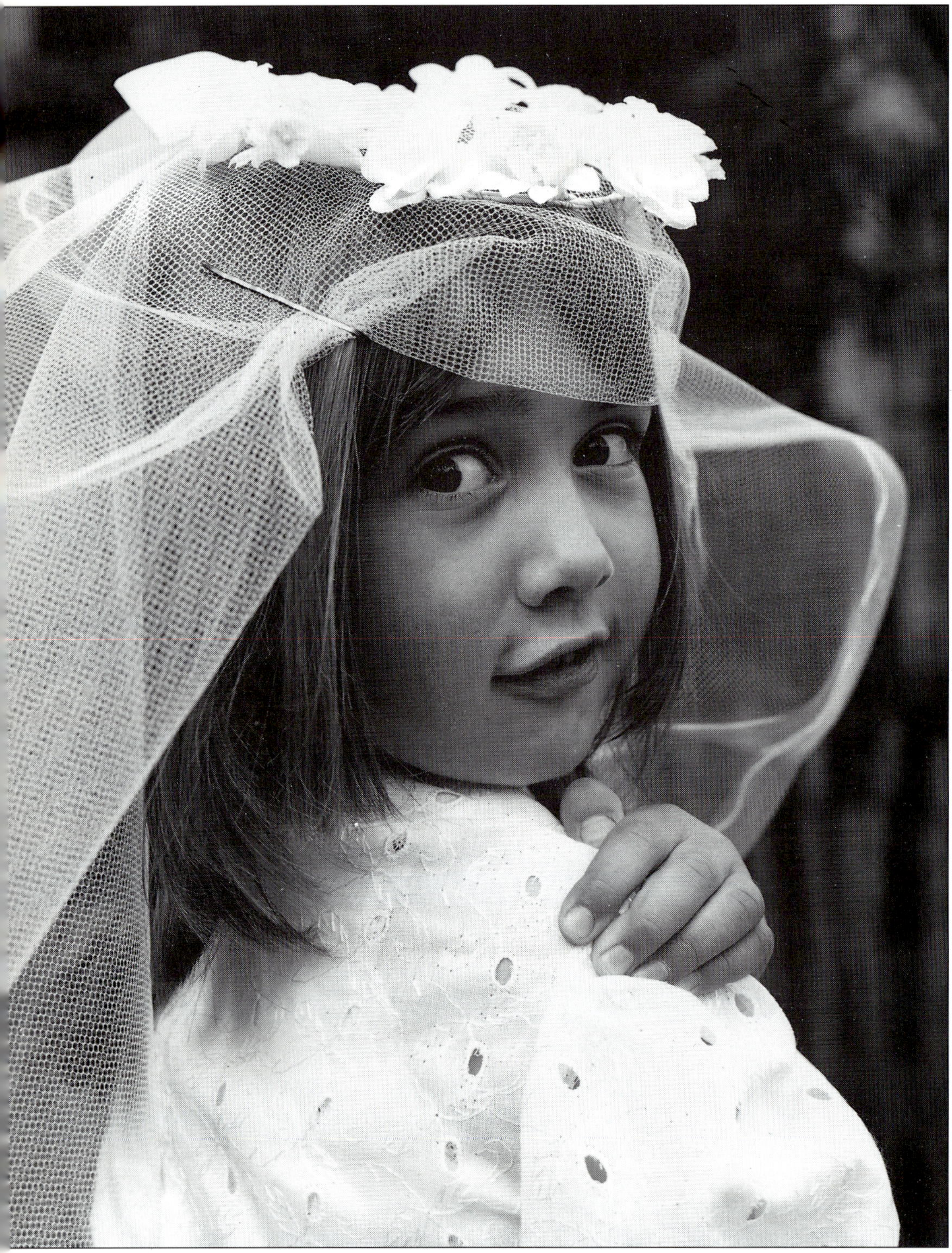

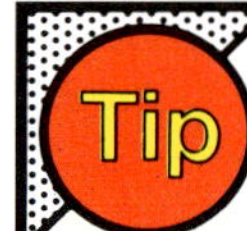

◀ *In overcast conditions like those in the picture here, the lighting is very even. Exposure is not as critical as for contrasty conditions, and a wide range of different exposures provides acceptable results. However, an exposure meter reading from the girl's hair – the darkest shadow area in which detail is essential – produces the best possible quality.*

Film speed

When you've determined an optimum film speed to suit your metering technique and equipment, use it flexibly. With very high contrast subjects, consider giving the film one stop extra exposure. Cutting development time by 15-20% will then keep contrast under control.

exposure in order to maximize detail in the shadows (in which case you will lose detail in the highlights) or you can give less exposure in order to maximize detail in the highlights (in which case you are bound to lose some detail in the shadows).

Either way, the best option is to give normal delvopment unless you want to increase contrast by giving extra development, or reduce contrast by decreasing development.

In practice, this may mean setting your camera's meter to a figure that is different from the film's nominal ISO rating. You can do this either by adjusting the camera's film speed dial or, on some cameras, by adjusting the exposure compensation dial.

Meters are set so that the area you measure from will be recorded as a mid-grey. If you take your exposure measurements from the shadow areas of the subject, the negatives will be overexposed. By moving the film speed, or exposure compensation, dial to a higher setting, you will avoid this, ensuring that the shadow detail causes a barely perceptible darkening on the negative. How much you depart from the film's ISO rating is a matter of experiment.

Filters for black and white

Using the right filter can transform a dull black and white shot into a fascinating study of mood, form and tone.

Black and white film records colour as tone, regardless of hue. This poses problems – what you see with your eye in great colour contrast may appear as uniform grey in print. For example, red and green turn out the same shade of grey if they are of equal brightness. So a red rose with green leaves of the same brightness are one shade of grey, with a dull, uninteresting print as a result.

Using a coloured filter over the camera lens lets you easily change the shades of grey in which different hues are recorded on film. With black and white film, a coloured filter lightens colours similar to that of the filter – and darkens those on the opposite side of the colour wheel. For example, when photographing a rose, a red filter darkens the leaves and lightens the flower. A green filter lightens the leaves and darkens the bloom.

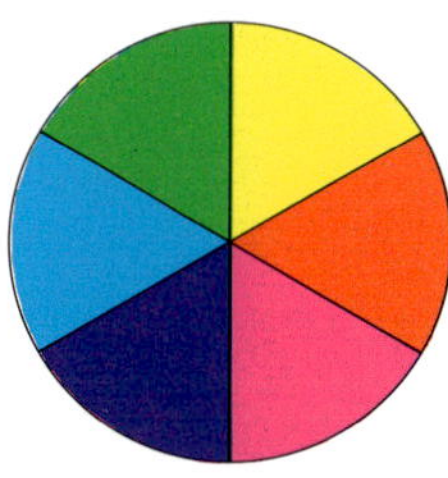

▲ *A coloured filter lightens colours on the same side of the wheel and darkens those opposite it.*

Tip Compact option

If your compact camera doesn't have a filter thread, you can still use a gelatin square mounted over your lens. Make sure it covers the meter window as well, or the camera won't compensate for light absorbed by the filter. Gelatin squares are not as long lasting as regular filters but they are useful when you can't get the right size filter for a particular lens.

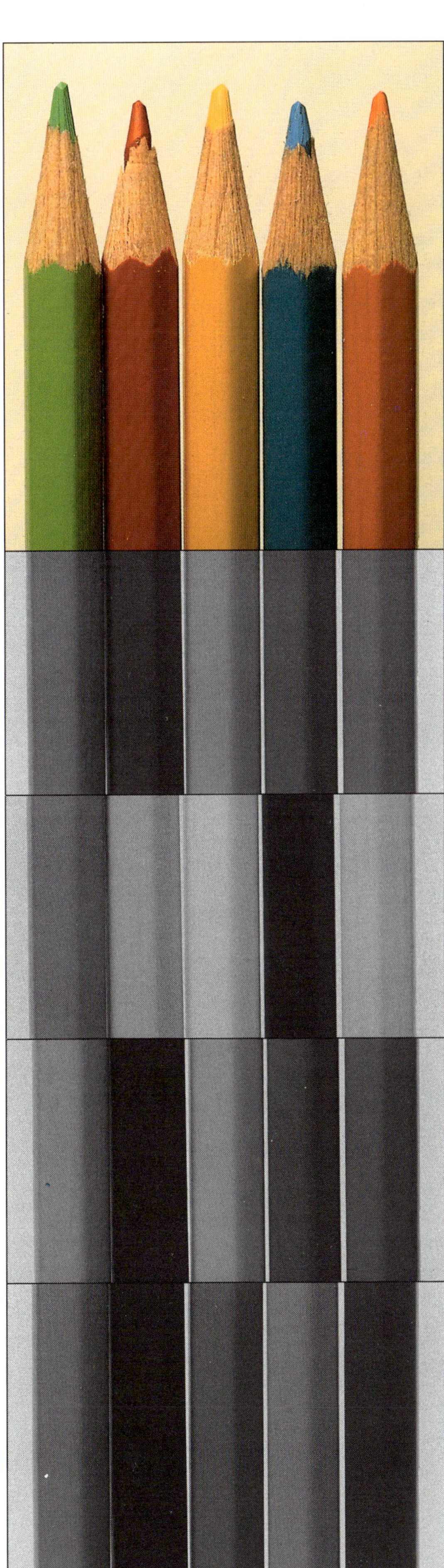

◀ *A range of coloured pencils as they appear to the eye. You can see the effect of photographing them in black and white, with and without filters (below).*

◀ *Without a filter the green, blue and orange crayons are similar shades of grey because they are of similar brightness.*

◀ *A red filter lightens the red, yellow and orange crayons. It darkens the blue crayon (an opposite colour).*

◀ *A green filter lightens the green crayon and darkens the red crayon.*

◀ *A blue filter lightens the blue crayon and darkens the red, yellow and orange crayons.*

The sky's the limit

The main use for filters is in landscape photography. With no filter, the sky is likely to record as pale or white and so clouds, especially white ones, are hardly visible.

The solution is to use a yellow, orange or red filter to absorb increasing amounts of blue light. This produces a darker tone to represent blue on the final print, so clouds appear light in contrast. Because they are blue tinged, shadows are darkened dramatically, too. The darker the filter you use the more exaggerated the effect.

❏ A medium strength yellow filter records blue sky as a light grey tone, which looks quite natural in print.

❏ For a more dramatic effect, try an orange filter, which records blue as a mid tone.

❏ A red filter records blue as very dark grey or even black.

Filter tip

Though warm-coloured filters darken green colours, grass, leaves and trees reflect so much yellow light that they do not suffer. Using a green filter lightens foliage but has only a slight effect on sky tones.

Used with care, darker filters can add bite to an otherwise flat photograph, juggle tone to give specific subjects more impact and add drama.

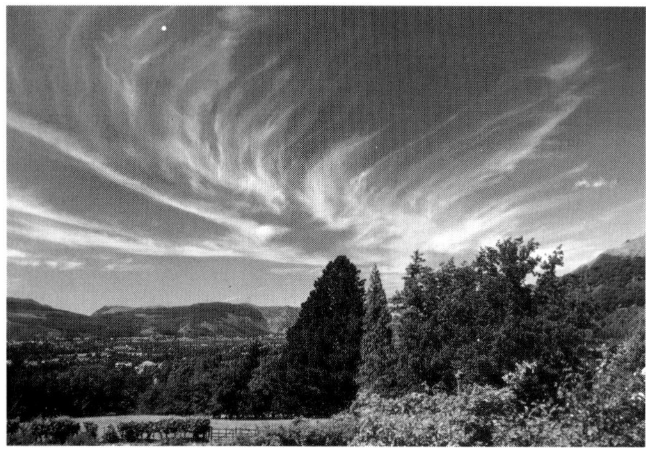

▲ In this landscape shot which was taken without a filter, the clouds look wispy and the trees in the foreground lack detail.

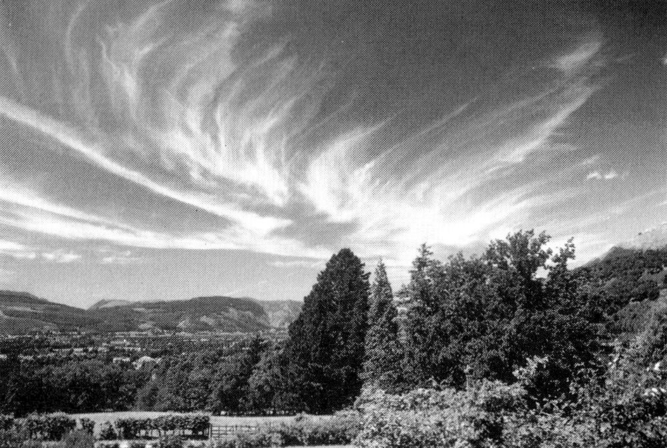

▼ A red filter darkens the whole picture considerably, increases contrast and brings out highlights in the hedge in the foreground.

▲ A yellow filter darkens the sky and draws attention to details of the clouds and leaves on the trees. Shadows under the hedges are strong.

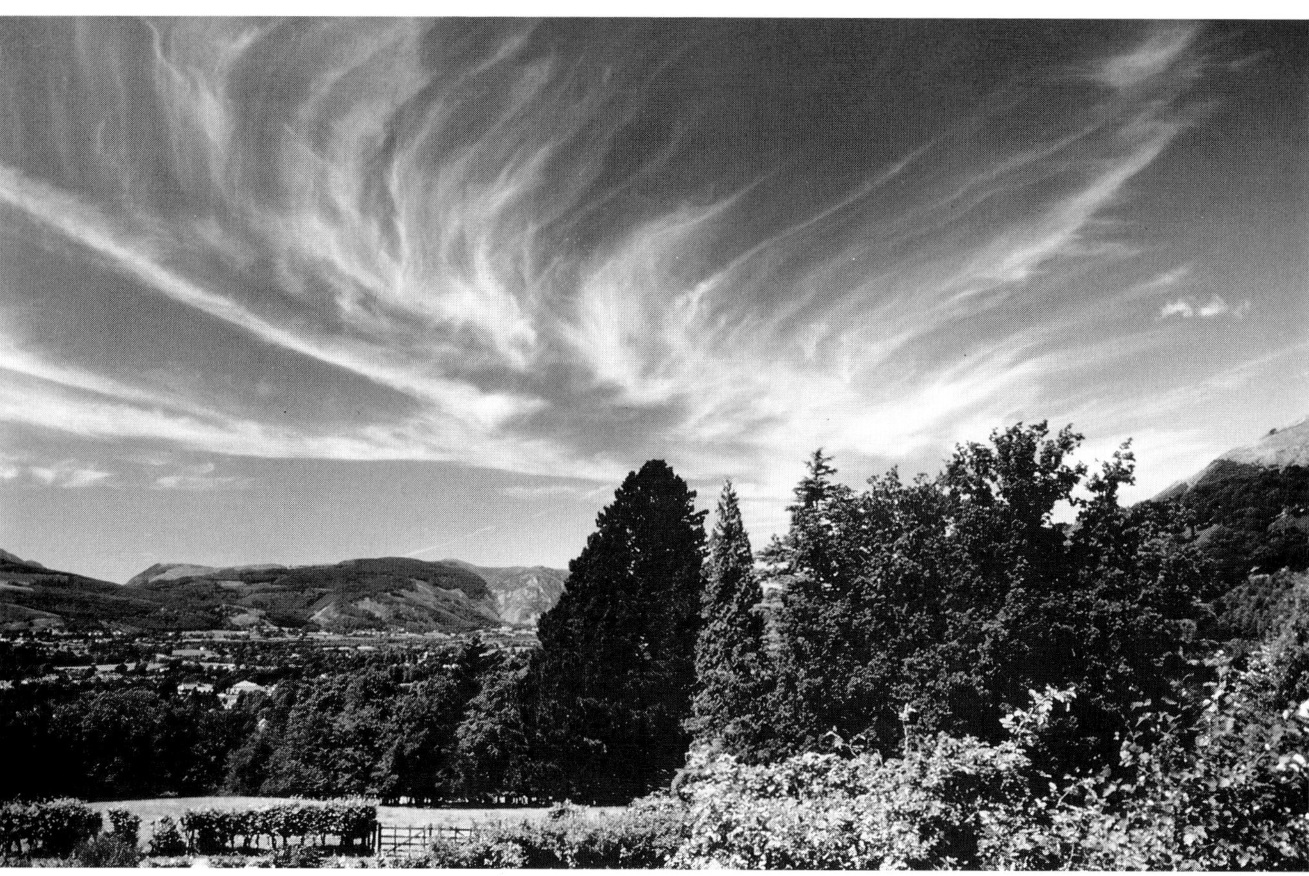

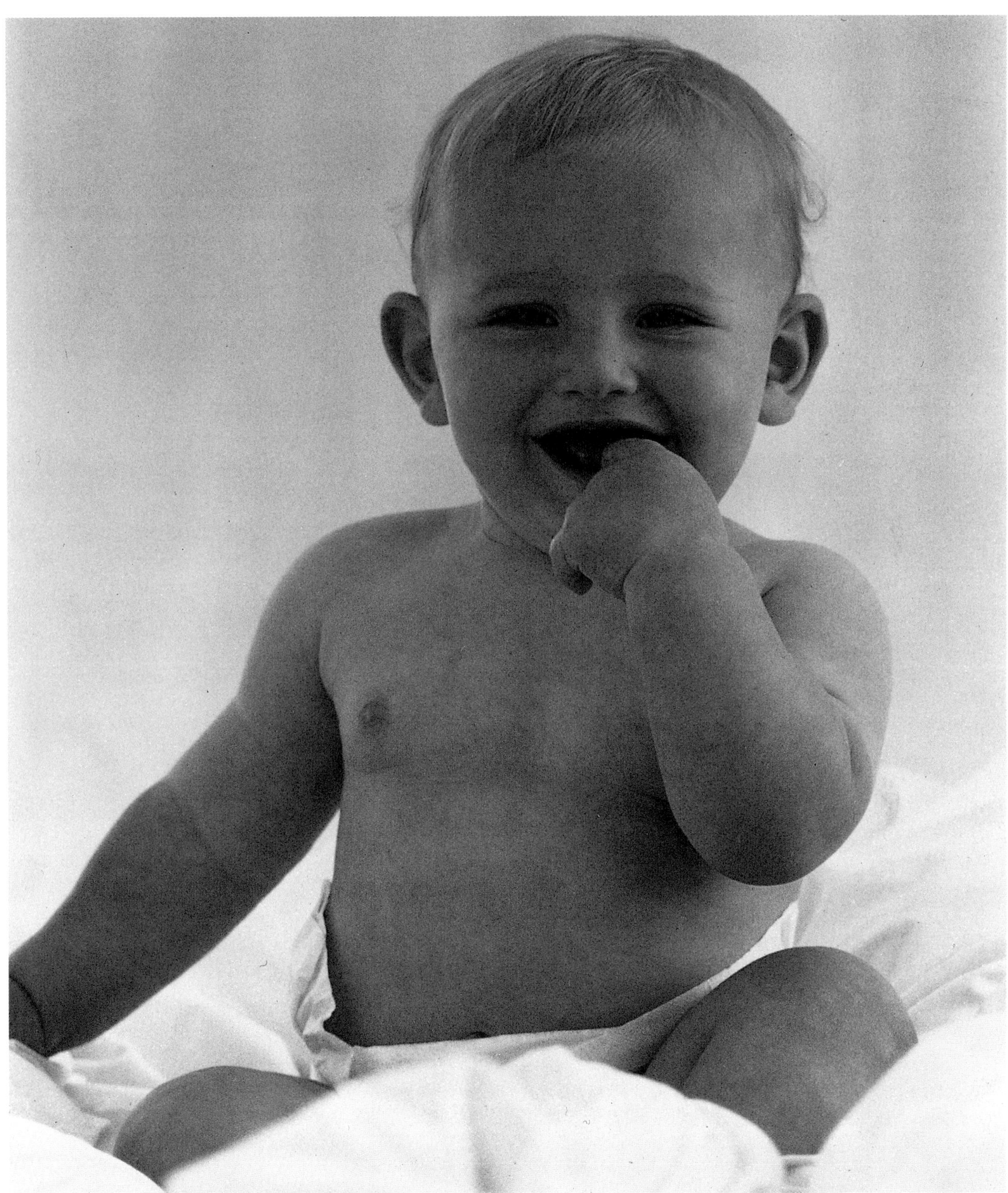

Portrait problems

In daylight, portraits sometimes suffer from pale, insipid skin tones. The solution is a pale green or yellow/green filter to darken both the skin tone and the blue tone of the sky.

Artificial light poses a different problem. Tungsten halogen lighting has a warm cast which has the advantage of hiding blemishes, but leaves flesh tones rather pale.

If you want true tones, correct the light with a blue Kodak Wratten 80A filter. A blue filter also prevents blue eyes from appearing too dark.

▲ *A young baby's skin can look deathly pale if photographed under tungsten halogen lighting . Fitting a blue filter over the camera lens restores the baby's natural skin tones for a more realistic photograph.*

Here, the photographer has captured the variety of natural tones in the infant's face to create a delightful portrait.

Filter factors

All filters for black and white film cut down on the light entering a camera. This interference is minimal in the case of some filters but others can considerably reduce the amount of light that reaches the film and so need an increase in exposure. Cameras which have TTL (through the lens) meter systems do not require any adjustment as the meter takes into account the reduced light, except with some deep orange and red filters. The amount of extra exposure needed on cameras *without* TTL metering depends on the filter and is known as the filter factor. The darker the filter, the larger the filter factor.

Most filters are marked with a factor which is expressed by a number preceded or followed by an x (see chart on right). A filter with a factor of x1 requires no additional exposure but a x2 filter requires an extra f stop, while a x4 filter needs an extra two f stops. An alternative method is to express the correction with a minus number. A filter marked -1 needs one extra f stop, -2 two stops and so on.

Filter factors vary with different light sources. The factor given on the filter is usually calculated for daylight, so check the instructions supplied before using any filter under artificial light.

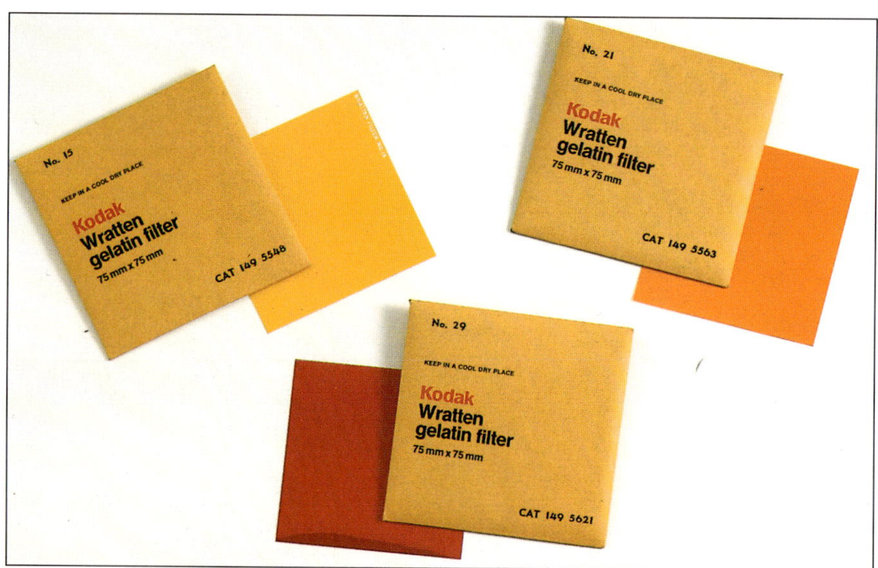

Filter factor (x)	Exposure increase (stops)
1.25	⅓
1.5	⅔
1.75	¾
2	1
2.25	1¼
2.5	1⅓
2.75	1½
3	1⅔
3.5	1¾
4	2
4.5	2¼
5	2⅓
6	2⅔

▲ *Gelatin filters are delicate, so handle them with care and store them in a cool place. You can use two at a time over the lens. It's best to use a filter holder, rather than tape.*

Types of filter

Modern filters are made from strong glass or acrylic plastic. These are either mounted in a metal ring which screws on to the front of the lens, or made to fit a universal holder.

Filters are made in different sizes – so take your camera along to a photographic shop and ask for the size you want.

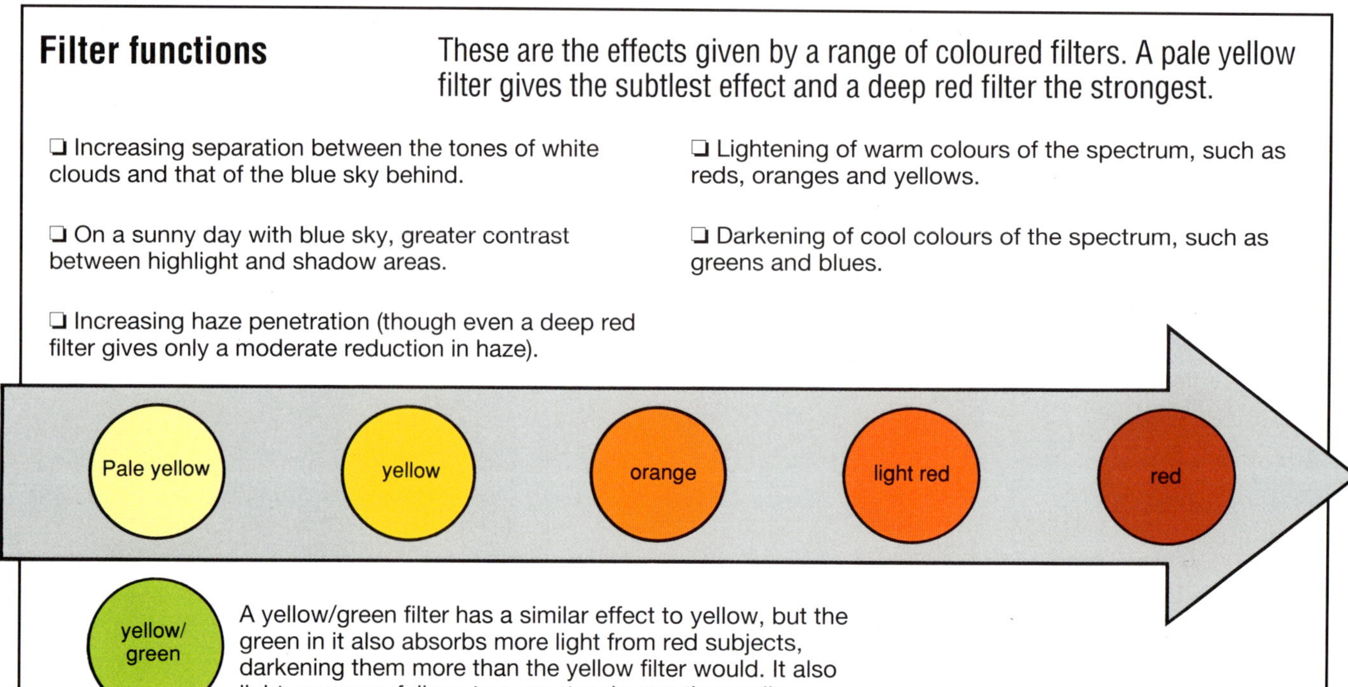

Filter functions

These are the effects given by a range of coloured filters. A pale yellow filter gives the subtlest effect and a deep red filter the strongest.

❏ Increasing separation between the tones of white clouds and that of the blue sky behind.

❏ On a sunny day with blue sky, greater contrast between highlight and shadow areas.

❏ Increasing haze penetration (though even a deep red filter gives only a moderate reduction in haze).

❏ Lightening of warm colours of the spectrum, such as reds, oranges and yellows.

❏ Darkening of cool colours of the spectrum, such as greens and blues.

A yellow/green filter has a similar effect to yellow, but the green in it also absorbs more light from red subjects, darkening them more than the yellow filter would. It also lightens green foliage to a greater degree than yellow.

Kevin Westenberg – Breaking the rules

Mixed light sources, out-of-balance film, deliberate camera shake and processing films in the wrong chemistry are only some of the techniques which make this Canadian's work so unusual.

'To take interesting pictures of a rock band', says Kevin Westenberg, 'you have to be prepared to take risks. If you just take a straight shot of a group against a backdrop it's going to look very boring. Most musicians aren't particularly glamorous looking people, so you have to make them look good on film. They're often very static subjects as well, so you have to try and build up an atmosphere around them.'

He employs a variety of techniques to make his studio portraits look different. He uses coloured filters, mixes flash and tungsten to achieve shadowy effects and reverse processes film to distort the colour and heighten the contrast. He is also very meticulous about printing. 'I do all my own black and white printing, and oversee all the colour. Printing is an extremely important part of the process, and I'll spend a long time making sure an image is exactly as I want it.'

His distinctive approach has made him popular with musicians, and recent subjects include Lou Reed, Primal Scream, Jane's Addiction, EMF, Sinead O'Connor, XTC, Ice T and Marc Almond.

Outside the studio, he often has to work very quickly.

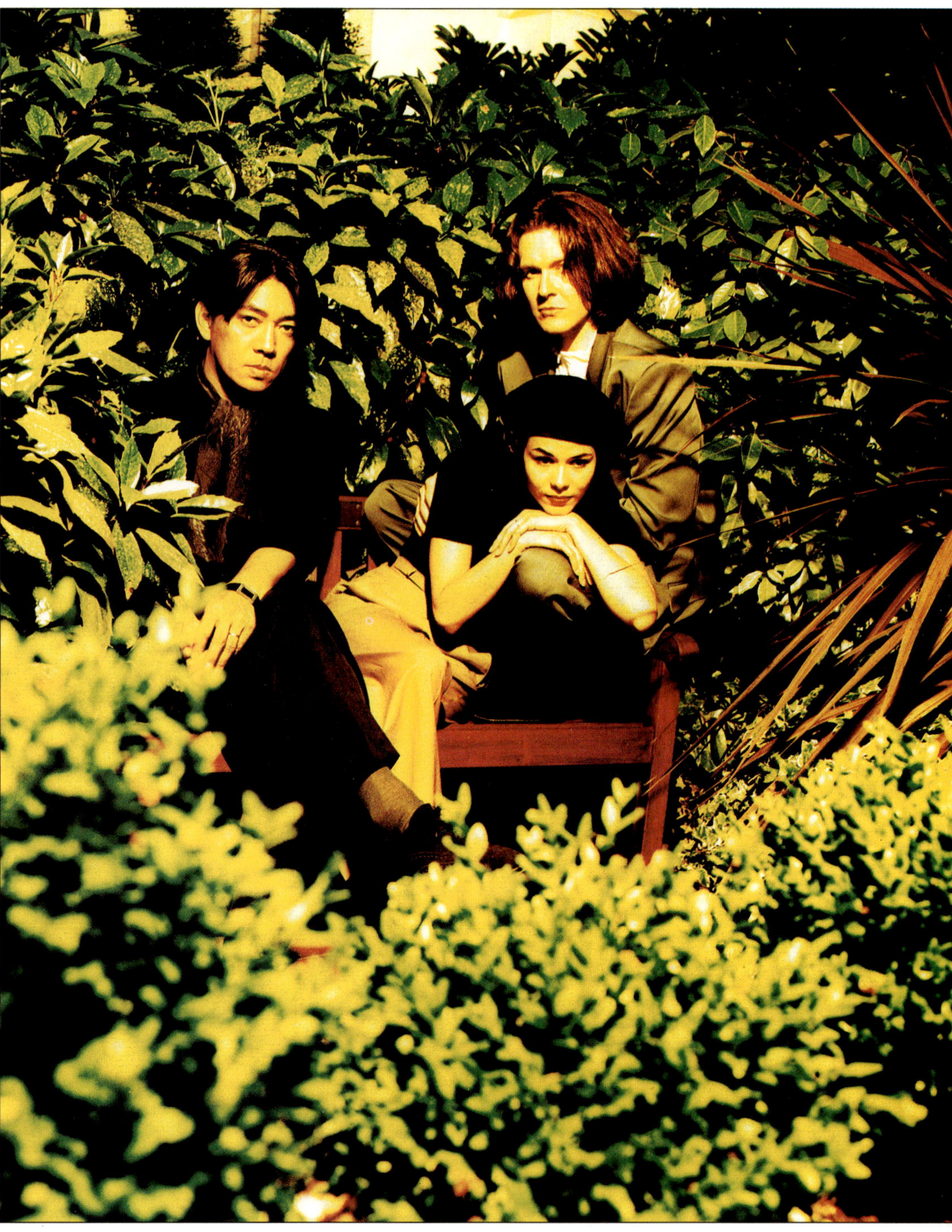

"I took this shot of Ruichi Sakamoto, David Sylvian and Ingrid Chevez outside a hotel in London. The sky was overcast so I had to resort to artificial light. I used one light underneath the bushes and a larger one above the shot. Reverse processing has exaggerated the unusual effect of flash outdoors." Taken on a Mamiya RZ67 medium format camera with a 90mm lens and flash on reverse processed Ektachrome ISO 100 slide film at 1/125th sec and f4.

Technical details

Kevin took this shot on slide film and then processed the roll in chemicals designed for colour negatives. This 'reverse processing' dramatically increases the contrast in an image and noticeably distorts the colour. The effect can be controlled by using filters in the printing.

Kevin's big priority when printing in colour is to get the skin tones right. 'I like skin tones to be as realistic as possible', he explains, 'and whatever happens to the colours around the face is less important to me. Reverse processing is a bit of a fad at the moment, but the technique will develop as time goes on.'

'I enjoy the challenge of only having ten minutes to get a rushed publicity portrait or a live shot', he explains, 'because it's a welcome change from spending eight hours in the studio trying to get a complicated lighting set up right. The pressure often brings out the best in you.'

Live work

Kevin's career began when he walked into the offices of the *New Musical Express* in London and showed them some travel shots he'd taken on his first visit to Europe. They asked him to go to a rock concert and take some pictures – he went to six in a week and came back with more than 40 black and white prints. 'I think they were impressed by my enthusiasm', he says. He began working regularly for them, and spent three years concentrating solely on live work. 'I found it very satisfying while it lasted', he explains, 'but doing concerts all the time became a bit wearing. There are some venues where the lighting's so bad that it's difficult to get decent pictures.'

'I tend to cover less concerts now', he says, 'but I still really enjoy the spontaneity of it. It's easier for me nowadays because being a bit more established means you get much better access at concerts.' He has recently begun experimenting with still life, and would like to get involved with stills for movies, but music remains his main concern. 'I get along with musicians', he explains, 'and I'm very interested in what they do, otherwise I wouldn't want to photograph them.'

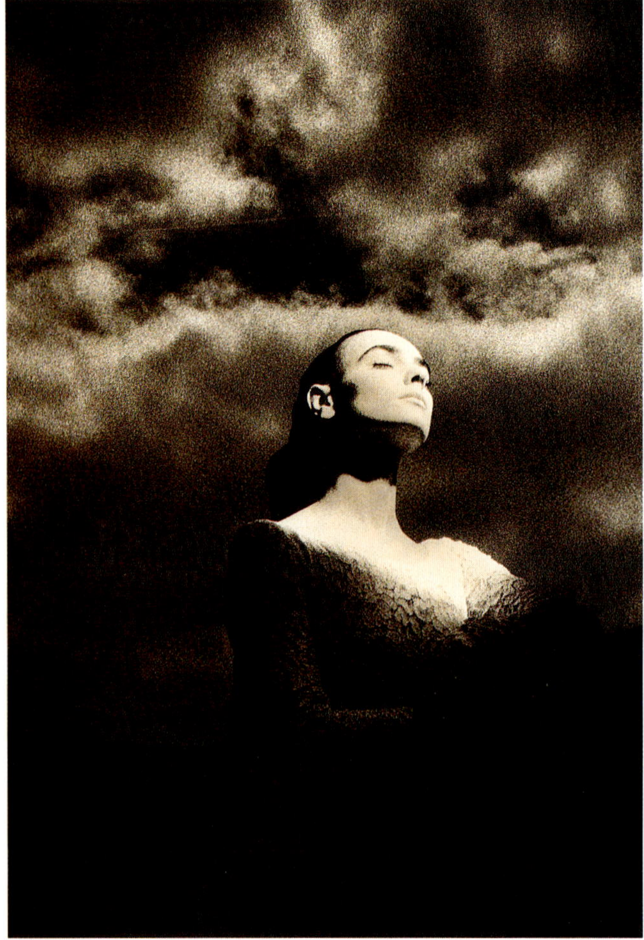

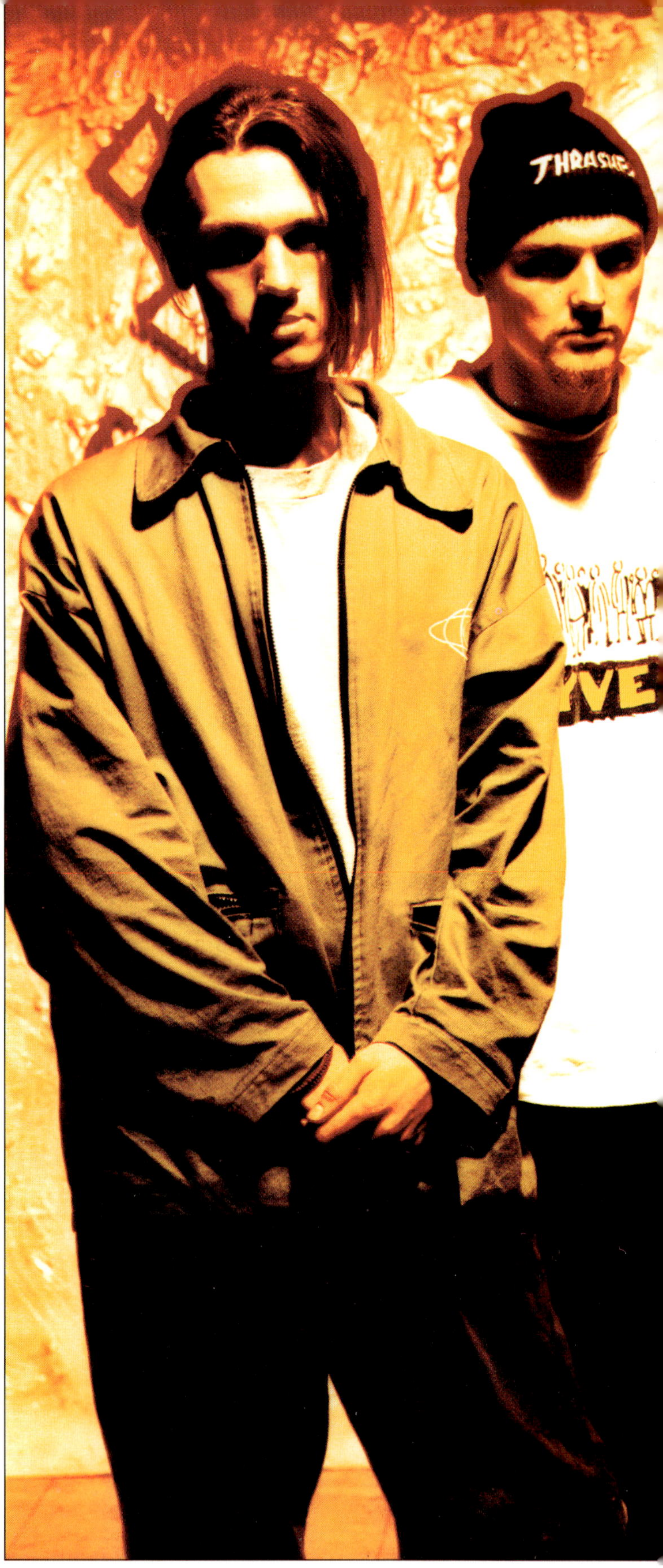

"This is Irish rock singer Sinead O'Connor. She has a lovely face, but she doesn't really enjoy having her picture taken. I had about 15 minutes to take a shot of her, so we went up on to the roof of the record company. The sky was very dark overhead but the sun was peeping through the clouds, so I got her to face right into the light and then exaggerated the overall effect in the printing." Taken on a Canon EOS 1 with a 28-80mm zoom lens on Kodak T-Max ISO 100 film at 1/60th sec and f8.

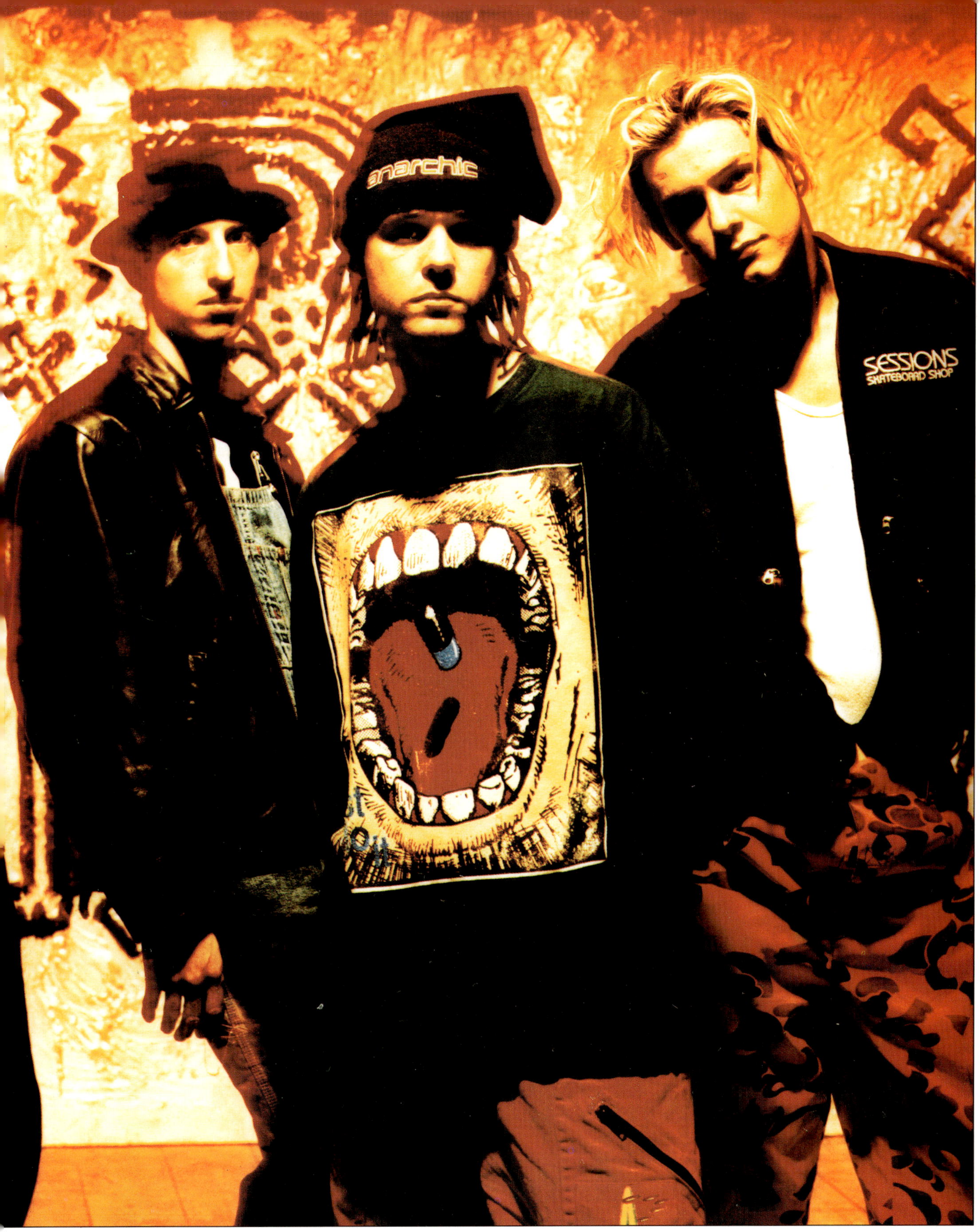

"I've worked with this band, EMF, since they started, and I really enjoy photographing them. This is my favourite shot of them so far, because all the different personalities come through. I lit the band with one flash above their heads and a bit of tungsten at the back of the shot. The red outlines were partly caused by the tungsten lighting and exaggerated in the printing afterwards."
Taken on a Mamiya RZ67 medium format camera with a 150mm telephoto lens and flash on Kodacolor Gold ISO 100 colour print film at 1/4 sec and f8.

"I took this shot of The Wonderstuff live at the Reading Festival. I had a good vantage point in the photographer's pit directly below the stage, and I used ambient light to capture this nice moment when the guitarist smiled up at the fiddler. I never use flash at concerts if I can avoid it. It tends to spoil the atmosphere."
Taken on a Canon EOS 1 with an 80-200mm zoom lens on Kodak T-Max ISO 3200 black and white print film at 1/250th sec and f3.5.

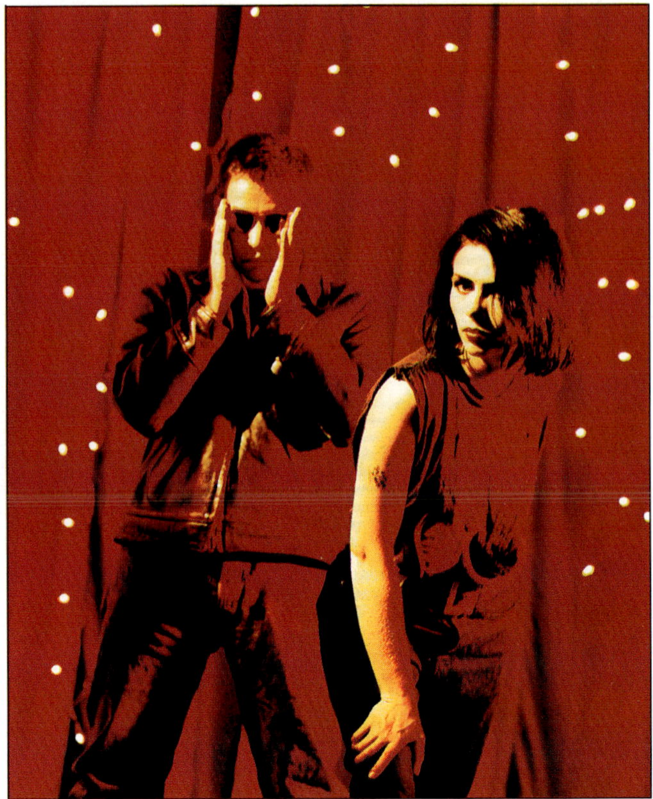

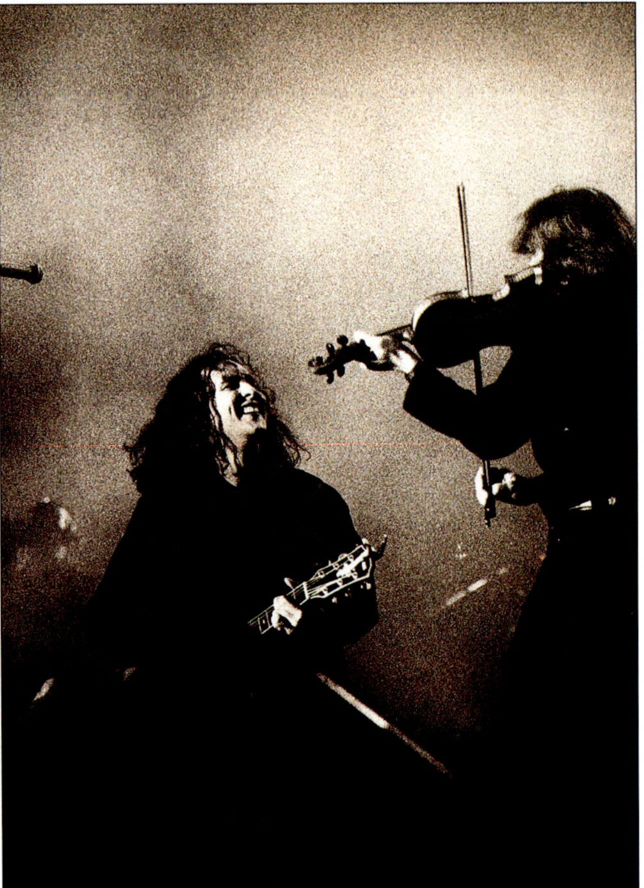

"There's a deliberate Christmas feel to this shot of Curve because it was taken at that time of the year. I used a red filter on the lights to give me the tint and flash to get the little dots of light on the background. It took a lot of Polaroids to get the whole thing exactly right. It was very difficult to keep her face from redding out in the printing."
Taken on the Mamiya RZ67 medium format camera with a 150mm lens on Kodacolor Gold ISO 100 print film at 1/125th and f4.

You can do it

To make your colour portraits more interesting, try using a mixture of tungsten and flash. On a long exposure your flashgun will freeze your subject when it fires, then the film will record the same scene lit only by tungsten. This can cause an outline around your model or a ghostly shadow if they move slightly. If you light the subject with flash and the background with tungsten they'll begin to disappear into it.

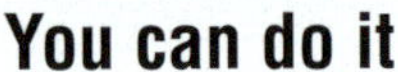

"I was asked to photograph this band, Ride, for the front cover of a magazine, so I had to make it look more interesting than just four blokes standing in front of a curtain. I used a combination of flash and tungsten, a coloured filter and some slight camera movement to create this unusual overall effect."
Taken on a Mamiya RZ67 medium format camera with a 150mm lens on reverse processed Ektachrome ISO 100 colour slide film at 1/4 sec and f8.

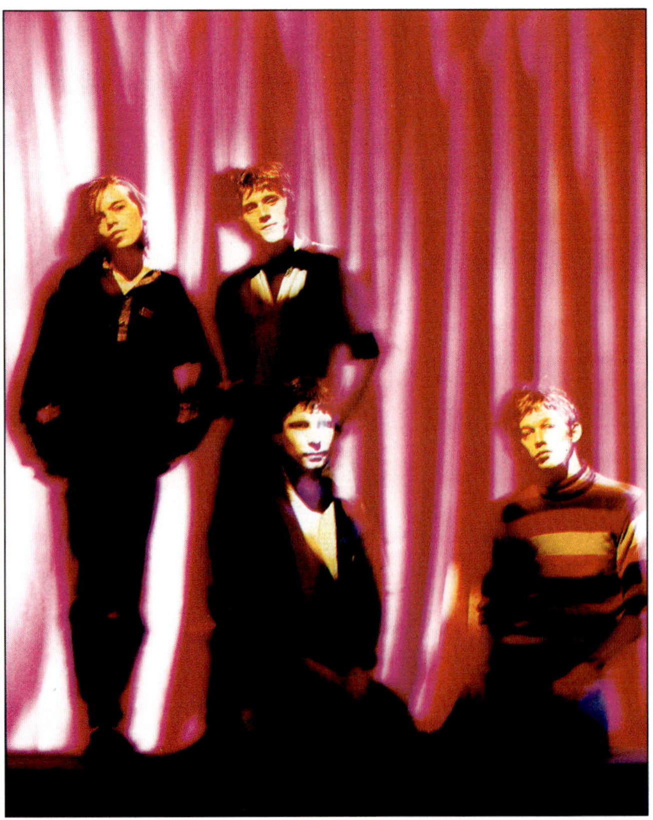

Creative use of wide angles

Kevin Westenberg manipulates film to get unusual images; another way of creating memorable pictures is by carefully selecting your lens.

The most obvious need for wide angle lenses is when you want to show as much of your subject as possible. They are invaluable when you are working within confined spaces or when you are trying to capture as much of a panoramic landscape as possible.

However, wide angle lenses don't simply mean a wider field of view – they have creative as well as functional uses.

For a start, wide angle lenses add impact to scenes by emphasizing depth. This is because they allow you to choose a closer viewpoint and by moving nearer you record foreground subjects at a larger scale.

A short focal length also gives you a large depth of field so you can take pictures which are sharp from foreground to background.

Variety of subjects

It's not necessary to limit yourself to conventional landscapes or cramped interiors when using a wide angle. These lenses can give you a fresh approach to a whole variety of subjects.

Architectural shots and portraits can be given extra impact with a wide angle lens. When you move in very close to your subject, this type of lens is also excellent for creating graphic abstracts. You can even add to the drama of sports events with a short focal length lens – so long as you can safely move near enough to your subject matter.

Additionally, it's possible to obtain some good candids with a wide angle lens. This is because people often assume you are using a standard lens and do not realize that they are in the frame.

Indeed, candids look particularly effective with a wide angle as they force the viewer into a nose-to-nose confrontation with the subject. Telephoto candids, although easier to take, often lack the sense of urgency of a candid taken with a wide angle lens.

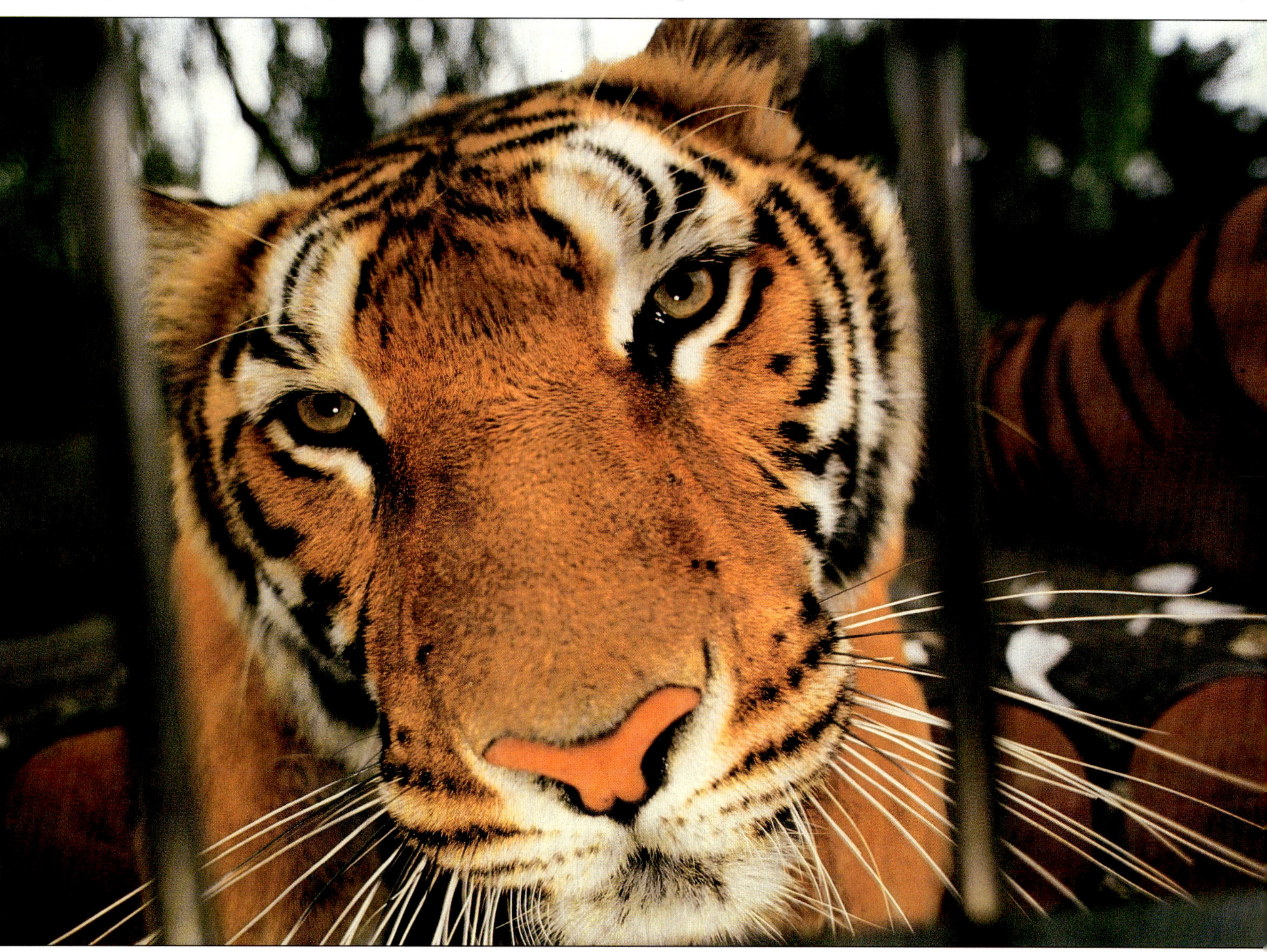

▼ *Wide angle lenses are one of the best ways to add impact to your pictures. A short focal length enhances the sense of depth in a photograph so that subjects close to the camera – like the tiger in this shot – seem to 'jump out' towards the viewer.*

Creative effects

Perhaps the most obvious quality of a wide angle lens – apart from the wider field of view – is that it gives an exaggerated sense of depth. Objects in the foreground will look much larger than objects in the background and this can inject a sense of vitality and dynamism into your pictures.

This characteristic is perhaps most obvious when you are shooting up towards tall buildings. The bottom of the building will appear much larger than the top. Consequently, the lines of the building will appear to converge at the top, giving an impressive sense of height.

You can shoot downwards as well as upwards to obtain this effect – and it's not limited to buildings. Take an unusual portrait by shooting from above with the subject looking up at the camera. As the face is nearest to the camera, it appears much larger than the rest of the body. Or 'stretch' faces creatively by placing them at the frame corners.

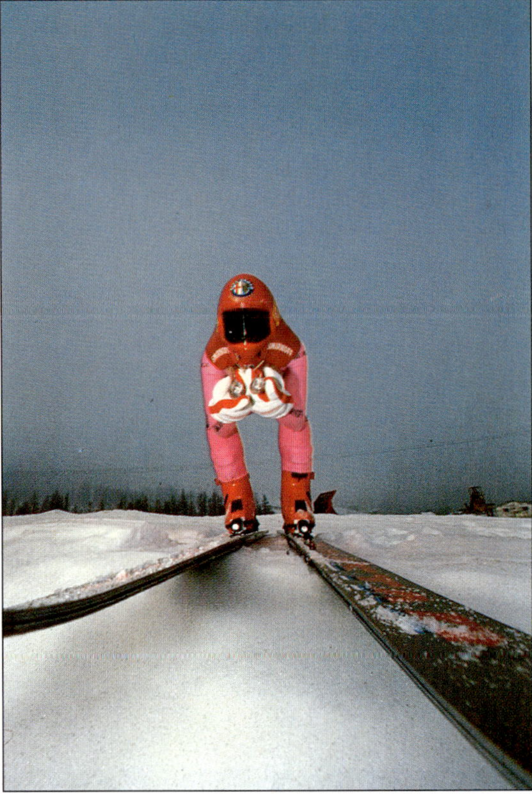

◀ *A wide angle lens was used here to emphasize the converging diagonals of the skis. It is particularly effective in this shot because the skis lead the eye to the skier. Note also that, as a result of the wide angle lens, the skier's gloved hands appear large in relation to the rest of her body behind.*

▼ *To emphasize the height of this building, a wide angle lens was used. The verticals of the building converge much more steeply than they would with a standard lens. To exaggerate the effect even more, the photographer chose a vantage point as close to the building as possible.*

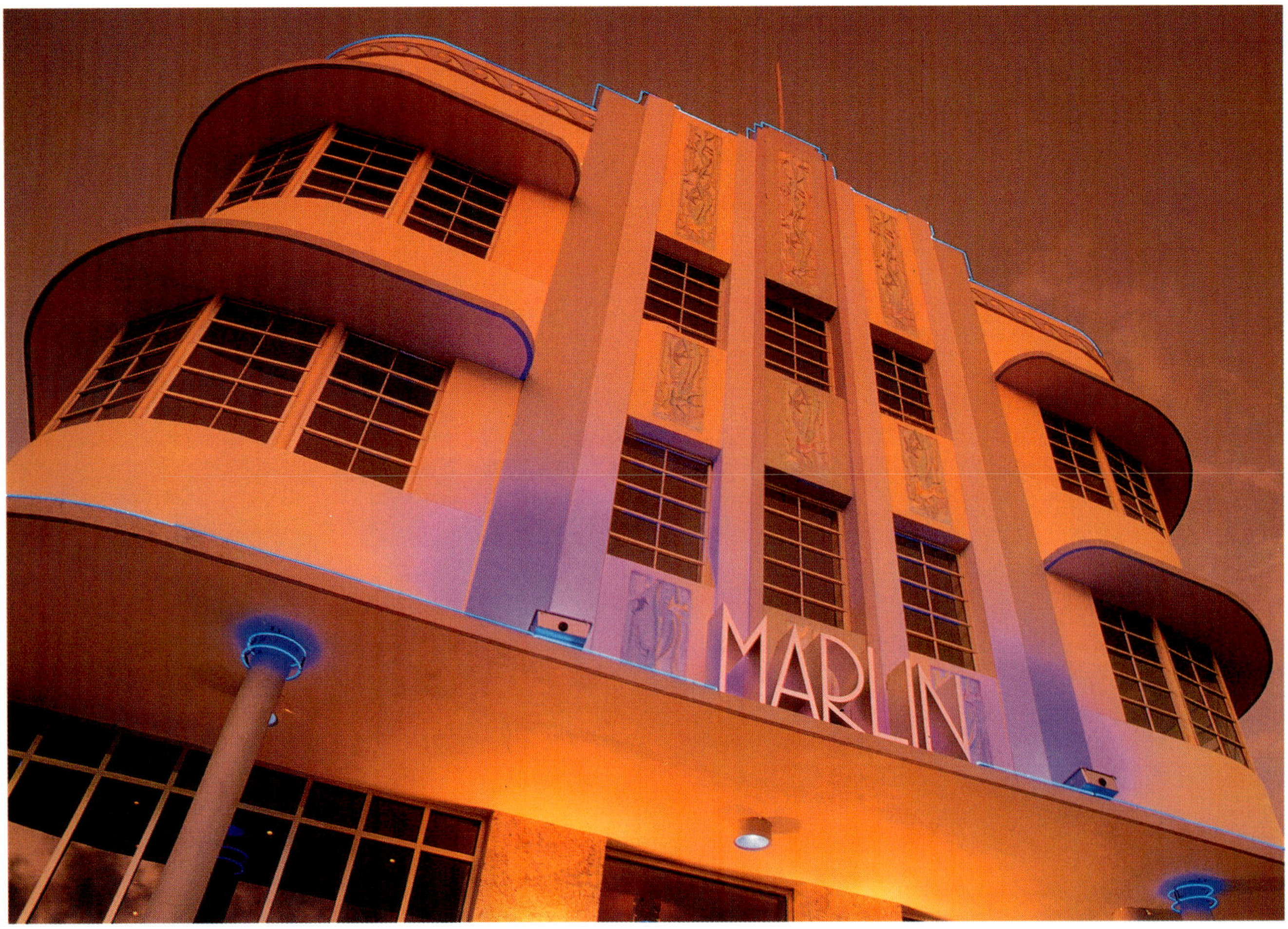

Exposure problems

Correct exposure can be difficult with extreme wide angles and fisheyes. This is often the case in landscape shots because you usually incorporate a large expanse of bright sky when using a wide angle lens. This can cause the shot to be underexposed.

To combat this, take an exposure reading from the land and then recompose to include the sky. You can do this easily by switching to manual exposure mode. Otherwise, if your camera has an exposure lock and spot metering, you can obtain even more precise exposures. Take a spot metered reading from an area that's neither in bright sunlight nor in deep shadow, lock that reading, and then recompose.

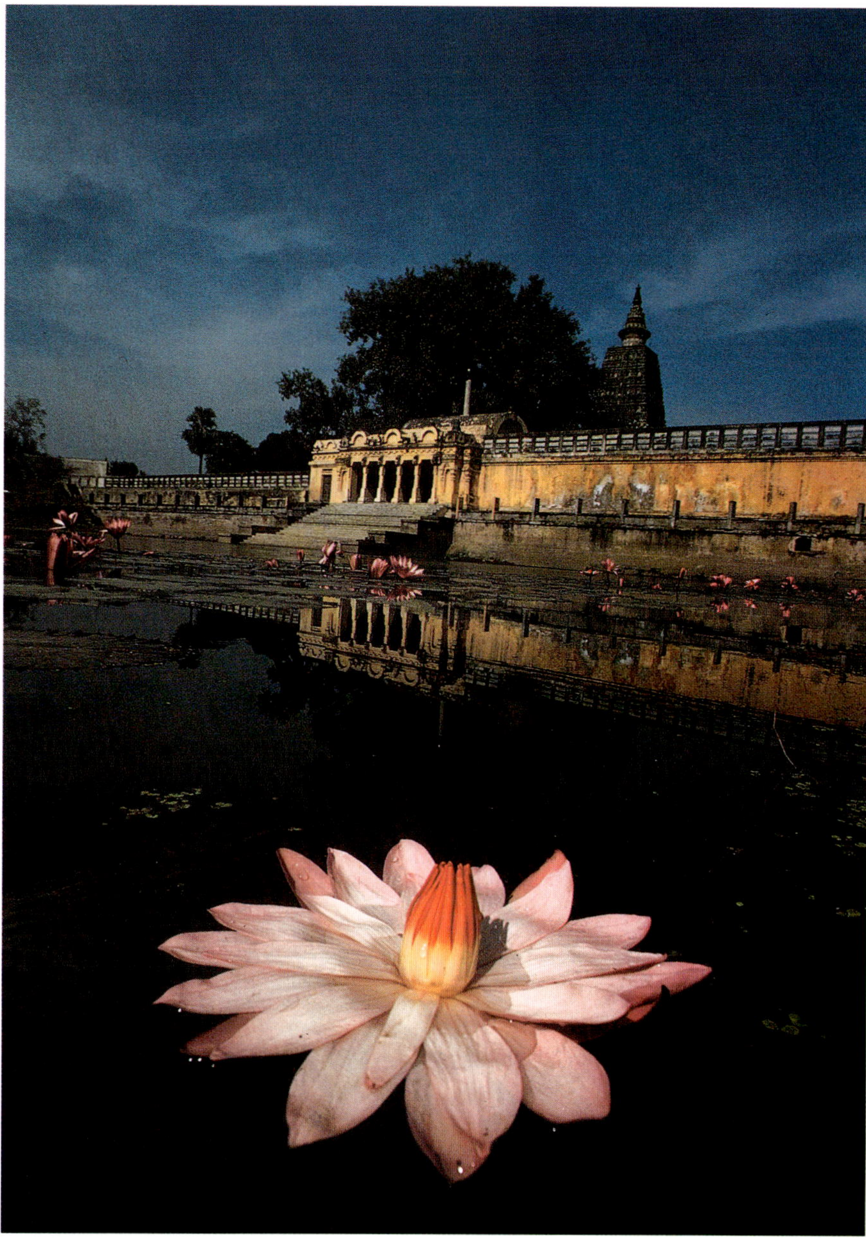

► *One of the advantages of wide angle lenses is their large depth of field. In this shot, everything from the lily in the foreground to the tower in the background is in sharp focus. Furthermore, compare the size of the lily with the size of the tower to see the dramatic distortion of scale caused by wide angle lenses.*

Foreground interest

With wide angle lenses, always try to compose so that you have interesting subject matter in the foreground. You may see a distant landscape and immediately think you need a wide angle lens to capture the whole view. However, remember that you will not be able to see the exaggerated sense of depth that a wide angle gives unless you introduce some foreground interest.

For a really dramatic landscape with a wide angle, try changing your angle of view so you can include some flowers or perhaps a stile in the foreground with the landscape unfurling behind.

Similarly, if you are doing a portrait you might want to incorporate some relevant accessories in the foreground. If you are photographing a group of musicians, for instance, you could compose the shot so that their musical instruments are arranged in the foreground.

Wide depth of field

Moreover, it's possible to get both your foreground subject matter and background subject matter in focus with wide angle lenses because of their very large depth of field.

To do this, you need to focus in between the foreground and background so that both points of interest fall within the depth of field. If you focus on the foreground, the background is liable to be out of focus and vice versa.

Check the markings on the barrel of your lens to make sure everything you want falls within the depth of field limits (or use the depth of field preview button, if your camera has one). Select a smaller aperture if you need to extend your depth of field.

Close focusing

Wide angle lenses also allow you to focus much more closely than normal lenses. For example, with a 28mm lens, you can focus down to about 0.3m whereas with a standard 50mm lens you can only focus down to about 0.45 or 0.5m.

Close focusing is useful when you want to isolate a subject in the near foreground, such as a wild flower in a field. By setting a large aperture on a wide angle lens, you could move right up to the flower and keep it in focus while letting the rest of the field fade out of focus behind.

Fisheye lenses

A fisheye lens is a specialist piece of equipment that gives you extreme wide angles. Photographs taken with a fisheye are immediately recognizable because of their circular, bulging distortion (although straight lines passing through the centre of the picture remain straight).

The name of the lens comes from the fact that it has a similar angle of view to that of a fish's eye. This design allows a field of view of 180° so that everything in front of the photographer is in the frame. Indeed, some fisheye lenses give you an angle of view as much as 220° – this means they can actually 'see' behind you.

There are two types of fisheye: circular image and full frame. The former will give you a circular image so that it appears as if you are looking into a goldfish bowl. A full frame fisheye gives you a conventional rectangular frame but still with the fisheye's characteristic curved distortion.

Fisheyes work very well when your main subject is centrally framed and close to the camera. The subject will appear to loom towards the viewer dramatically. Also, the curved distortion will lead the eye to the centre of the frame.

Fisheyes also give you an enormous depth of field. If you use a fisheye on the smallest aperture – usually f22 – virtually everything in the frame will be in focus. On f22, you can put your hand in front of the lens, and both the hand and the horizon will be in focus.

Off the wall shots

You can use this characteristic of the fisheye lens to achieve some really unusual shots. If you are photographing a clocktower, for example, you could get both the watch on your wrist *and* the clocktower in the frame and in focus for an interesting comparison.

Similarly, if you are taking a photo of a field of wheat, you might also want to include an individual ear of wheat held in the palm of your hand close to the lens, for a general view of the wheat field and a close-up of the wheat itself.

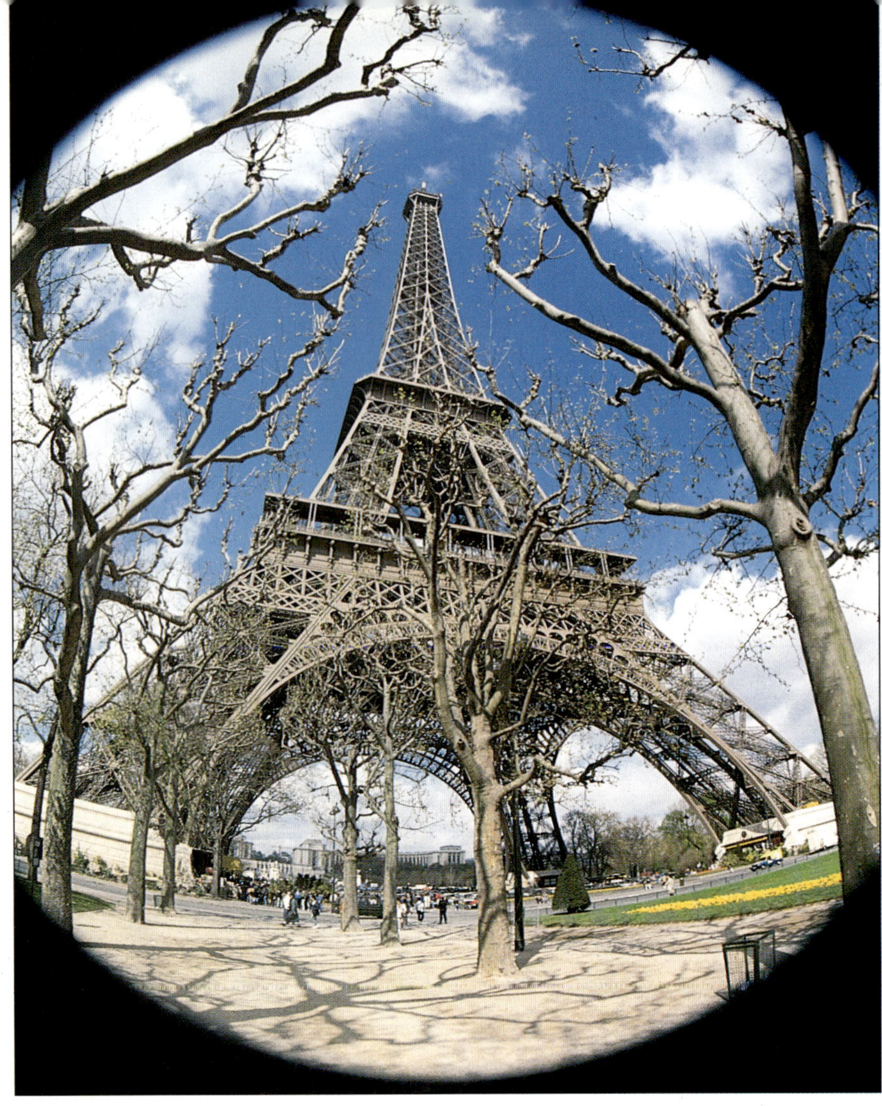

▲ *When you are using a circular image fisheye lens, a centrally framed subject looks particularly effective. Note how, because of the fisheye distortion, the trees bend inwards here to frame the Eiffel Tower.*

▼ *The photographer chose a full frame fisheye here to include as many people as possible in the shot. The curved distortion of the fisheye seems to emphasize the crowded nature of the scene.*

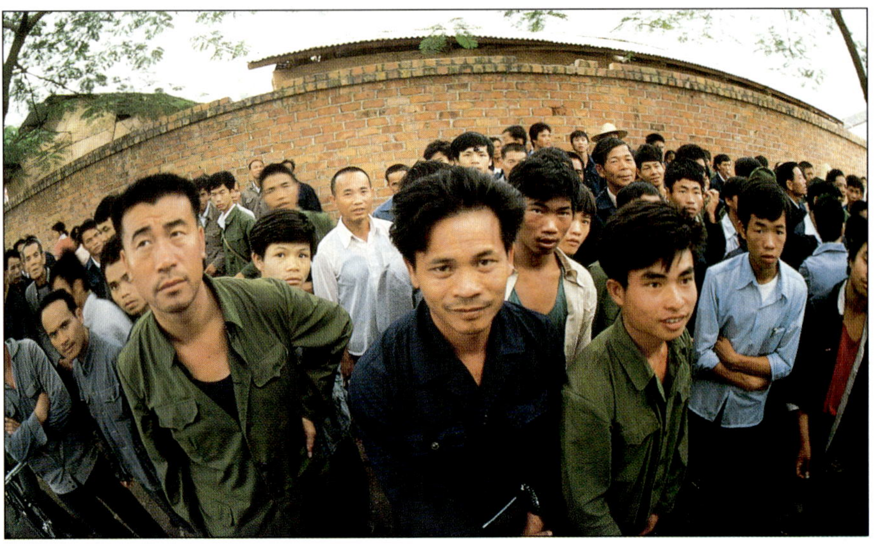

Front projection effects

With just a few slides and a projector you can create unusual and effective 'trick' pictures in a home studio. Find a suitable subject – and let your imagination do the rest.

Without moving from home, you can set up stunning location shots, print a pattern on a plain coloured subject, or superimpose one image on another. You can achieve any of these effects with a method called front projection.

All you have to do is place your camera, a slide projector and a subject in front of a screen. Then you project a slide either on to the subject, or on to the screen behind to provide a backdrop, and take a picture on tungsten balanced film.

Projecting on to a subject

You can make all sorts of unusual pictures by projecting an image on to your subject, then photographing the result. The picture you get is not particularly sharp since you aren't projecting on to a flat surface. But this doesn't matter, because the creative aspect of the final picture is what counts, not its technical merit.

Slides Bold, colourful, or easily recognizable subjects work best. If you copy existing pictures, remember

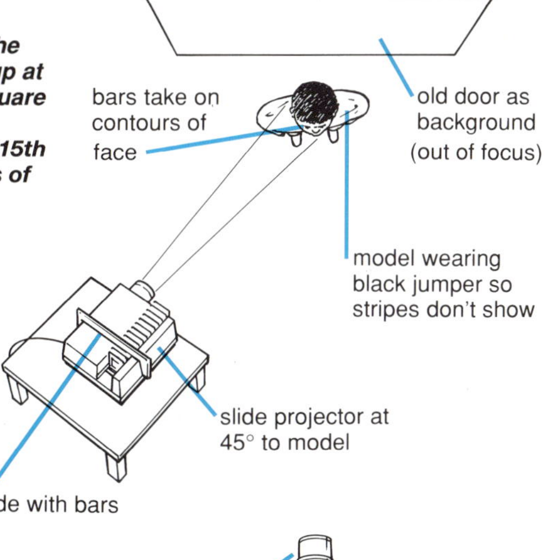

▶ *Position your model in front of the background with the projector set up at 45° to the model and the camera square on.*

For this shot the exposure was 1/15th sec. The slide was made from strips of tape stuck on acetate.

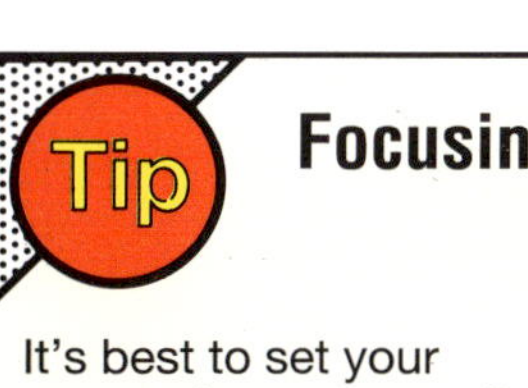

It's best to set your camera lens to a small aperture so that the whole of the subject is in focus. This helps to minimize any blurring in the final picture.

▲ ▼ *Bars projected across the face distort the model's features and create a sinister look. The effect varies depending on the colour of your model – it is more subtle on the black model than on the white one.*

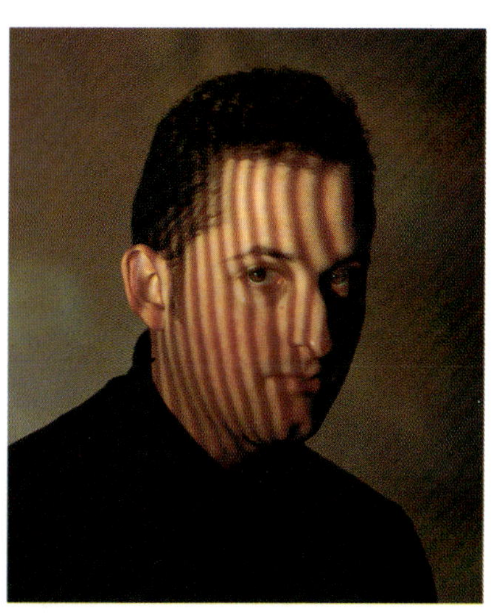

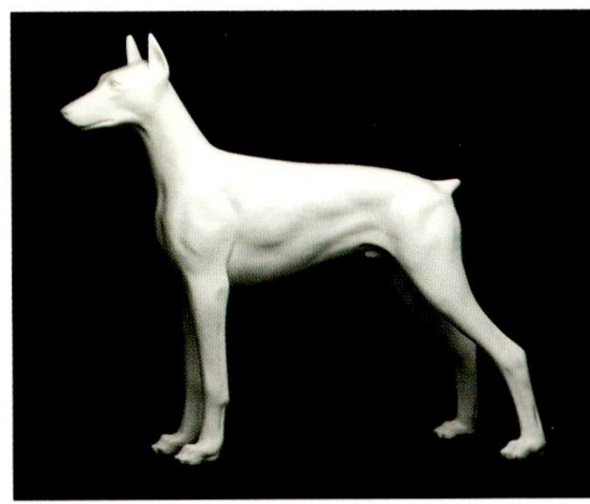

▲ *When projecting a pattern on to a white object, a dark background (such as black velvet) absorbs the colour.*

that they are subject to copyright.
Shutter speed Because the only light on the subject comes from the projector, there will not be very much light around and you will need to set a slow shutter speed. Also, since many surfaces, including skin, are not very reflective, the image of the slide is rather dim.

The slow shutter speed may mean that you have to use a tripod. It also limits your choice of subject to those with minimum movement. For this reason it is a good idea to start off with still life subjects.

Projecting backgrounds

You can also project backgrounds behind normally-lit subjects, but as the subject is the same side of the screen as the projector, it may cast a shadow on the background.

Professional photographers get round this by using a special mirror

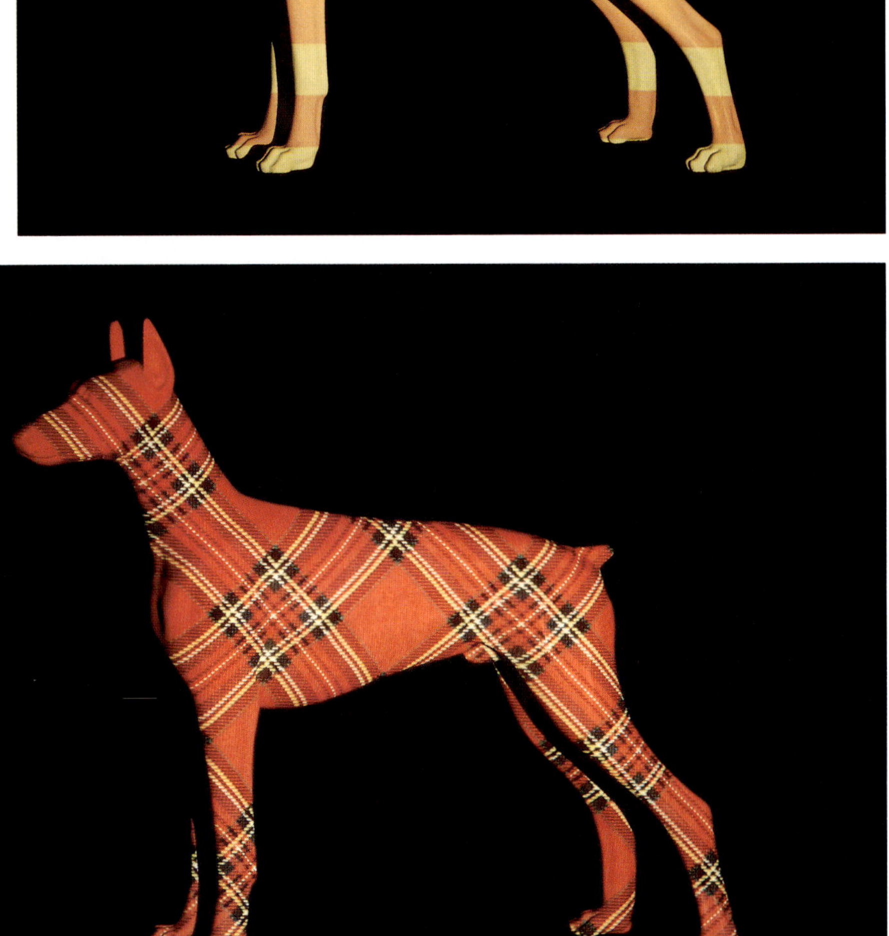

▶ *A pattern of stripes was photographed on slide film, then projected on to this white plaster dog – an easy way to transform it into an amusing image.*

▶ *Changing the look to tartan is a simple matter of swapping slides. Because the surface of the dog is quite smooth, the pattern looks even. The rougher and more uneven the surface, the more distorted the pattern will be.*

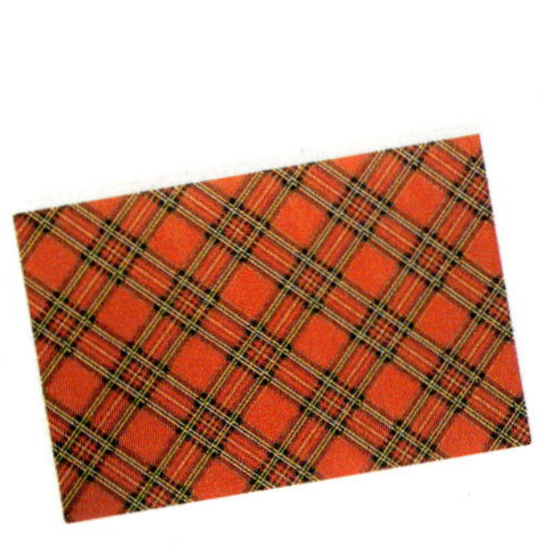

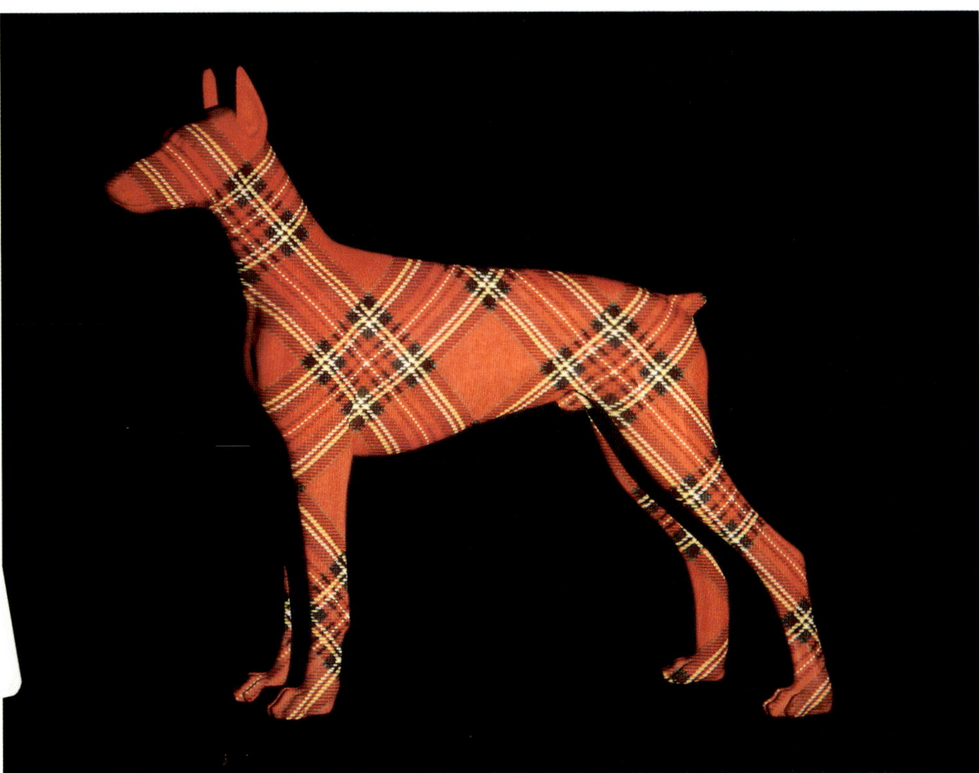

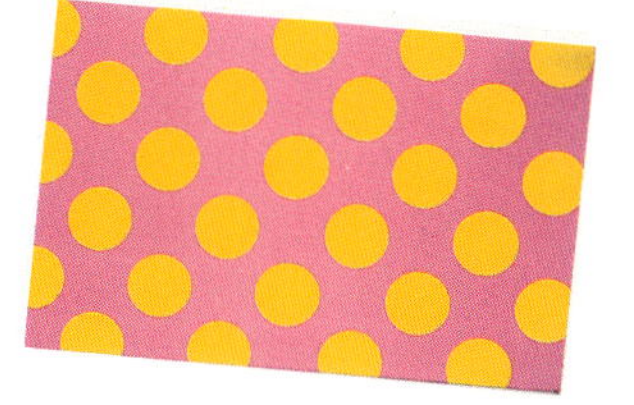

arrangement so the camera and projector are effectively in the same position. This means that the subject automatically hides its own shadow. The equipment to do this is costly but you can hire it at some studios.

However, you can achieve excellent results in a home studio by arranging things so that either the camera or the projector is at an angle to the screen. The subject has to be positioned so that the projector beam doesn't hit it.

Back projection

You can also project slides on to the back of the screen by placing the projector *behind* it. This method is called back projection. Although much used in the past to relocate actors in both movies and on TV, it is seldom used today and very rarely by stills photographers.

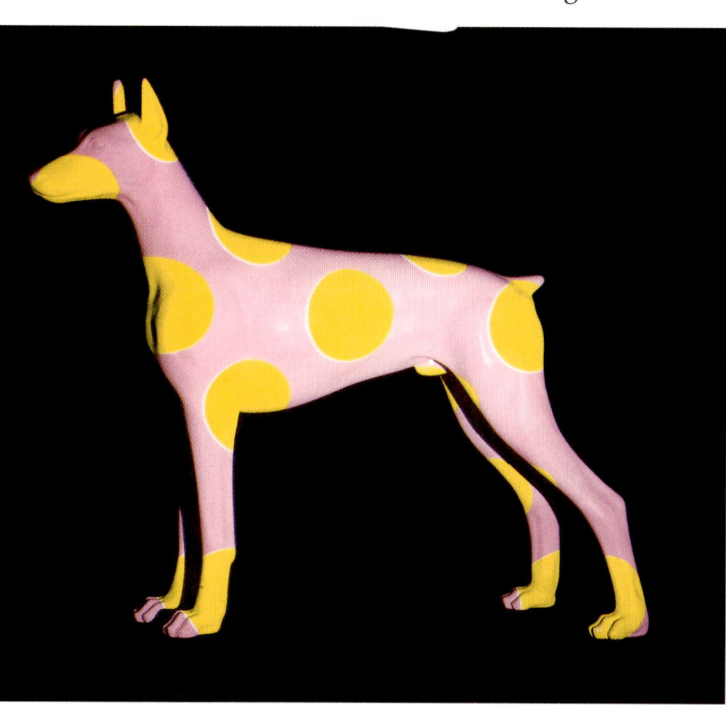

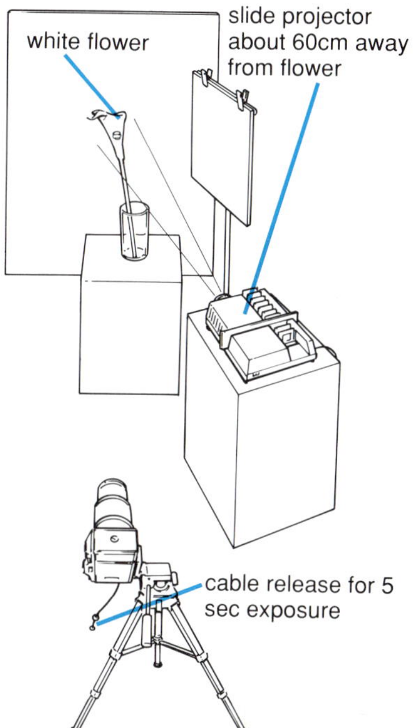

▼ ▶ **The photographer shot the perfume bottle against white paper which wouldn't show up when he projected it on the white flower. He used a small mirror to reflect light on to the flower, to improve modelling. He placed the projector close to the flower, so the image of the bottle was small enough.**

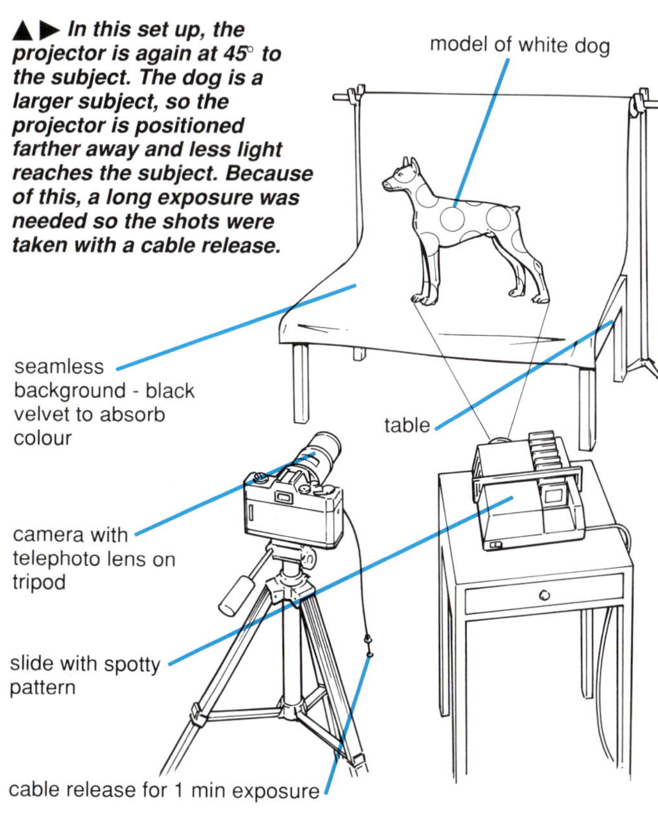

▲ ▶ **In this set up, the projector is again at 45° to the subject. The dog is a larger subject, so the projector is positioned farther away and less light reaches the subject. Because of this, a long exposure was needed so the shots were taken with a cable release.**

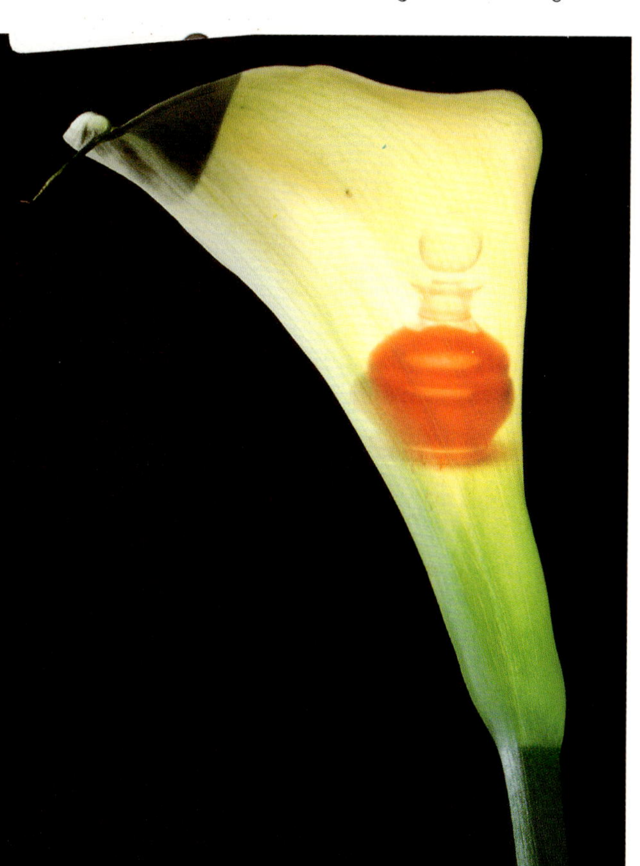

Using a screen

The main problem when projecting backdrops is that the subject casts a shadow. One solution is to position the subject to one side of the projector and far enough forward for the projector's beam to miss it. It's best to use a wide angle lens on your projector. Then you can place it close to the screen yet still throw a large image.

Another way of doing front projection with a screen is to project the slide from one side instead of square-on to the screen. This allows you to have the subject in front of the screen without it casting a shadow.

Position your subject

Once the background slide is projected satisfactorily, you can position your subject about a metre away from the screen without it blocking any of the beam (and so casting a shadow). Place the camera on a tripod square on to the screen.

Attach masks made from black card to your tungsten lamps to prevent any light spill on to the screen. Finally, move the lamps closer to or further from the subject until both the subject and the screen need the same exposure.

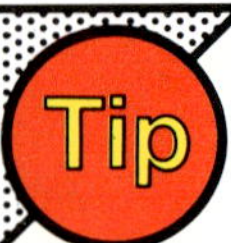

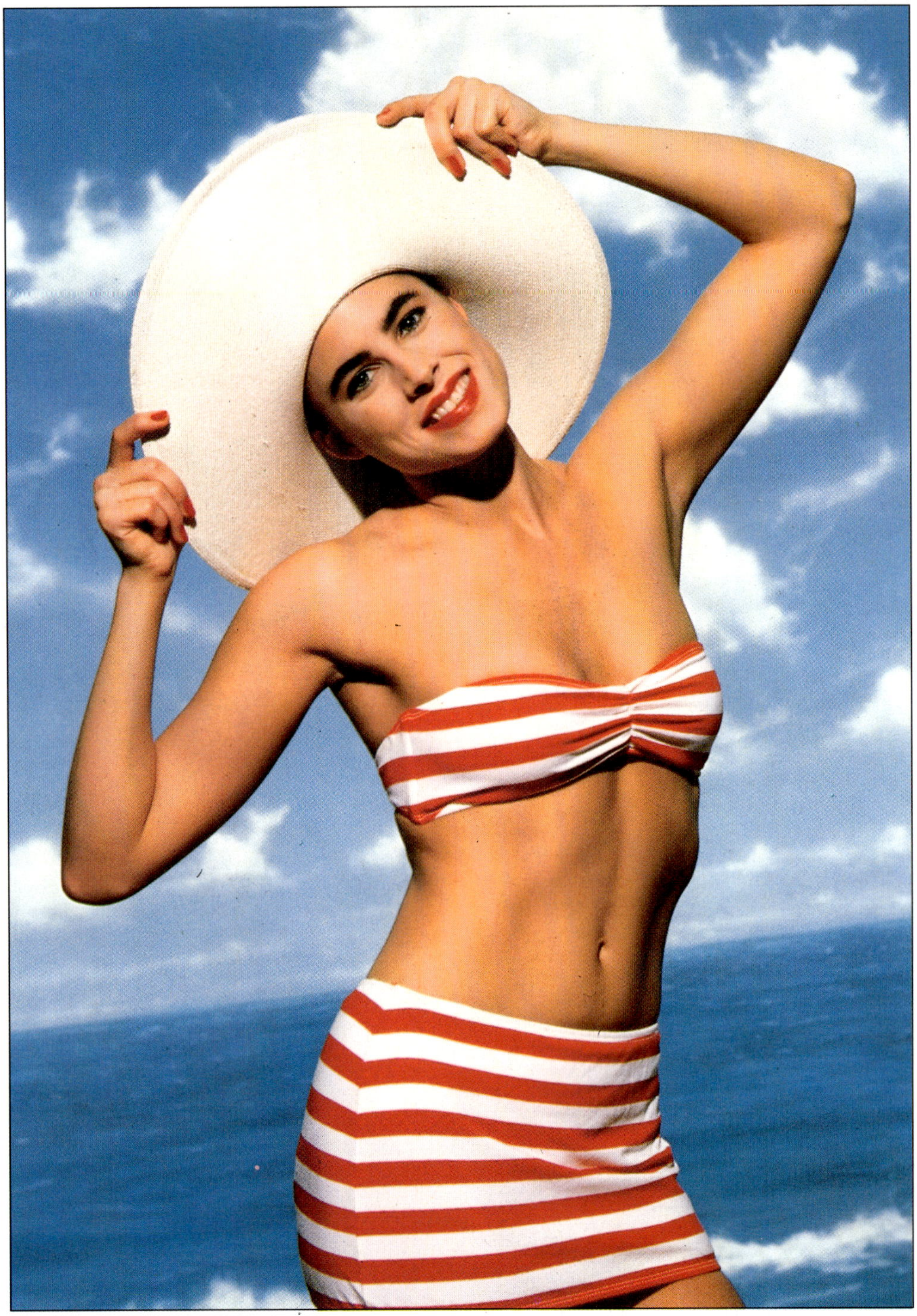

A new angle

Tip

When you project a slide at an angle, it can appear 'stretched' on the screen. To keep this effect to a minimum, use the longest projector lens you own (or the longest setting if it is a zoom) and keep the projector as close to perpendicular to the screen as you are able to do.

Foil and mirror tricks

With just a mirror or a piece of foil to hand, you can create all sorts of interesting and bizarre trick shots designed to deceive the eye.

You don't need expensive gadgets to create a range of special effects. The highly reflective surface of foil or a mirror can produce extraordinary pictures, such as mirages or weird distortions.

Mirrors You can use ordinary glass mirrors. Front-silvered ones give better results but they are more expensive and harder to find.

Mirrofoil and reflective Mylar are metallic coated flexible plastic sheets with a perfect mirror finish. They are available in rolls from art supply or stationery shops. When you lay them flat the sheets are like ordinary mirrors, but when bent they give a distorted effect, like a fairground mirror.

Chrome-plated steel sheets can be used as an alternative, but you must check for scratches.

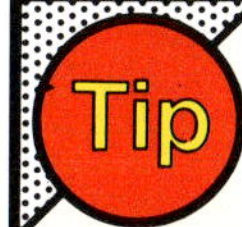

Distortion option

If you find that your friends are unwilling to pose for their features to be distorted, you can give a 'fairground' effect to a photo you already have. (The photo edges will show in your shot.) Hold the Mirrofoil and board close to the light source, at an angle so you can see the photo's reflection in the curved foil. Point the camera lens at the foil and shoot.

Fairground freak

To take a distorted shot like this, you need a flat board and a piece of Mirrofoil twice the size. Tape the board to the back of one half of the Mirrofoil. Gently bend the other half of the foil. Hold the foil at an angle to your subject's face so the flat half of the foil reflects one side of the face perfectly. The curved half of the foil reflects the face's other side with an elongated, streaked effect. Tiny movements of the foil give a lot more distortion.

You could also try bending the foil to give a vertical distortion.

The bent foil changes the apparent camera to subject distance, making the subject go quickly out of focus. So when you shoot, focus on the reflection of the face, not on the foil surface, and use a small aperture to give a big depth of field. Don't use camera mounted flash, as the foil reflects it.

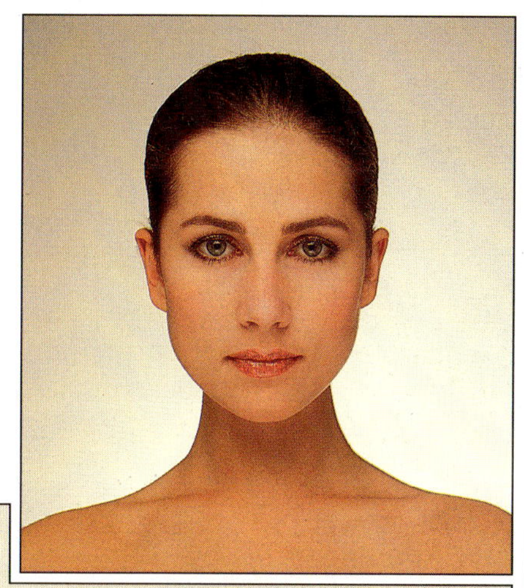

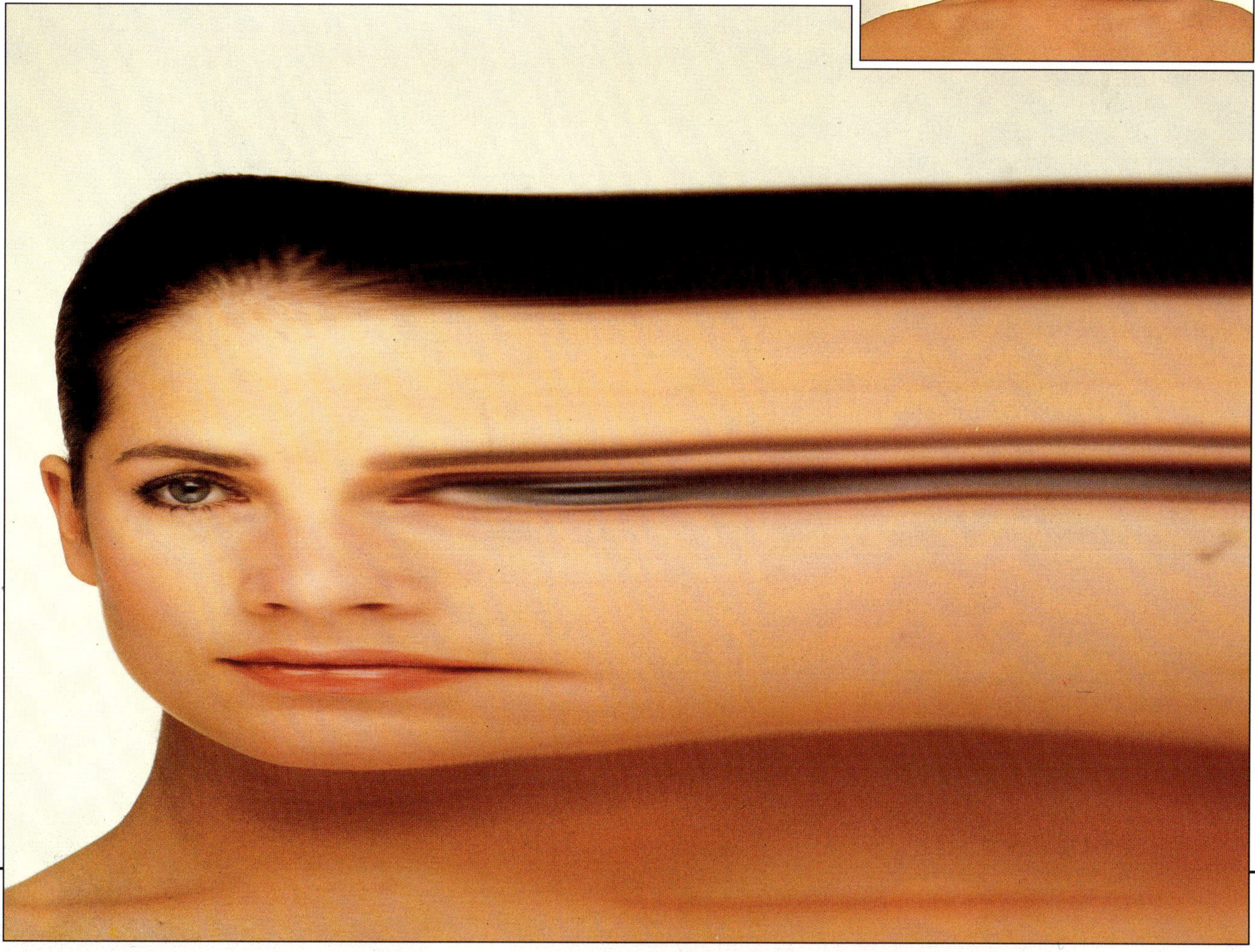

Foil tube

One way to use Mirrofoil creatively is to construct a tube, through which you can take your photo. Make a foil tube by fixing Mirrofoil to a sheet of flexible card bent into a tubular shape. This should fit snugly over the lens (or fix it with tape). The length of the tube depends on the lens' focal length – shorter for a wide angle lens and longer for telephoto.

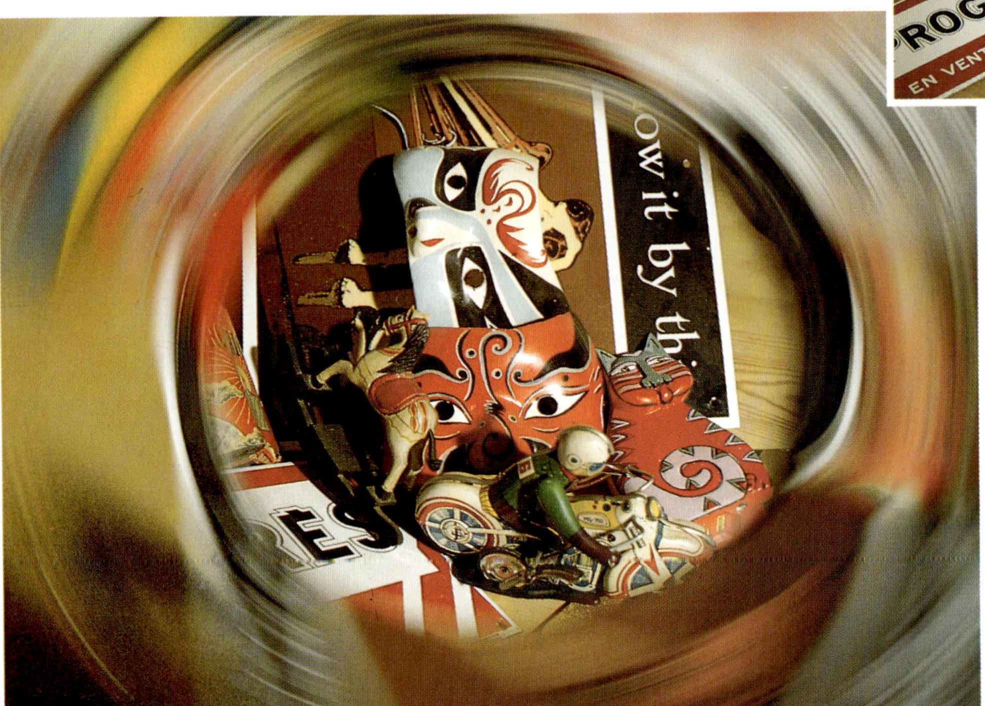

▲ *When selecting subject matter for a shot through a foil lined tube, choose really strong colours and bright, bold patterns.*

◀ *Photographing through a foil lined tube produces a circular central image surrounded by reflected patterns. This shot was taken at f4.*

Lighting up

You can use a mirror for a dramatically lit outdoor portrait. For best results choose a sunny morning or late afternoon, when the sun is low in the sky. Ask your subject to stand with his or her back to the sun, holding the mirror so the light shines on to it and is reflected into the subject's face. Set the exposure to the illuminated area of the face.

You could try out different shapes and sizes of mirror – a round mirror produces a circular spot of light, for example.

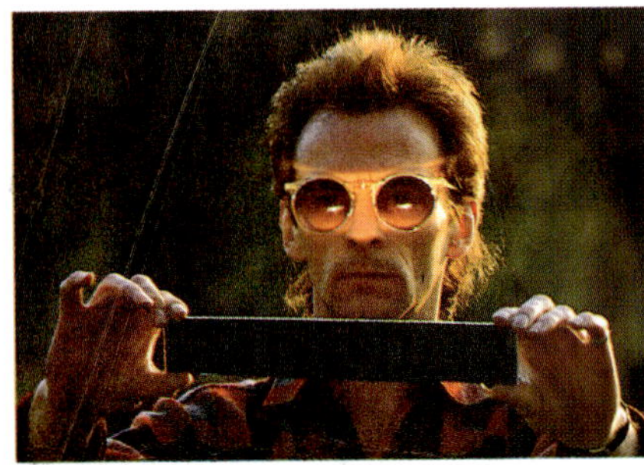

▲ ▶ *The shaft of light shining across the subject's face gives this portrait a sinister look.*

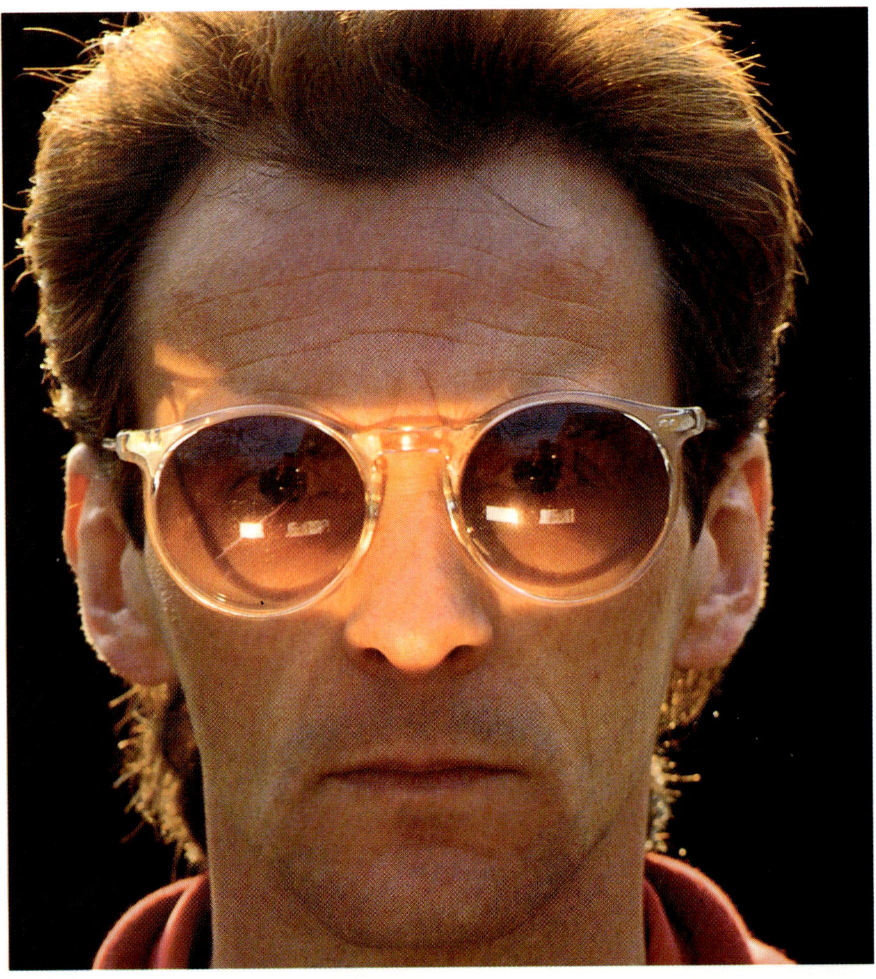

Kaleidoscope

It isn't difficult to make your own kaleidoscope – all you need is some hand mirrors of equal size, strong cardboard and masking tape. For the best results use front-silvered or anodized mirrors, available from specialist glass or hardware shops.
Number of mirrors Three is the easiest number of mirrors with which to achieve perfectly reflected images.
Width Mirrors about 7.5cm in width suit most lenses.
Length A wide angle lens needs mirrors about 15cm in length. Longer lenses may need mirrors 30cm long. It's a matter of trial and error to find the right size.
Glass-cutting tool If mirrors of the right size are not available, you could use a glass-cutting tool to cut a large mirror to the sizes you want – but make sure the edges are straight and even, so that the mirrors fit together snugly.

A glass-cutter is not difficult to use – but it is a good idea to get someone in a glass shop to show you how.

Making a three-sided kaleidoscope

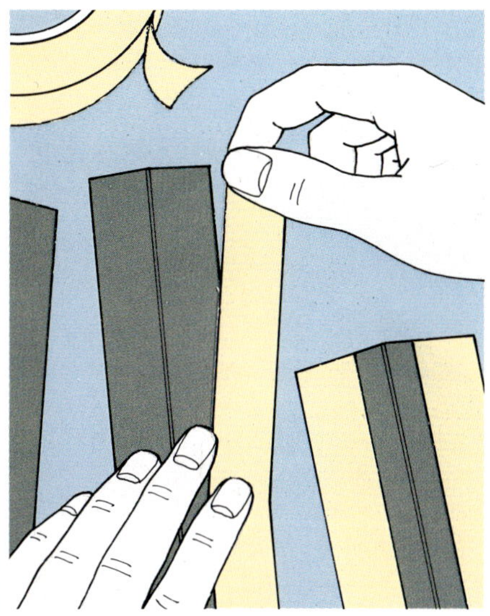

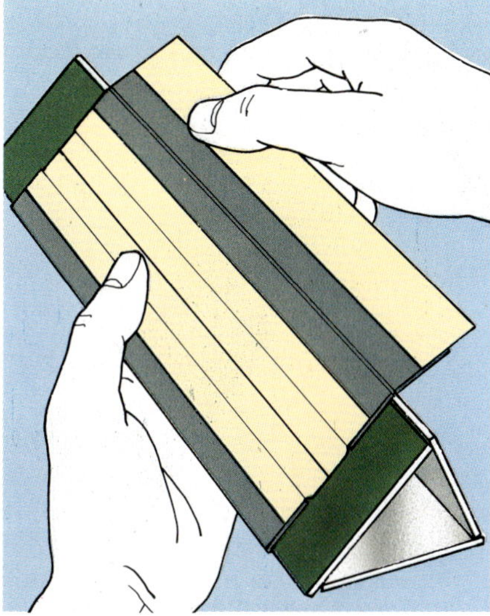

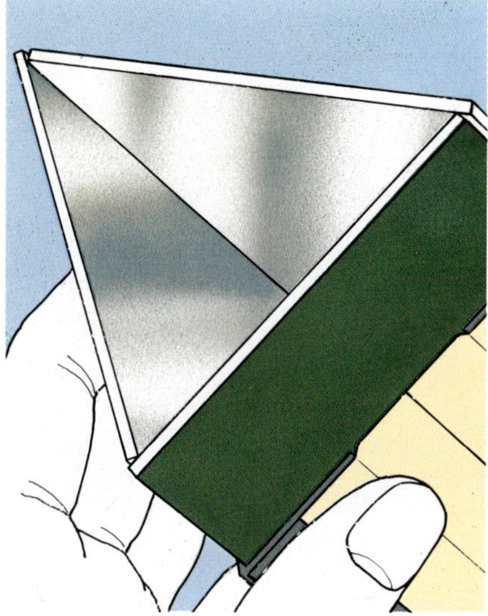

1 CUT CARD STRIPS
Cut three strips of cardboard slightly shorter than the mirrors and about 5cm wide. Score the strips with a knife down the centre and fold in half. Stick masking tape along the long sides of each strip so half the tape extends over the edge.

2 POSITION THE MIRRORS
Slide a mirror into one cardboard crease, leaving a gap at the crease for the next mirror to fit into. Press firmly on to the tape. Position the next mirror in the gap and secure. Stick another length of board into its other edge, leaving a gap for the third mirror to slot into. Use the last strip of board to join the first and last mirrors.

3 PRESS THE TAPE DOWN
Smooth the tape down firmly to hold the mirrors securely in place. The kaleidoscope is now ready for use. If you have a metal lens hood slip the kaleidoscope on to it – otherwise hold it separately.

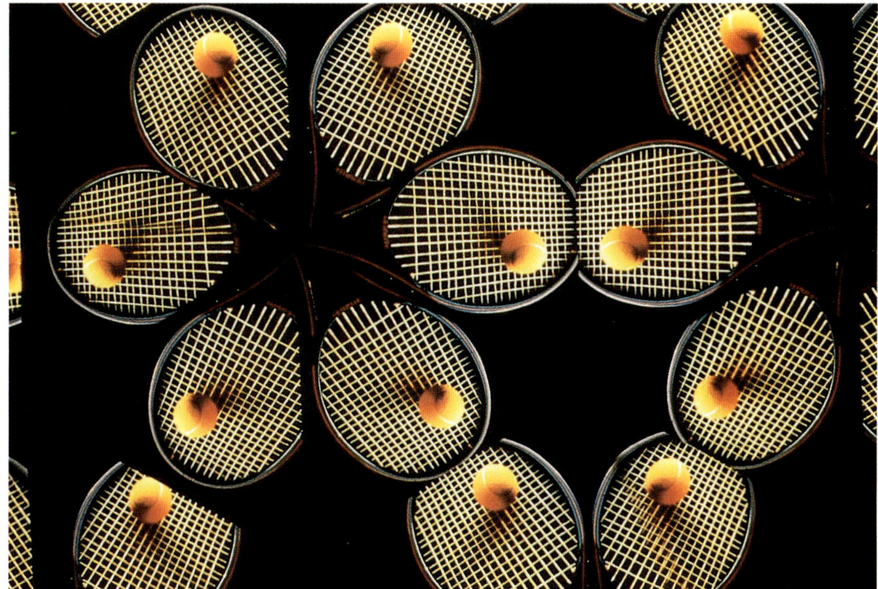

Using the kaleidoscope

Position the kaleidoscope in front of the lens and aim it at your subject. Rotate the kaleidoscope until you achieve the effect you want. With wide angle lenses the subject should be quite close to the kaleidoscope so you don't get any outside areas reflected.

You need good light for city or landscapes so the details are clear because they will take up a relatively small proportion of your final picture.

◀ *Symmetrical subjects, such as this tennis racquet and ball, show the kaleidoscopic effect dramatically.*

Moody mirage

You can create a realistic 'lake' effect by holding a hand mirror under the camera lens. This usually works particularly well for naturally atmospheric landscapes such as hills, fields or trees. If you can, choose a subject with a bold outline, which will create a dramatic shape when reflected in the mirror.

Use a tripod, if possible, so you don't have to hold the camera still as well as the mirror.

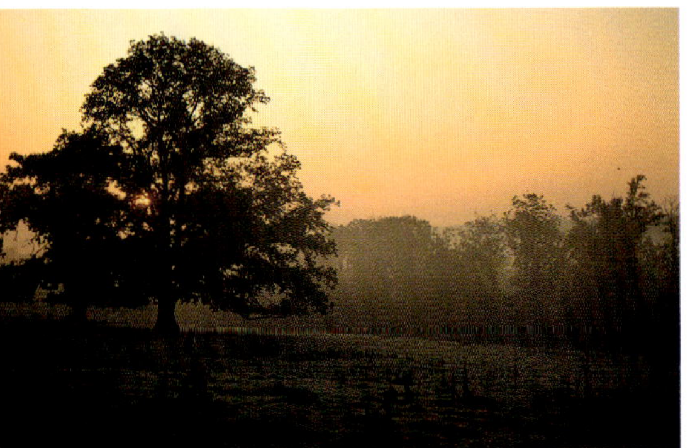

▲ ▼ *The simple device of placing a mirror under the lens transforms an early morning shot of trees in a field (above) into a tranquil scene of mist on a lake (below).*

Focusing

Mirrors are a useful way of breaking your picture up into two or more distinct areas – objects and their reflections. But the first thing to decide is on what you are going to focus – just the reflected image or both the mirror and the reflection?

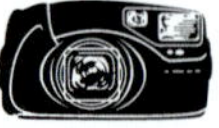

Compact tip

To focus on the reflected image, simply point and shoot, as the camera will focus on the image automatically.

Getting both the reflected image and the mirror in focus is harder. Your best chance is to shoot in bright light so the camera sets a narrow aperture. This increases the depth of field which may stretch to include the mirror frame and its surroundings. Placing the subject near to the mirror also helps to keep the focusing distance to a minimum.

▶ *The photographer wanted both the mirror and the reflection in focus, and so used a small aperture setting. Tall buildings obscured the light, making the edges of the photo dark.*

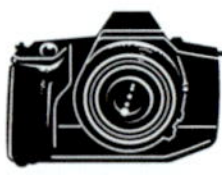

SLR tip

Focusing is much easier if you are using an SLR camera. To get the reflected image in focus, make sure it fills the viewfinder frame and focus on the image.

To include the mirror frame and background detail, just focus manually and check that both mirror image and subject are sharp enough, using the depth of field scale on the lens barrel or, if available, the preview facility.

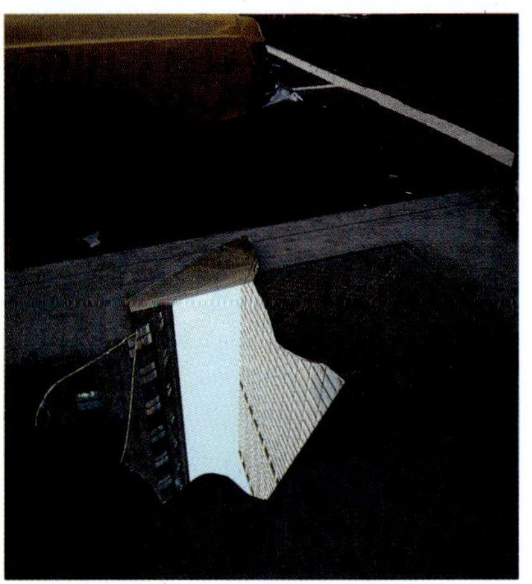

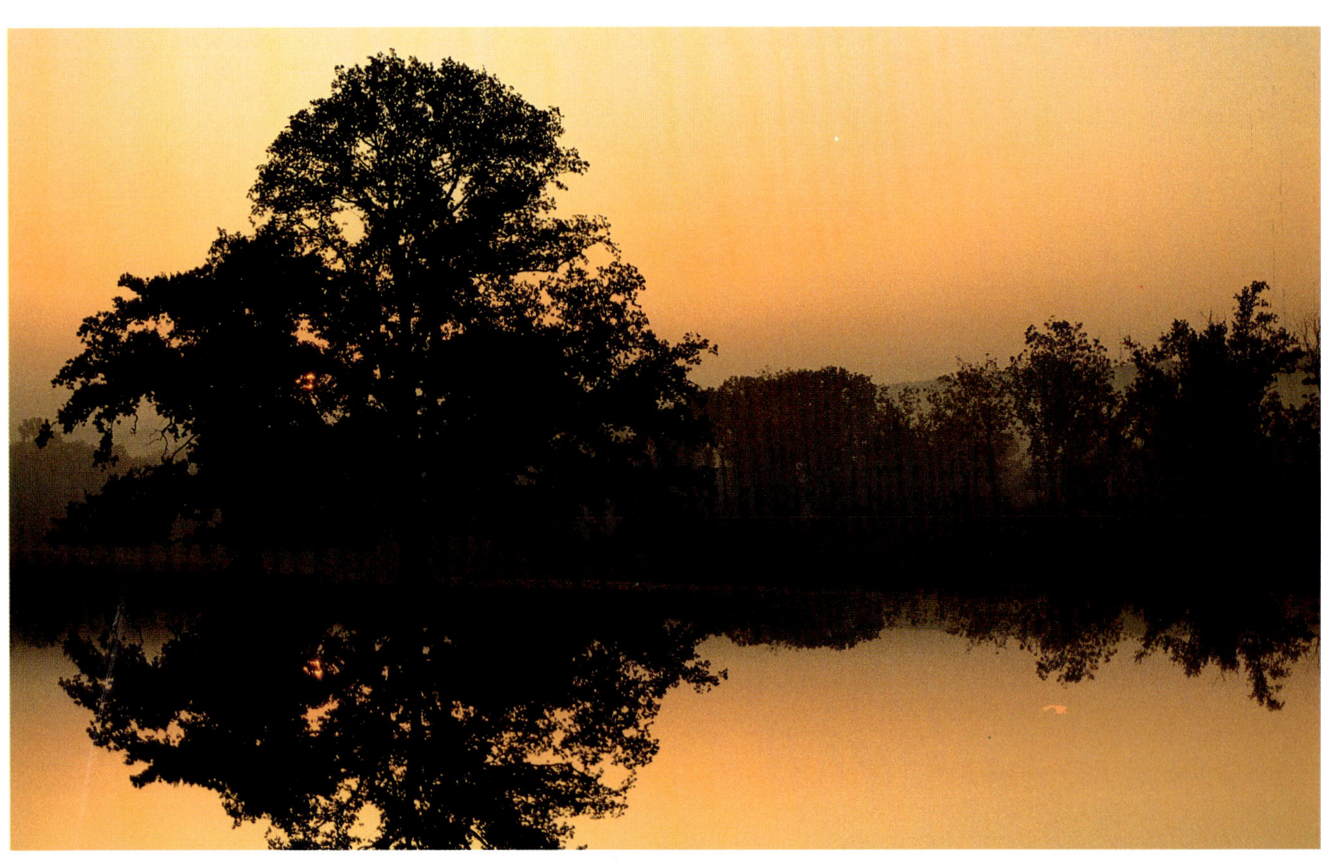

Creating a double exposure

Next time you see a spectacular photo where the photographer seems to have caught exactly the right moment, look again – it may be a double exposure. This fun technique lets you greatly extend the range of creative effects possible with your camera.

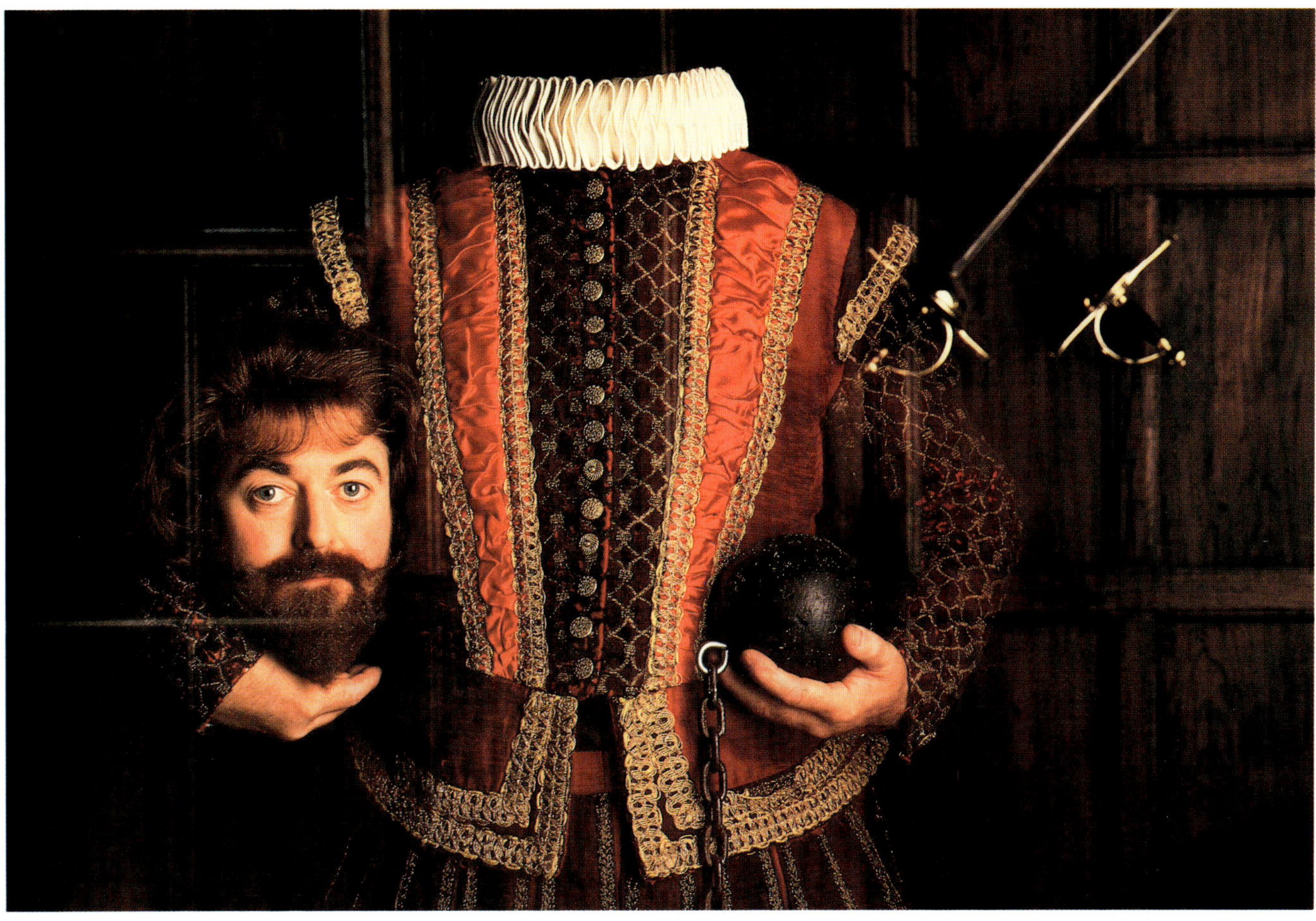

▼ *Double exposure lets you achieve fantasy shots. Too much wood panelling overlaying the 'ghost' would have spoiled the picture, so the photographer made sure that the head and body were strongly lit. Paler areas in one exposure always hide darker areas in another, so here the panelling can be most clearly seen through the arms. With a shot like this you may need to bracket your exposures of each image to be sure of achieving the effect you want.*

Double exposure is just what it says – you make two exposures on the same frame of film, so that two separate images are recorded on the same photograph. If you make more than two exposures, it is called a multiple exposure.

Two ways of making double exposures are to run the whole film through the camera twice or to make selective double exposures.

A series of images

You can expose an entire roll of film twice with all 35mm cameras, even compacts. Take one set of photos as normal, and rewind the film. Then take a second set of photos.

This technique is best if you want to merge images of subjects that are far apart (whether in place or time), because you can take the film out of the camera between the two series of exposures. Do remember to label your film, so you don't forget what's on it later. If the image is at all complicated, it's worth making a sketch of where the subject is on each frame.

If your camera lets you rewind mid roll, you don't need to shoot a whole roll of double exposures. Simply expose a few frames, rewind to the beginning, and start the roll again.

Only the first few frames will have gone through the camera twice, so only these frames will be double exposed.

Individual frames

You can even double expose individual frames on the roll of film. If you have an SLR or compact where rewinding can be done by hand, you can hold down the rewind button while winding on the film. You must make your second exposure directly after the first, so it's not as flexible as running the entire film through the camera twice.

Double exposure button

Alternatively, use your camera's double exposure button. Look in the spec to see if it has one – many of today's cameras do.

Check what type it is, too. Some multiple exposure buttons are self cancelling – with others, you need to return them to their normal position, or you'll continue to take all your photos on the same frame!

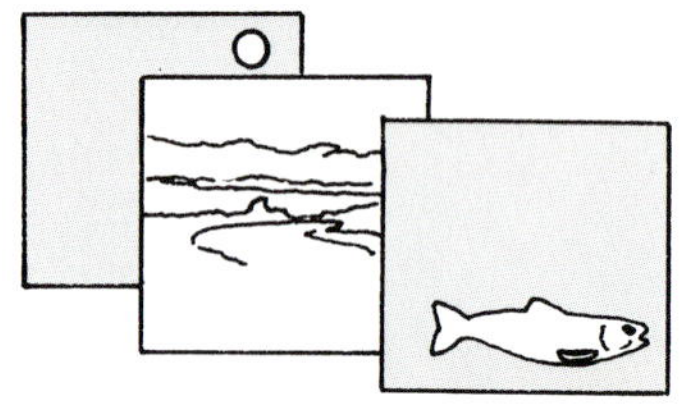

▶ *The most unlikely mixtures are relatively simple using multiple exposure techniques – but for complex combinations like this one, careful control is essential. The photographer first sketched each element on a tracing paper overlay for the camera's focusing screen. This made it easier to position the fish, moon and river scene precisely.*

▼ *With unpredictable subjects like cats, it's best to expose your secondary image – the moon, in this case – before tackling the main shot. To enlarge the moon, switch to a long lens, perhaps with a teleconverter as well.*

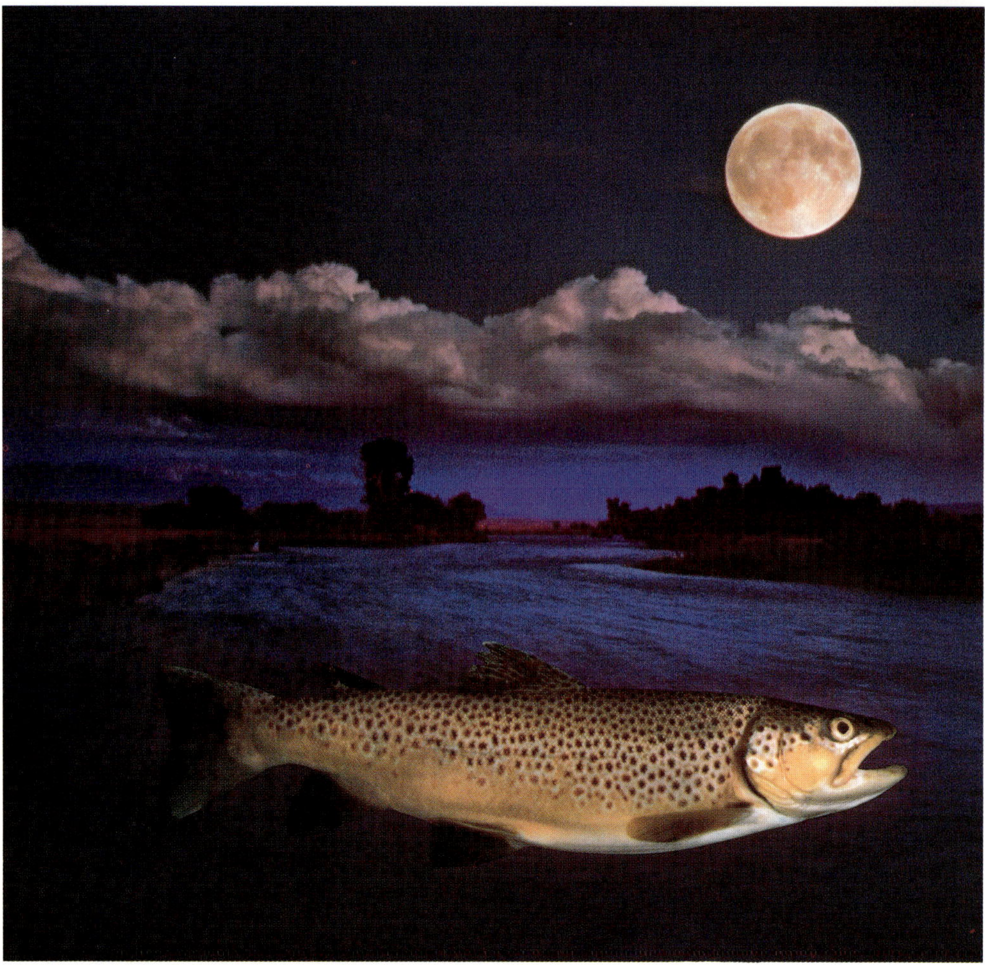

Lining up the film

For a series of double exposures, it's essential to line up frames exactly. This is quite tricky, and takes a bit of practice.

Many cameras have a loading index mark on the camera back to indicate how far you need to pull the film out of the cassette when loading. You can use this mark as a reference for aligning the film.

If there's no mark, just write one on the camera with a marker pen, or stick a small label on to the camera back close to the take-up spool.

Mark the film (see below) and either press the shutter release or crank the lever wind.

If your camera has motorized film advance, operate the shutter release. This ensures that the film advance mechanism has completed a full cycle before you continue.

Loading up

Load the camera normally and take pictures as usual. Once you've reached the end of the film and rewound it, follow the same loading procedure as before, making sure that you carefully line up your mark on the film with the index mark on the camera.

Finally, take a few extra pictures of your chosen subject to allow for some failures.

Marking the film

When you first load the film, draw the correct length of leader (film end) out of the cassette. Lay it across the camera back as if you are loading the film normally. Then use a pin to scratch a fine mark on the film at exactly the same place as the loading index point or mark on the camera back. (Make sure no bits of film drop inside the camera.)

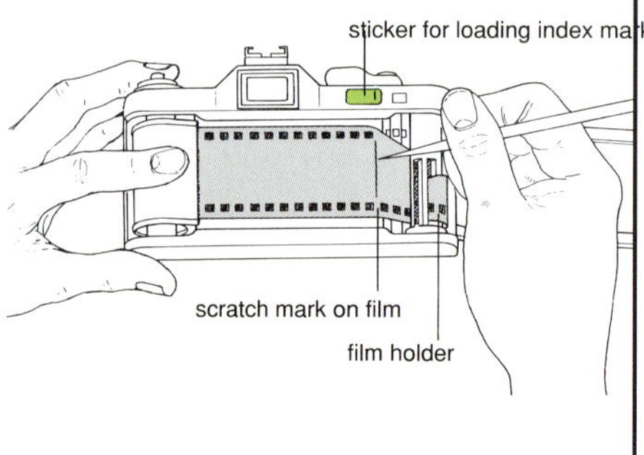

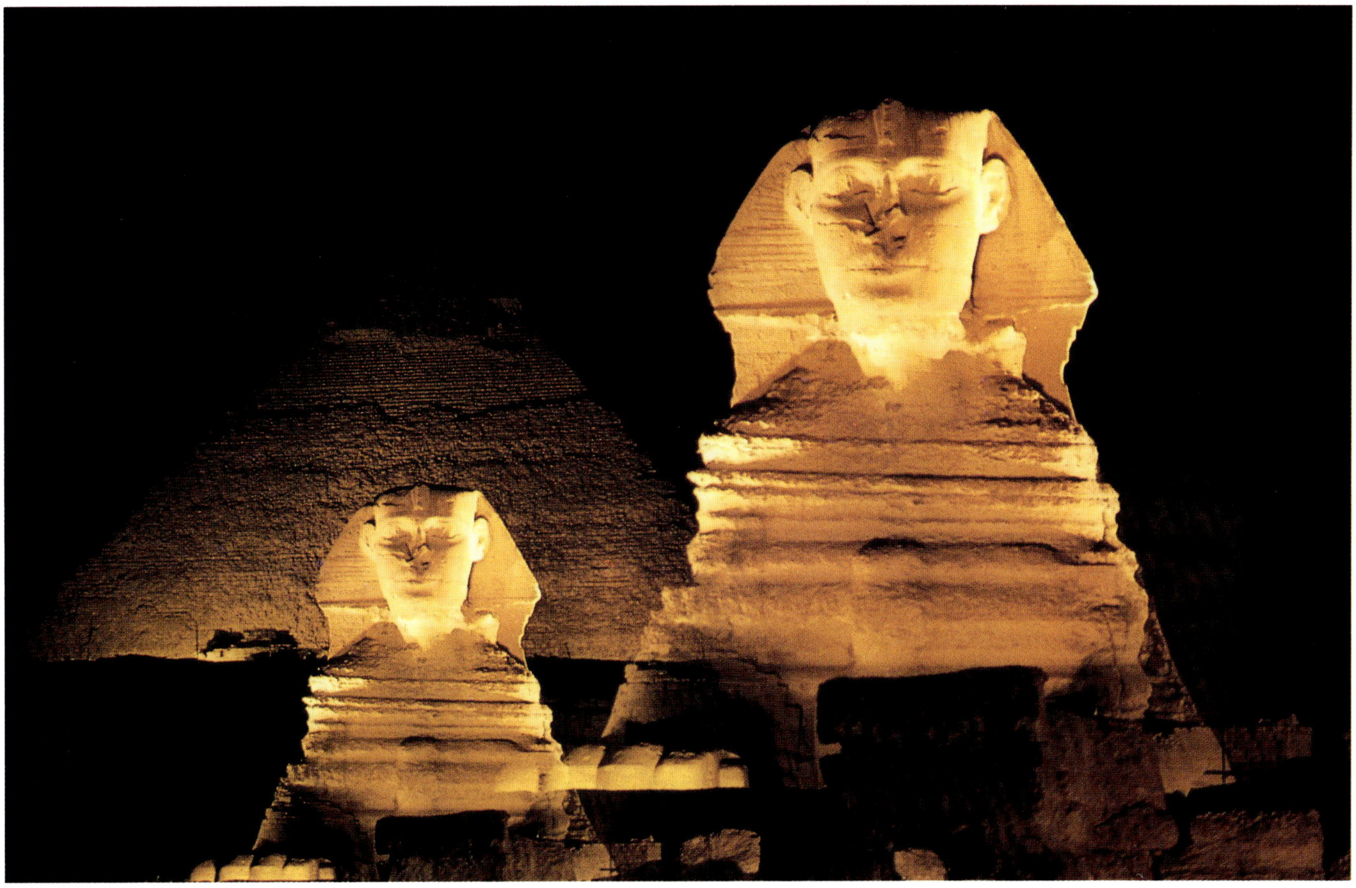

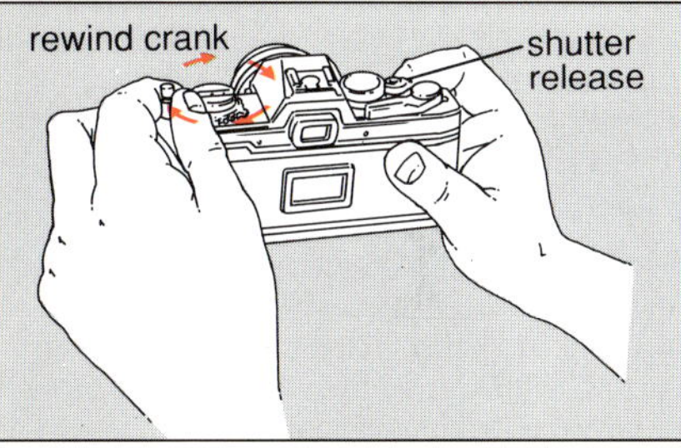

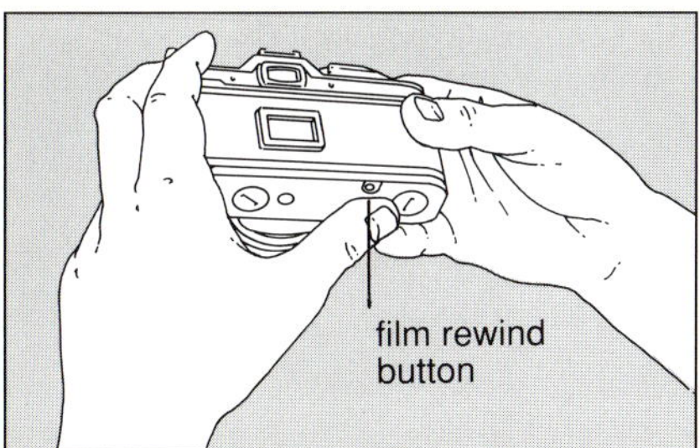

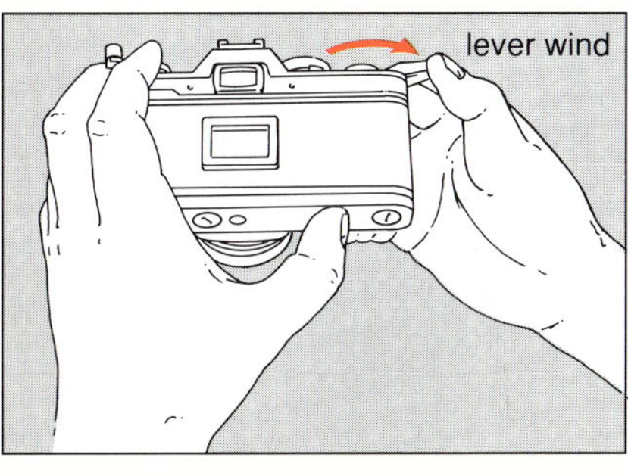

▲ *Night time offers special opportunities for double exposures, because black backgrounds make it easy to avoid the second image showing through. Here the photographer had limited time to take pictures, and has cleverly used double exposure to make an original view of a hackneyed landmark.*

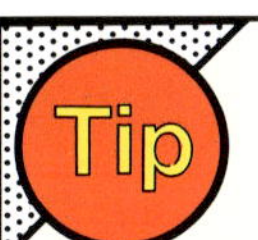

Recovering the film

If your camera rewinds automatically, the film end (leader) is often completely wound inside the cassette. Buy a film retriever and use it to recover the leader.

You can improvise by attaching double sided sticky tape to one end of a piece of thin cardboard. Carefully push this end 2cm through the film cassette's opening slit, with the side the tape is on facing towards the film. Rotate the spool counter clockwise so that the leader presses against the tape. Gently pull out the cardboard – the film end should be stuck to it.

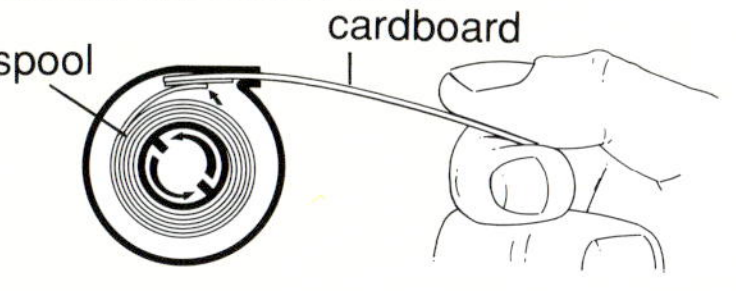

Holding down the rewind button

1 TIGHTEN THE FILM
After taking the first picture, turn the rewind crank (usually found on the top left of your camera) clockwise or in the direction of the arrow marked on it until you feel a slight resistance. This tightens up the film inside the cassette.

2 PRESS IN REWIND BUTTON
Keep hold of the rewind crank to maintain the tension, and press in the film rewind button (on the base of your camera).

3 COCK SHUTTER RELEASE
This stage takes a bit of practice. Operate the lever wind to cock the shutter release without advancing the film, while still holding the two other controls. You're now ready to take a second exposure.

Setting exposure

When you take more than one picture on a single frame, you increase the amount of exposure to light that the film receives. Your photos could be overexposed. The simplest remedy is to use colour print film. Any mistakes in exposure can usually be corrected at the printing stage.

If your image areas overlap, and you're using slide film, set a smaller aperture or faster shutter speed for each exposure. Set one stop less than the meter shows.

There are several ways of altering exposure settings – one of these should be possible unless your camera is totally automatic.

If you can't change the aperture or shutter setting on your camera by hand, use the exposure compensation dial to reduce the amount of exposure. On non-DX coded cameras, you can fool the camera into thinking it has faster film inside by turning the film speed dial to a higher ISO number.

▶ *Double exposure is a technique much used by advertising photographers. In this studio shot, after the first exposure the photographer masked off most of the picture with black card, and then closed in on the bottle to show a sidelit detail of the label.*

▼ *Think about exposure control as well as positioning. Here the photographer set one stop more than recommended for the window so the uncoloured glass is white. The passage way is underexposed for deeper shadow.*

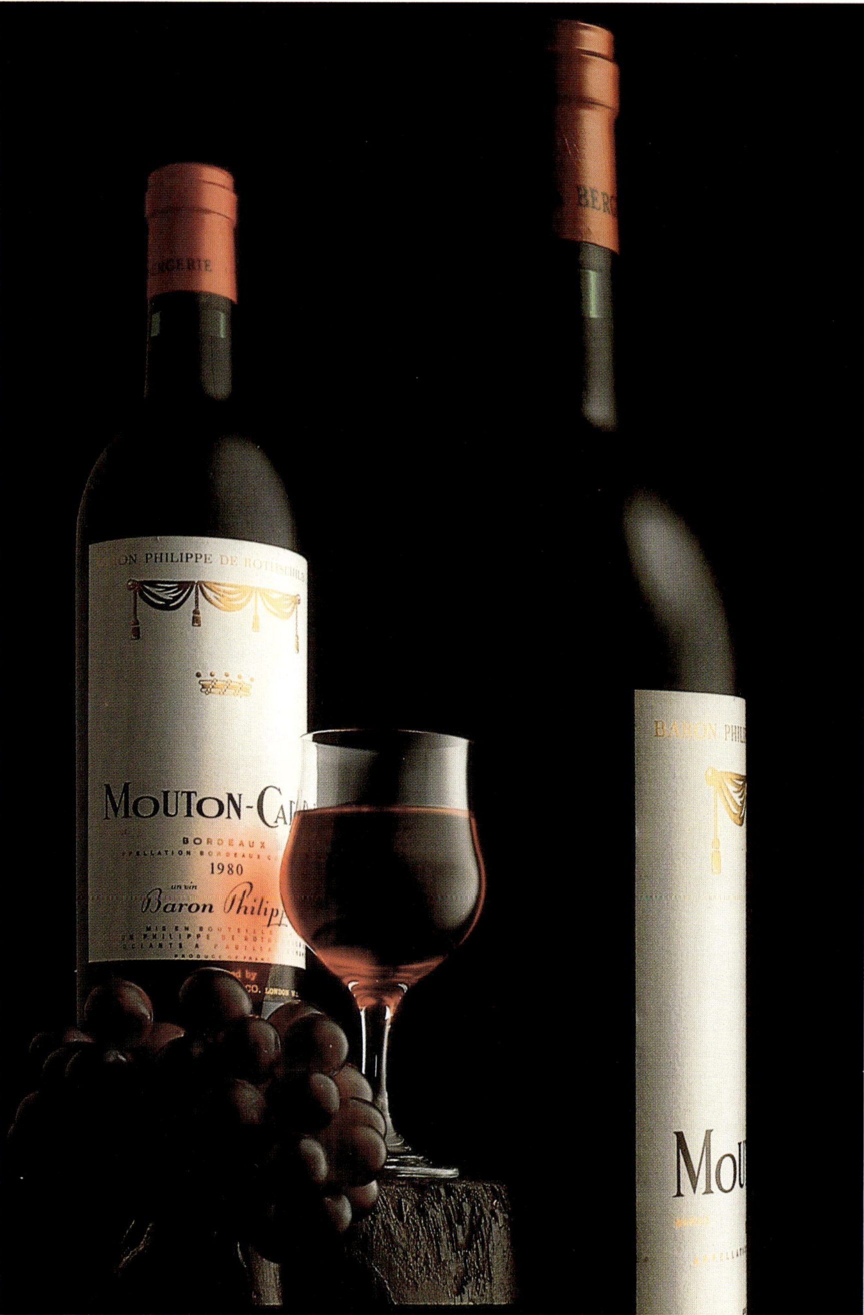

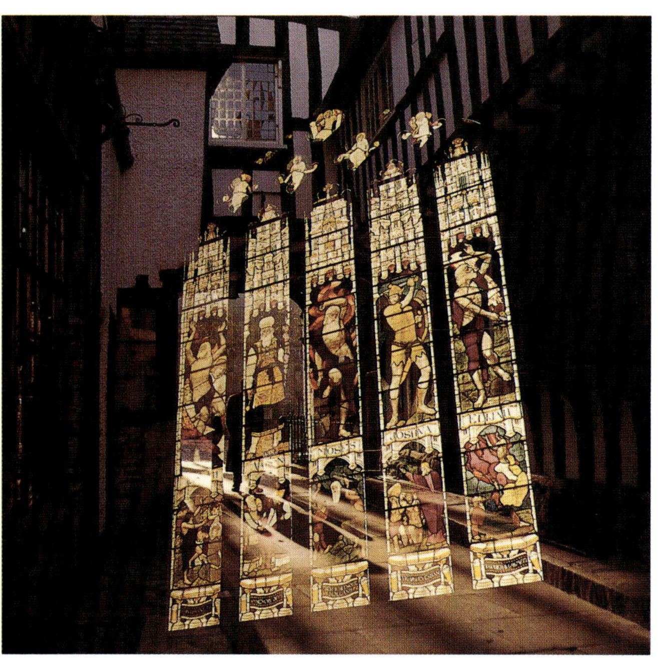

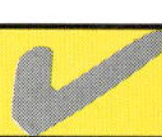

Points to remember

❑ The camera's frame counter usually records the number of exposures, not frames, so keep a separate record of how many frames you have left.

❑ Tell your lab that some frames are double exposed, so that they don't think you've made a mistake.

❑ If you run the whole film through the camera twice, frames may not line up exactly, so keep important parts of the subject away from the picture edges.

❑ If you're taking the same subject and positioning is critical, use a tripod.

❑ Make a note of the exact position of your subject as you take the first exposure, so you know where to position the second image – you could make a sketch.

❑ If you're using slide film, note the exposure settings as well.

❑ Be prepared for a few failures at first – don't stint on film.

Michael Fong – The power of Polaroid

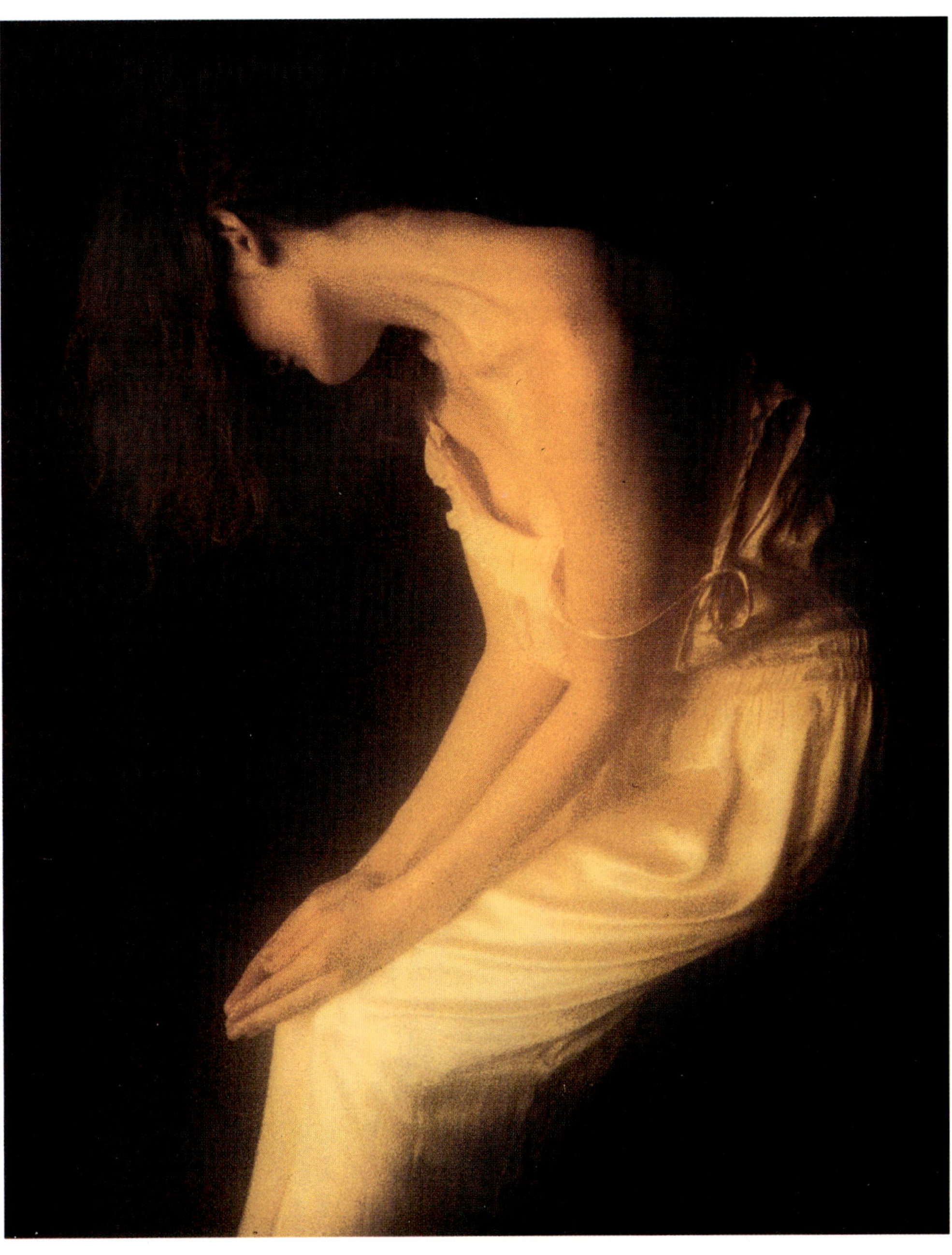

Most professionals use Polaroid film only for checking lighting and exposure, but as Michael Fong shows, it can also be used as a powerful creative medium.

'I like to keep the content of my photographs simple', says Michael Fong. 'I tend to light them simply, avoid unnecessary clutter and concentrate on trying to create an atmosphere. I wanted to suggest a dreamy mood in all these images of women, so I used reflected light and soft focus in all of them.'

Fong originally had the idea for this unique series while taking landscapes several years ago. 'I'd been photographing hills and rock formations, and I began to notice the similarities between landscapes of this kind and the contours of the female form, so I decided to try and relate the two in the studio.' Ignoring the traditional glamorous approach to photographing women, he concentrates instead on using light and shadow to highlight the natural shape and curves of the female body.

A simple set up

He generally uses a very simple lighting set up to achieve the look he wants in the studio. Most of these pictures were lit with one main light source and either one or two polystyrene reflectors to throw a gentler light back on to the subject.

Fong achieves the dream-like softness in his photographs with a combination of soft focus filters and Polaroid film. He uses either an Image Polaroid camera or an MPP 5 x 4 large format field camera for his studio work, then softens the image by placing a piece of fine gauze or a Cokin soft focus filter in front of the lens. The Image camera is totally automatic and uses $3^{1}/_{4}$ x $4^{1}/_{4}$ Polaroid colour film.

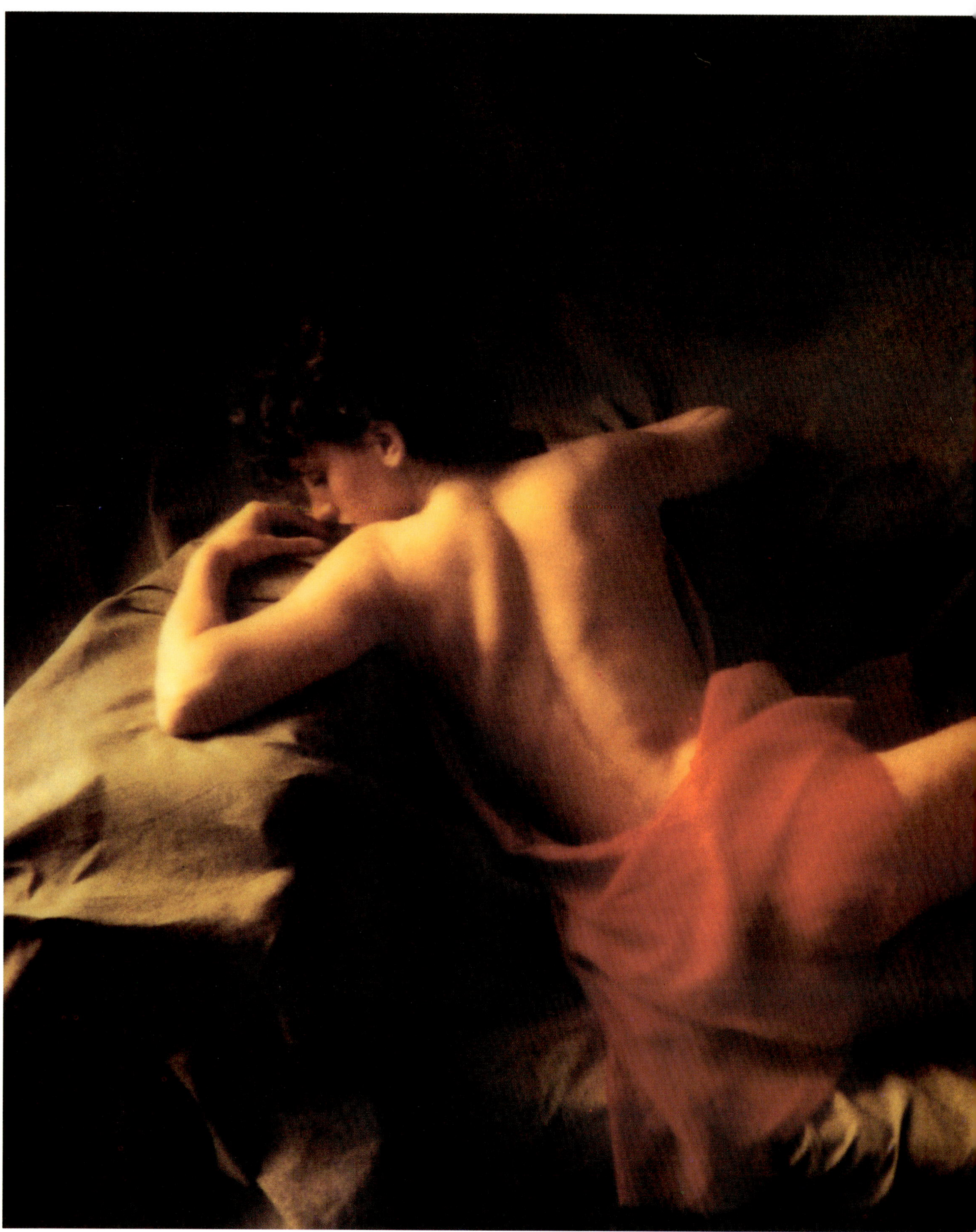

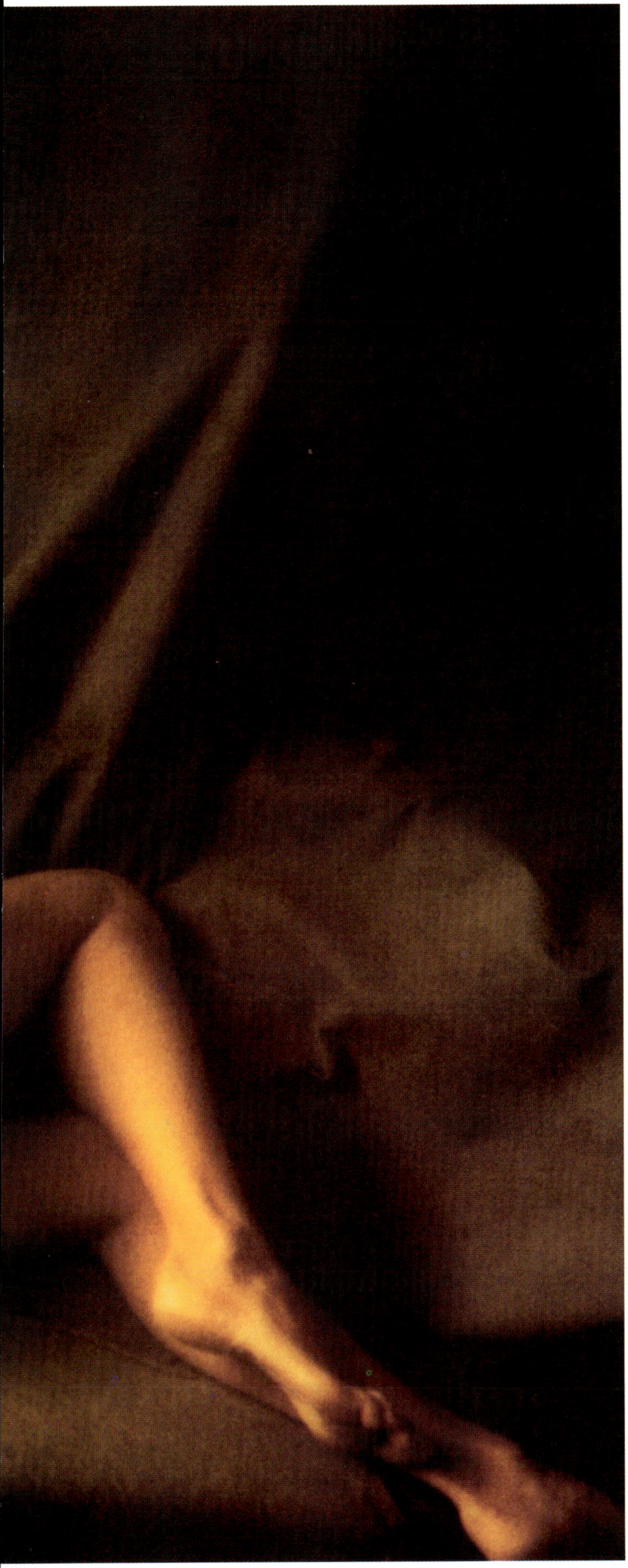

"I'm sure this was a difficult pose for the girl to hold, but it makes a dramatic picture. It was lit from the left again, with two reflectors on the right of the shot. I like the way the lighting has picked out the curves of her body and the muscles in her back and arms."
Taken on an Image Polaroid Camera with a 35mm lens on ISO 600 Polaroid film with an Elinchron flash system at f22.

"The combination of this girl's striking hair colour and her orange dress looked very effective, and I ended up photographing her in a variety of poses. For this shot I needed quite a strong light in the middle of the frame to make it work, so I bounced a strong light off a group of reflectors."
Taken on an Image Polaroid camera with a 35mm lens on ISO 600 Polaroid film with an Elinchron flash system at f16.

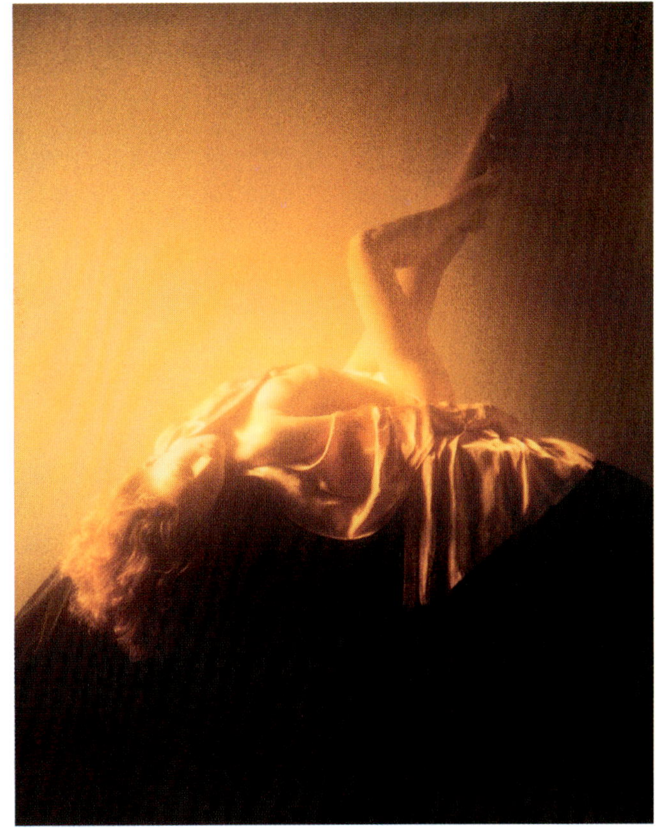

Technical details

Michael Fong likes to shoot on Polaroid film in the studio because of the extra contrast it provides. 'Most photographers only use it for lighting tests', he says, 'but I really like the dramatic look you can achieve with Polaroid in certain lighting conditions. It's an adaptable film, and has different effects in different situations – I think it allows a more individual interpretation. It certainly makes you look at lighting in a totally different way.' When Fong shoots on Polaroid, he always transfers it on to slide film afterwards to create a more contrasty, saturated and stable image. Fortunately, Polaroids are much more stable than they used to be, and the colour doesn't fade with time as it used to.

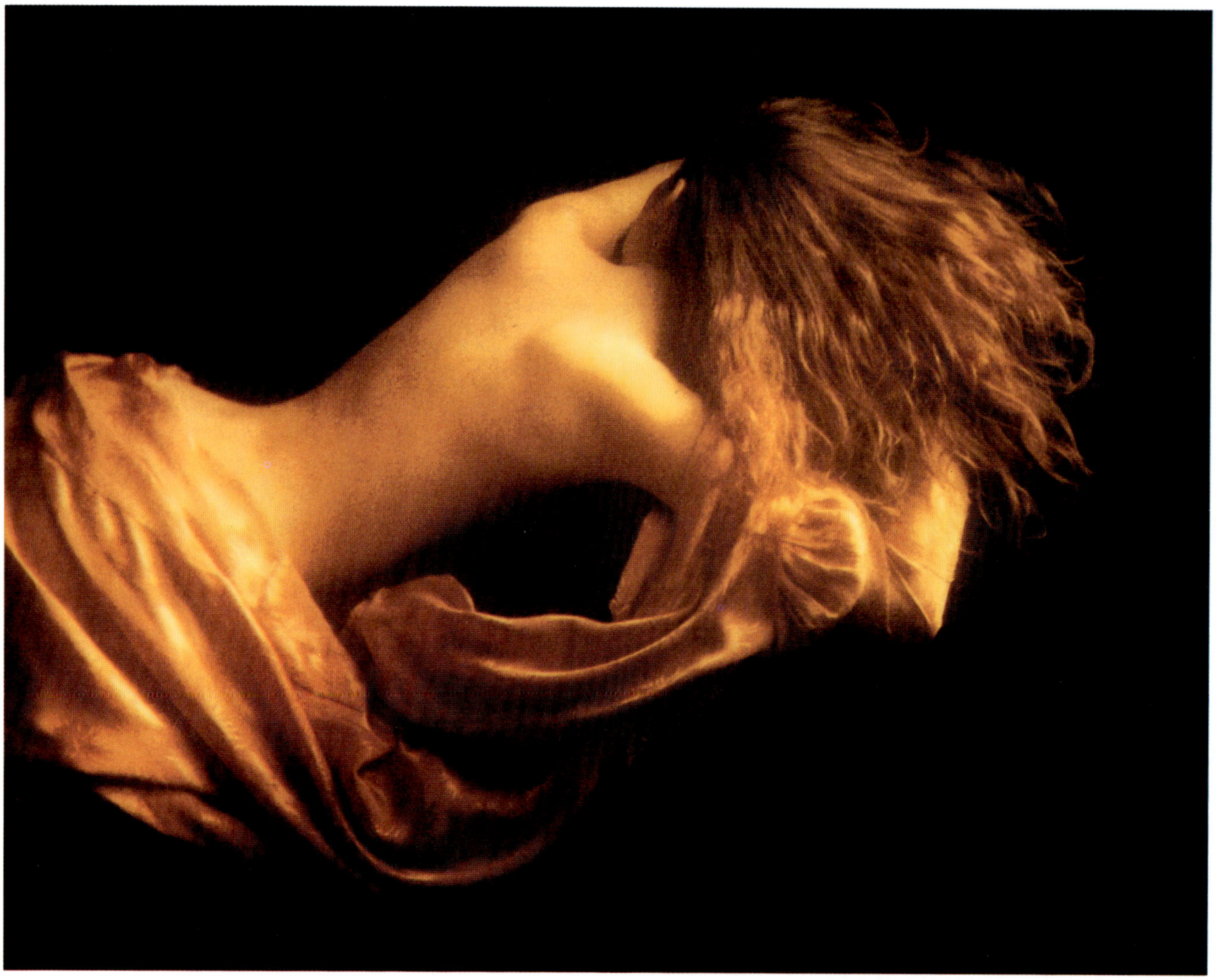

"This is another shot of that red-haired girl. I lit this from above to get a more even light across her back, and used spotlights to highlight certain areas. A warm up filter has given this shot an overall warmth that I really like."
Taken on an MPP 5 x 4 camera with a 150mm lens on ISO 100 Polaroid film with an Elinchron flash system at f11.

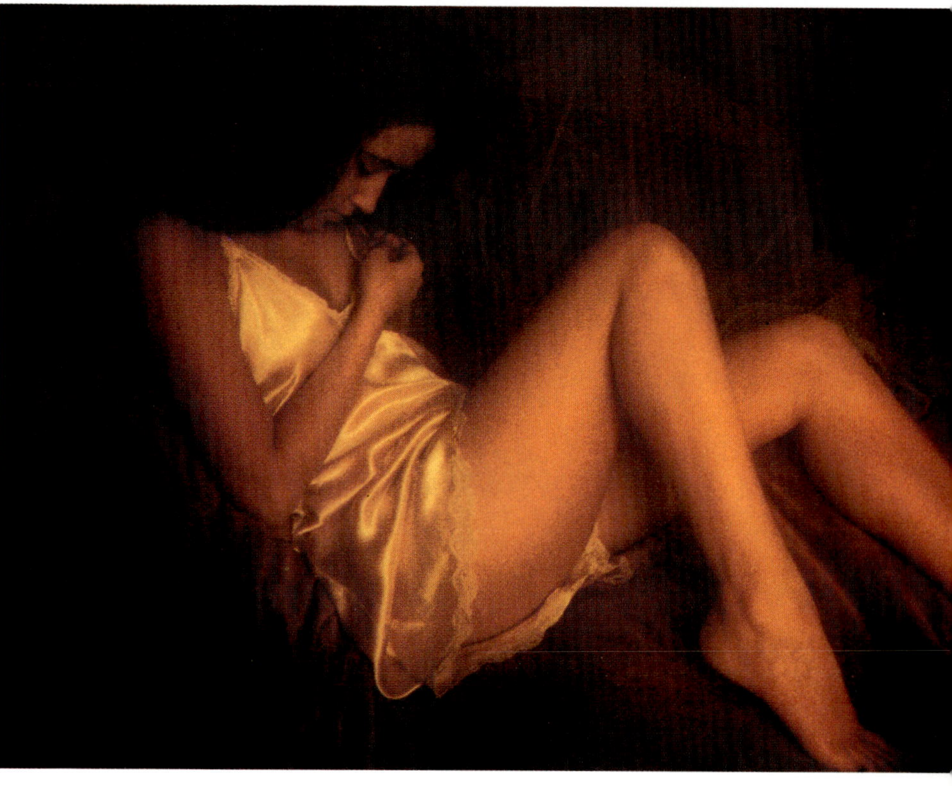

"I wanted this picture to have a particularly dreamy look, so I used Cokin soft focus and warm up filters together to accentuate the effect of the film. This hazy effect combined with the girl's pose makes it a very intimate photograph."
Taken on an MPP 5 x 4 camera with a 150mm lens on ISO 100 Polaroid film with an Elinchron flash system at f16.

Simon Donnelly – Experiments in fashion

Experimenting with different films, exposure and filtration, and then changing filtration again in printing or copying, allows you to experiment without costly new equipment.

Age is no restriction for British photographer Simon Donnelly. At 19 he set up his own photographic company and studios. Within three years he had already earned commissions from clients in the European fashion centres of Berlin and Paris. Now he's poised to take Europe by storm with his fresh and inspiring portfolio of fashion and beauty shots.

Simon's progression from complete novice to professional fashion photographer is inspiring in itself. He left school with little or no experience of photography, but managed to land a job as an assistant in a large studio. Having bought an old Pentax SLR, he set about teaching himself the basics of photography. 'You should always show other people your work when you're starting out,' he suggests, 'because you learn from their comments. Also, gaining good responses to

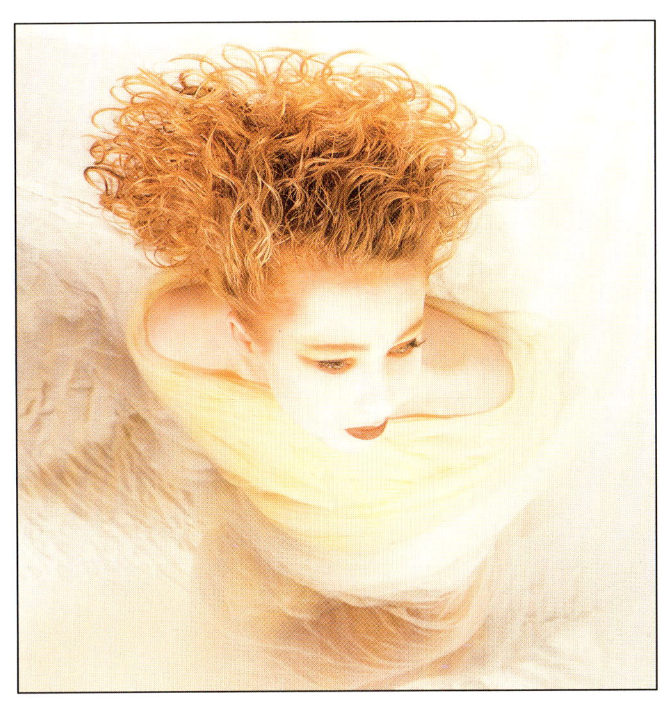

"I tried shooting these twins in a variety of poses before I settled on this one. I like its simplicity and their closed eyes give the image an ethereal feel.

The shot was taken on Polaroid black and white instant slide film, which can be processed using a portable processing unit. I printed it on to Cibachrome paper, which enhanced the film's blue tone.

I used a flash strip light over the twins and a reflector laid at an angle on the floor in front of them. I stuck a length of silver foil along the bottom edge of the reflector to throw highlights on to the girls' lips."
Taken on a Nikon F2, with a 105mm f2.5 lens, using an aperture of f8 on Polaroid Polapan CT ISO 125.

"This picture was commissioned by a hair products manufacturer. I was asked to focus attention on the model's hair, but also to make her face look as interesting as possible.

The model was lying on a low table and I cocooned her in metres of pale coloured silk fabric. I used a large softbox above her head and two other softboxes – one on either side of her body. I also placed white polystyrene boards all around her to bounce back any stray light.

I deliberately overexposed the shot by 1/2 stop to give it a light, airy feel. The image is printed upside down to make it look more dramatic. Photographed on a Bronica SQA, with a 150mm f4 lens at f5.6 on Fujichrome 100D slide film.

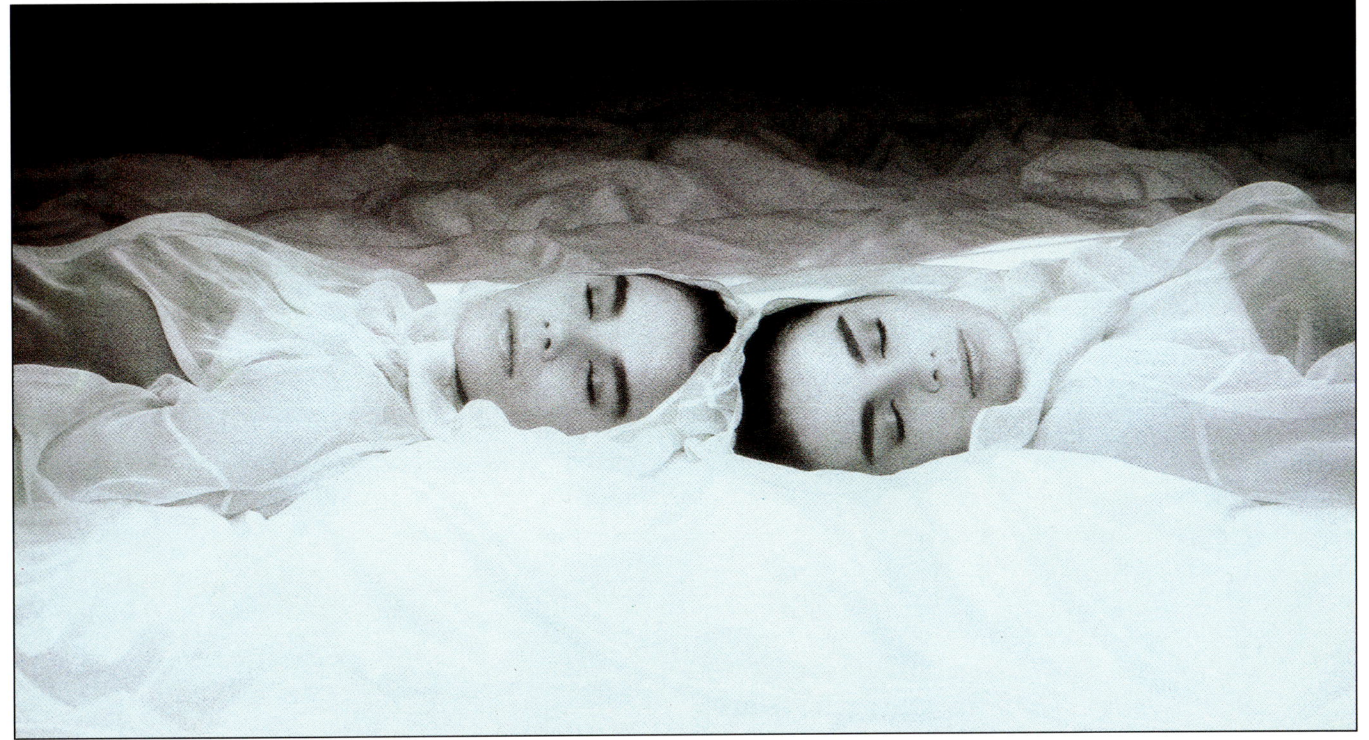

your work is the best way to build up your self-confidence.'

Clued up

After only two years assisting and learning the ropes Simon struck out on his own. His experimental approach to fashion and beauty shots soon attracted clients, and proved especially popular abroad – he now has his own photographic agent in Berlin. 'It's too easy to copy other photographers' work – so now I avoid looking at fashion magazines and photographic books. Instead, I tend to work closely with stylists and make-up artists to come up with truly original images,' he confides.

Simon's advice to budding fashion and beauty photographers is to learn about printing and processing. 'It's essential to get 'clued up' on the printing side. It's one thing to record an image on film, but the way in which it's printed is just as crucial to the finished look.'

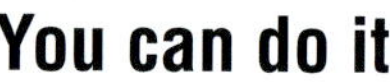

"This promotional shot was taken inside a nightclub. I chose the models especially, because they had known each other for a long time. It would have been difficult to create the intimate feel of the shot if the two models had been strangers.

I loaded up with Kodak's high speed T-Max ISO 3200 black and white film so that I could record background details using the dim available light. A hand held Metz flashgun lit the foreground."
Shot on a Nikon F2, with a 70-210mm zoom lens at f5.6, a Metz 60CT1 flashgun on Kodak T-Max 3200 film rated at ISO 1600.

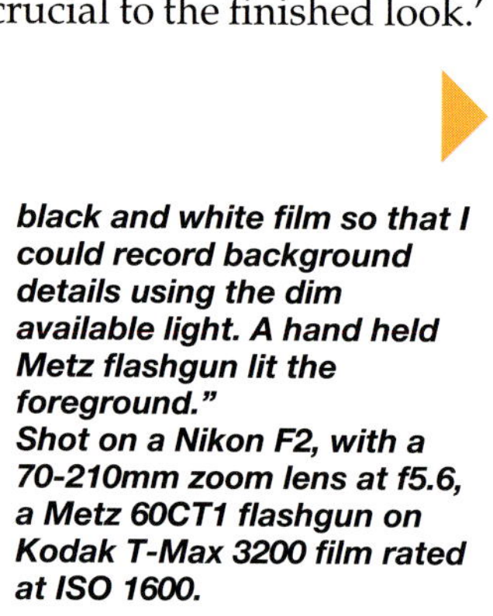

"The most difficult aspect of this shoot was arranging the head scarf. It took two hours to get the natural look I was after.

The portrait was lit using a single softbox and a reflector to bounce light back into the model's face.

I projected the image on to a piece of coarse canvas using an old Gnome projector. The projected image was photographed on 5 x 4in sheet film, and then enlarged to 10 x 8in.

An artist made a mask with streaks in it. This was placed over the slide and I made a print on to Cibachrome paper."
Taken on a Bronica SQA, with a 150mm f4 lens at f11 on Fujichrome 100D.

You can do it

Why not try projecting some of your favourite slides on to textured surfaces and rephotographing them? All you need is a projector, a well exposed slide and a suitable surface, such as a whitewashed brick wall, or a piece of light coloured canvas.

Projectors use tungsten bulbs, so to record colours correctly you need to shoot on tungsten balanced film. Alternatively, you can shoot on daylight balanced film and fit an 80A filter over the projector lens. However, for his picture Simon preferred to shoot on daylight film and leave the light unfiltered. This gave the picture a pleasing warm tone.

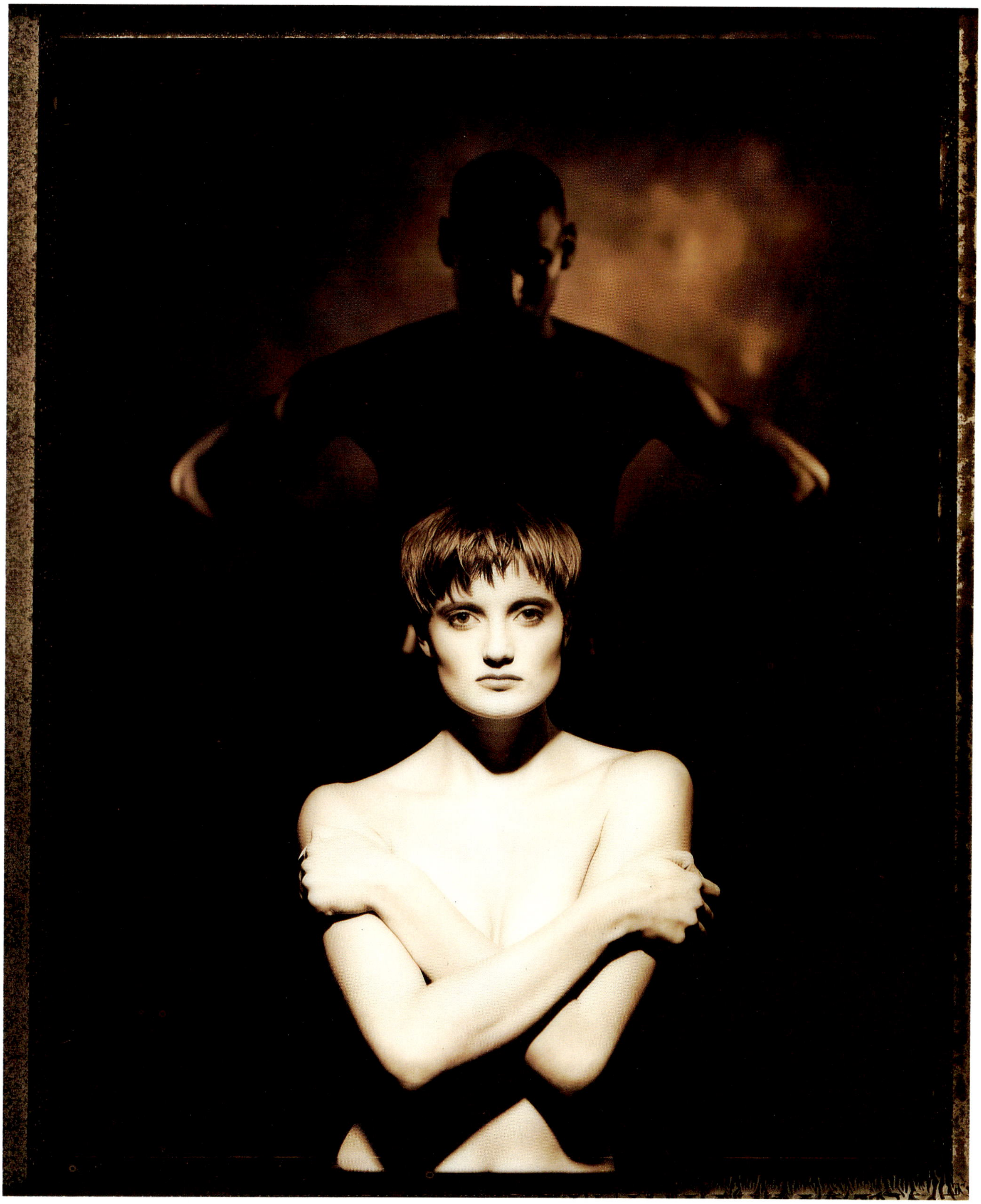

"I tried out Polaroid 55 film on this shot. It's a black and white sheet film that gives an instant print and a negative. The negative gives a high quality enlargement with an attractive border.

I made a print on to colour paper from the negative and used the enlarger's filtration controls to get the rich brown tone.

I lit the model with a spotlight and a softbox. The man at the back was lit with two softboxes and I focused a tungsten spotlight on the background."

Shot on a Sinar 5 x 4, with a 210mm (standard) lens at f5.6 and a shutter speed of 1/60th sec on Polaroid 55 instant print film.

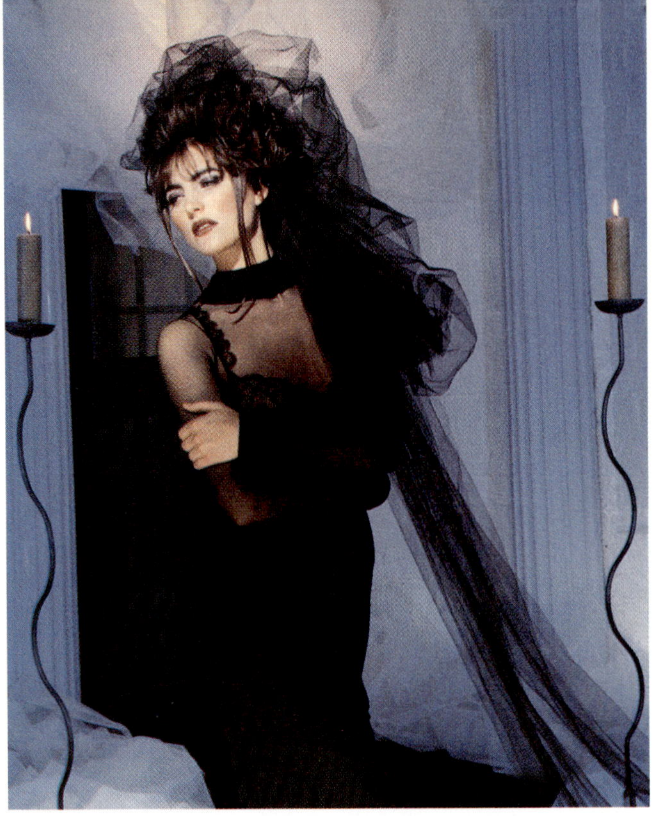

Technical details

For beauty shots Simon often lights his models with a spotlight and a softbox. 'Spotlights help define the face, revealing the shape of the jaw and the cheekbones. But the light from a spotlight is too harsh on its own,' he explains. 'This is where a softbox comes in. You can use it to fill in the hard shadows.'

Simon positions the softbox high above and slightly in front of the model, making sure that it doesn't create a catchlight in her eyes.

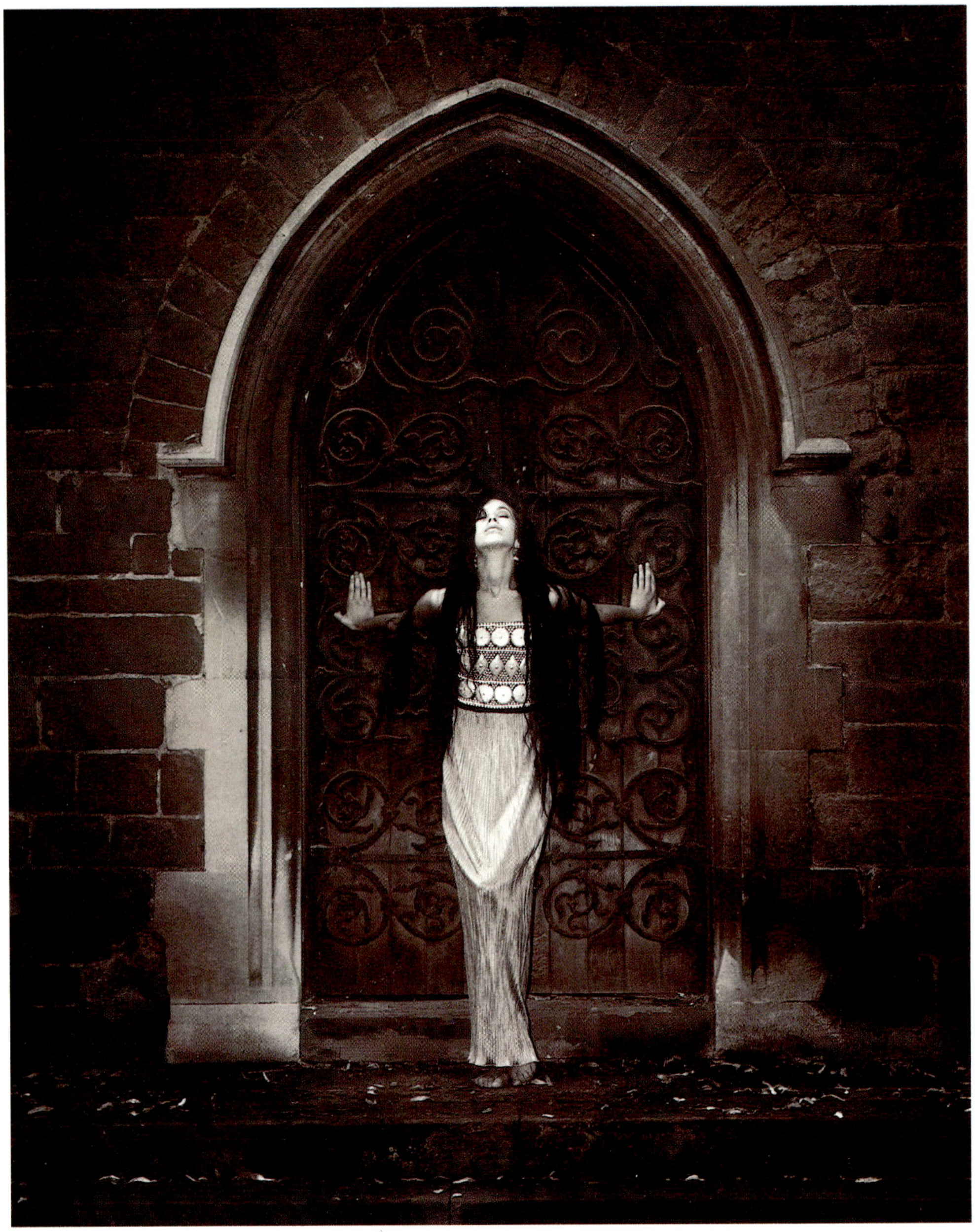

"I noticed this church door on my way home from work one night. The next day I saw the dress and immediately saw the two together in my head.

The dress was made from metallic materials, so I used fill-in flash to bring up the details.

I printed the image on Ilford Multigrade resin coated paper and then sepia toned it. I also burnt in the edges to emphasize the shape of the arch."
Photographed on a Bronica SQA, with a 80mm f2.8 lens at f5.6, with a shutter speed of 1/30th second, using a Metz 60CT1 flashgun on Ilford FP4 print film.

Presenting prints

Once you have taken a memorable picture, it isn't worth much unless people can see and admire it. Thoughtful framing can make an immense difference to the way in which people perceive and enjoy your pictures.

A good style starting point is the decor of the room in which you wish to display your prints. For example, with pine decor you could choose natural wood frames – or go for contrast, such as an ornate frame in an uncluttered room or choose frames in a contrasting colour to the walls.

Frame style can be modest and functional, simply protecting the print from dust, or a powerful design statement in its own right. 'Purists' may prefer a plain frame, which doesn't compete with the image, while others see a photograph as an excuse for an elaborate frame. Neither approach is the 'correct' one – it's just a matter of what you like.

Cost is an important consideration. Inexpensive modern and reproduction frames are widely available in shops. For a more unusual frame, explore secondhand and junk shops.

▼ *This tubular frame is perfect for a desk or table top. It blends in with desk accessories and it's sturdy, able to take accidental knocks.*

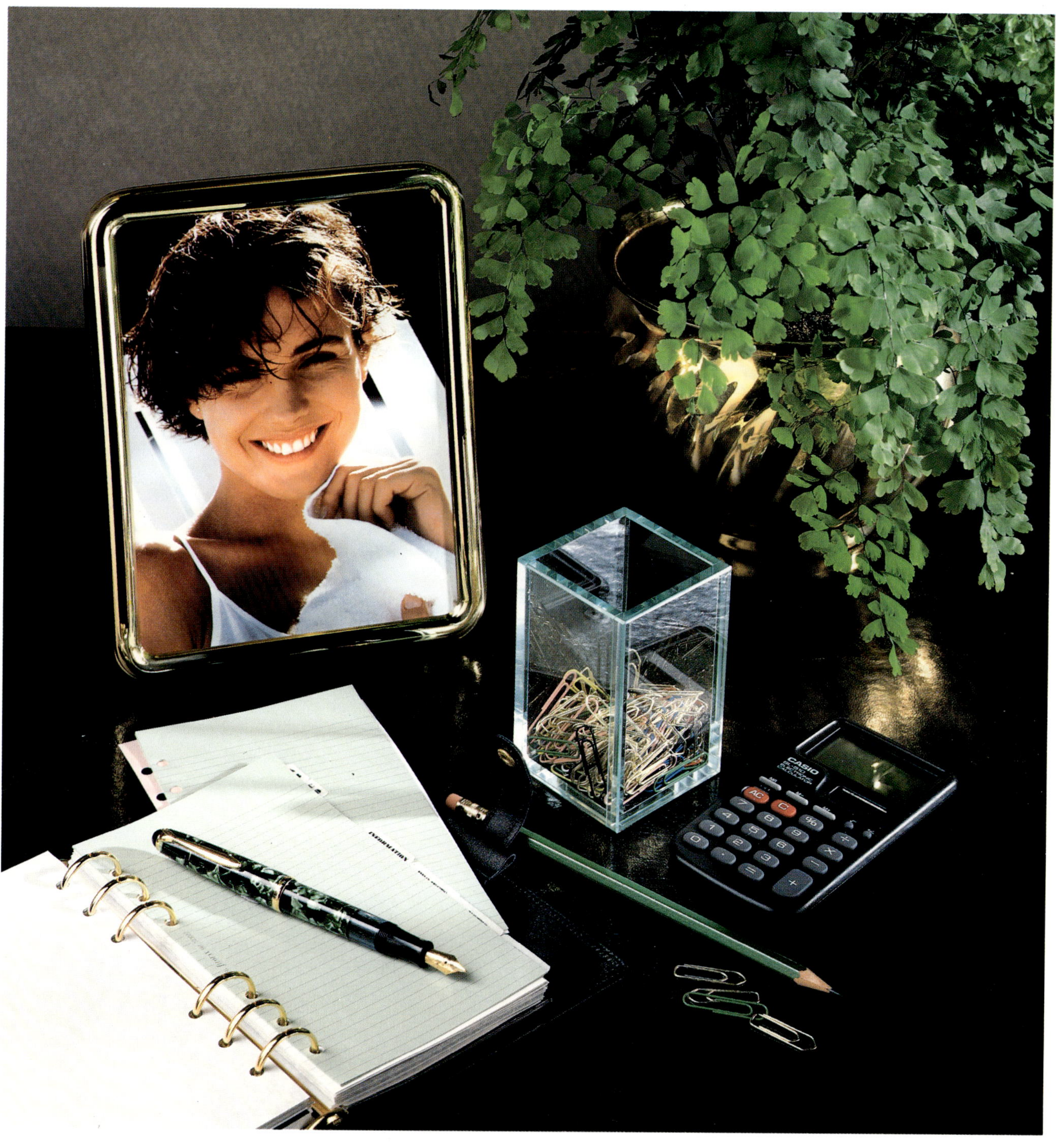

Mounts

A thick card surround between the print and the frame is optional but increases the size, shape, colour and texture options. A mount can give a small print more visual impact or transform a large print into a magnificent focal point, for a wall above a fireplace, for instance.

You can make your own mounts – this is ideal if you'd like a personalized mount covered with decorative paper or fabric, for example. Alternatively, buy them from a shop – look in the telephone directory under 'Picture framers'.

Most shops have samples of mounts plus wood and metal sections of all descriptions to make into frames. Be sure to bring the print along for reference before ordering the materials. Take as long as you like trying out different combinations.

Multiple displays, on a wall or dressing table, for example, can feature identical frames, perhaps varying in size. Or you can use frames with a basic overall theme, such as several styles and shapes of silver gilt frames, or a genuine mix and match – potentially the most exciting.

1 TONE ON TONE
Monochrome prints look stronger when they don't have to compete with the frame. A silvery frame and white mount, edged with a drawn line, complement the subtle tones of this study of a viaduct.

2 REPEATING COLOURS
The crisp, blue-white atmosphere of this enchanting wintery study is echoed by the blue band on the mount and again by its classic wooden frame.

3 EASY DOES IT
Glass clip frames are cheap, widely available in a range of sizes, easy to use and unobtrusive. The print can fill the whole frame or can be set in a mount. Most clip frames come with a reversible paper mount on which the print rests, so no measuring or cutting is involved.

4 FAMILY PORTRAITS
Pre-cut multiple mounts make it easy for you to display several portraits of your family or record a child growing up, in a single frame.

5 GEOMETRIC STRENGTH
The plain black frame and the bluish mount repeat the simple geometric theme and powerful colours of this beach hut study.

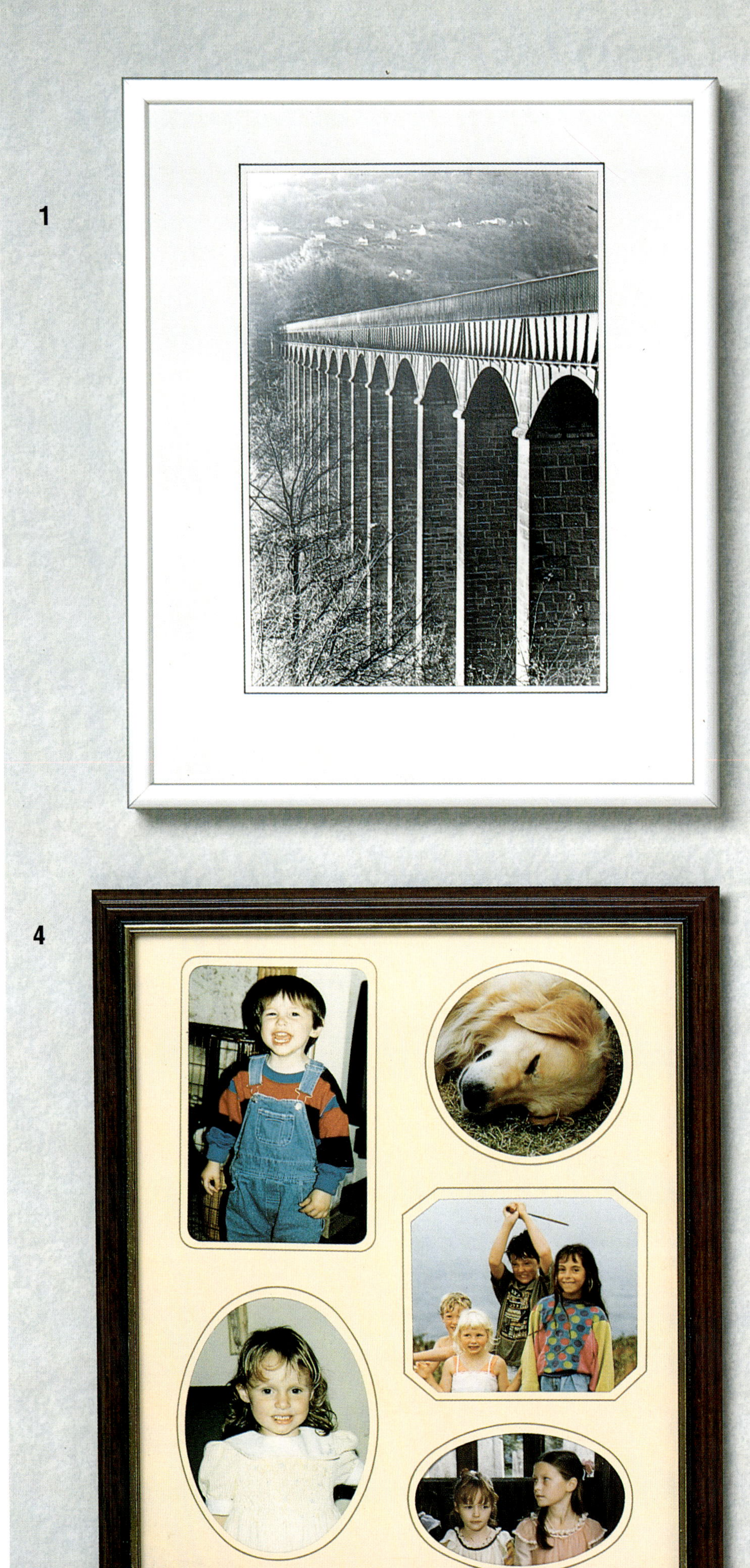

2

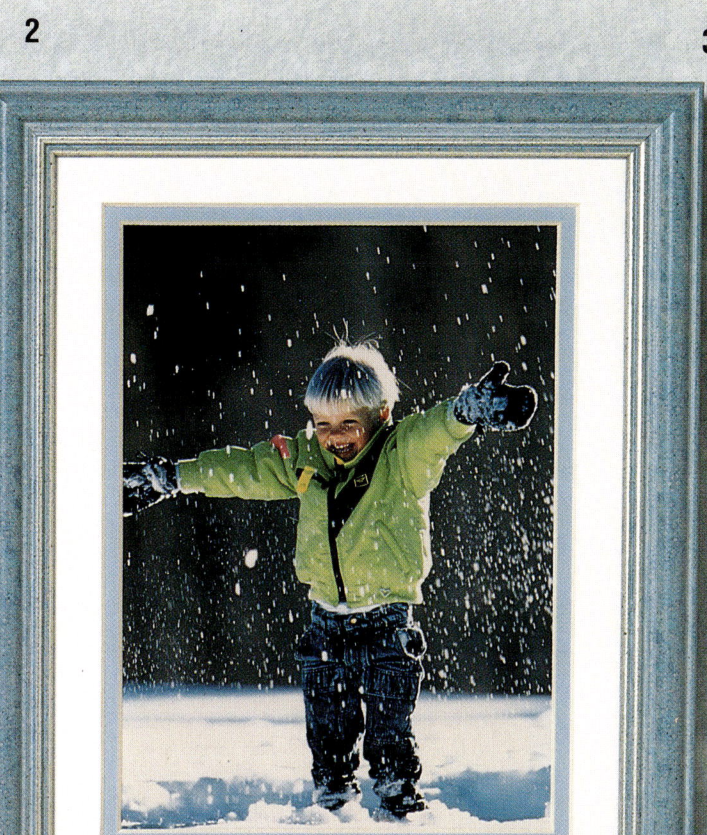

3

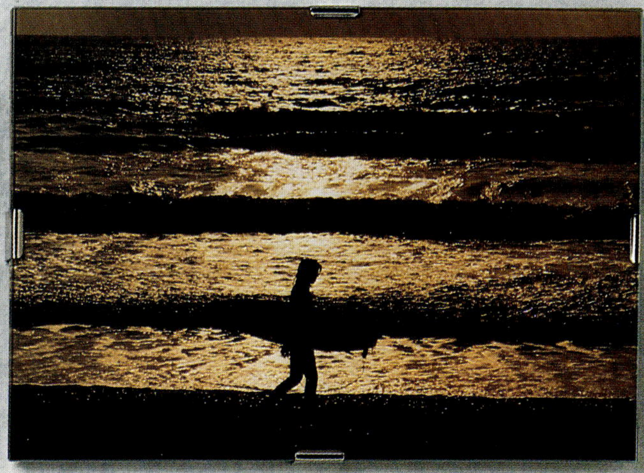

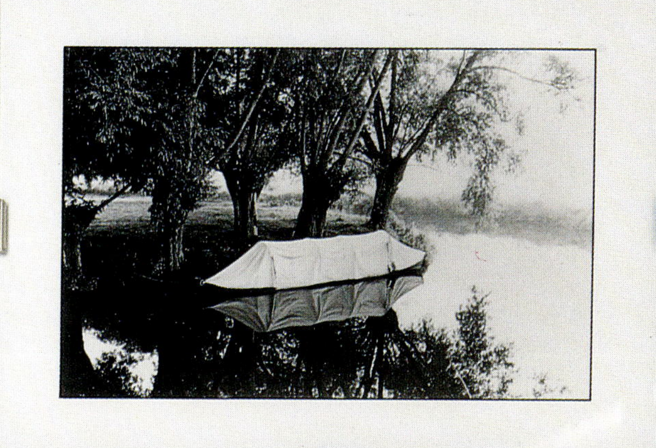

5

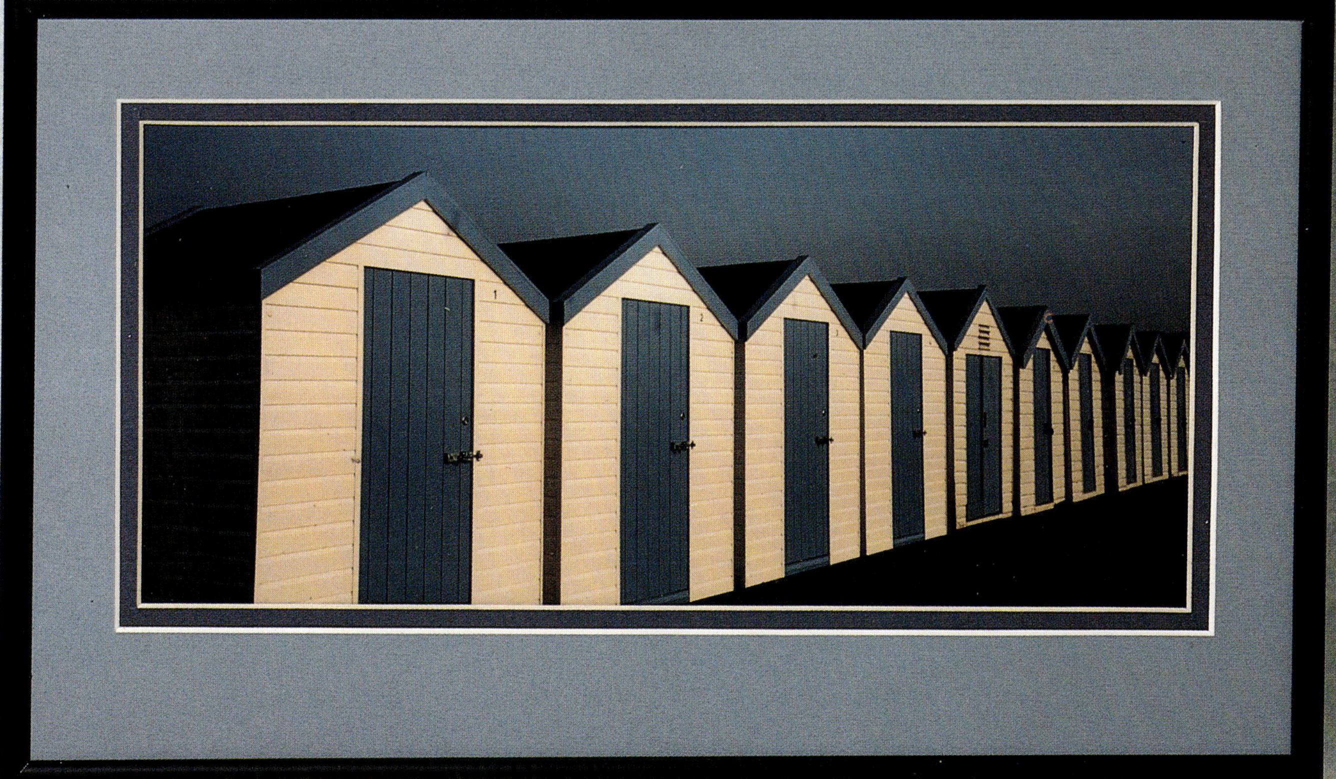

Placing the picture

Your border should be large enough to give the print plenty of space. For example, if the print is 25 x 20cm (10 x 8in), an appropriate size for the outer edge of the mount is 38 x 30cm (15 x 12in).

When you position the picture in the frame, make the bottom border wider than the top one. If both borders are equal, an optical illusion often makes the print look as if it's slipping down in the frame.

Make sure the bottom border is at least 1cm wider – the amount is tiny, but makes all the difference visually. The borders either side should be the same width as the top one.

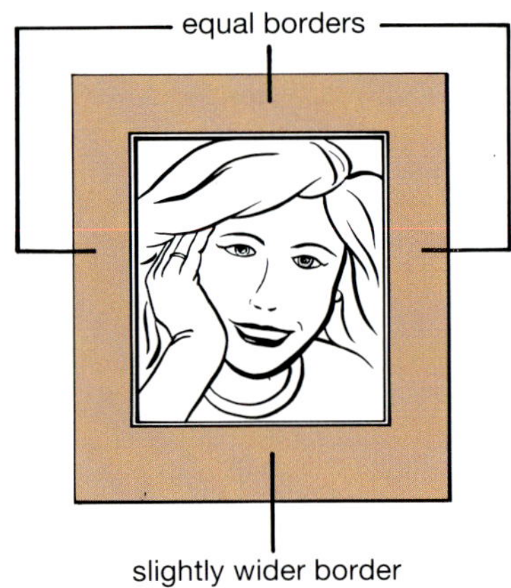

Choosing and changing a border

A carefully chosen border can transform a good photo into one that's eye-catching. Its thickness also protects the print from the glass. You can buy or make a cardboard border to surround the photo.

The surround is often a neutral colour like white, cream, grey or beige, but other colours can work well if they tone with the picture's shades. A photo with red detail in it, for instance, can look really striking if its border matches. But beware of two colours that are not quite identical – they can clash.

Embellishing the mount

To make your print stand out more, you can add thin lines near the edge of the mount. Black and silver lines work well. Use a ruler and set square and lightly mark out the lines in pencil first. Then carefully draw along these lines with ink.

Another option is to colour in the cut edges of the mount nearest the print with felt tip pen. Neutral colours like grey work well. You can also use a colour that matches the frame. Test the pen on a scrap piece of card first.

Whichever method you choose, work slowly to avoid mistakes. Draw lines or colour in any areas on the mount before you have inserted the photograph.

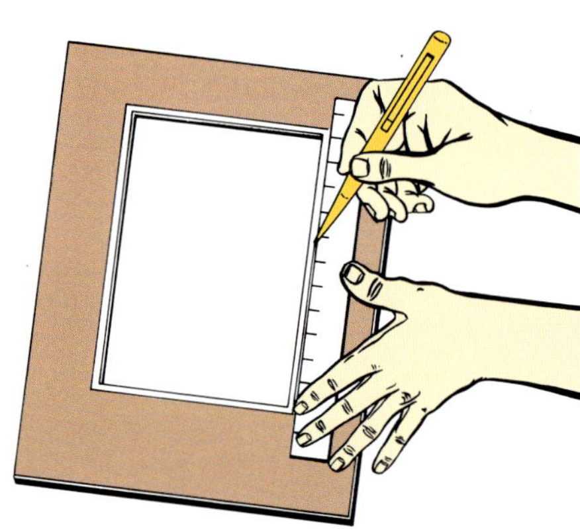
ruled ink line adds impact to picture

Making a tape hinge

If you'd like the option of removing your photo from its mount at a later date, fasten the print to the card with tape instead of permanent adhesive.

1 POSITION PRINT

Place the border face down on a flat surface, with the print face down on top. Carefully position the print in exactly the right place. Fix the top edge of the print to the border with a strip of masking tape.

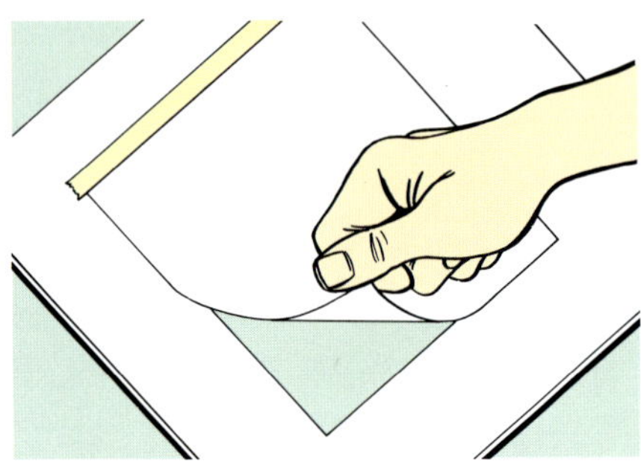

2 ATTACH HINGE

Place the windowed card face down alongside the backing card. Join the two pieces together with a strip of 3cm wide gummed brown paper down one side of the card to act as a hinge.

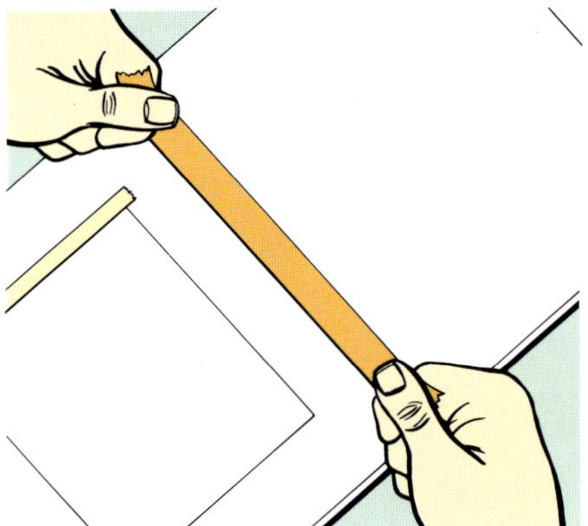

3 COMPLETE MOUNT

Bring the two pieces of card together. Carefully remove any marks on the card with a soft eraser.

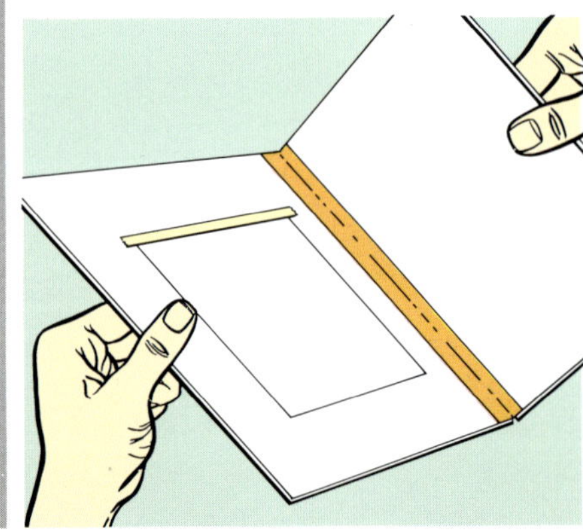

Changing mounts

Tip

You don't have to buy a new frame to transform your print – swapping mounts can make all the difference. If you're not sure what colour would be best, cut several L shapes from scrap card and hold them between the frame and the print. You can then see which shade is the best match.

different coloured L shapes cut from scrap card

Cropping prints

Trimming the edges of your prints (cropping) is an easy way to sharpen up their impact. From prints you might otherwise discard, you can make pictures to be proud of.

Some photographers disapprove of cropping. Obviously it is better to frame the picture to advantage when you take it, because when you print from the whole negative area you obtain the best quality print. However, if you can occasionally improve a picture by cropping one or all of the edges, you should do so.

With a pair of 'L's' to hand (see L-plates tip) you can try various ways of cropping around the image. Sometimes you have to crop off a large part of the picture to get a really effective composition. Sometimes merely cropping a fine line off one side does the trick.

Once you have decided on where to crop your print, use a guillotine or a scalpel and metal rule to make a sharp, straight cut.

Cut it out

Experience teaches you certain problems of composition that are best avoided unless you are using them for a specific reason. Small bright areas in an otherwise dark scene inevitably draw the eye and

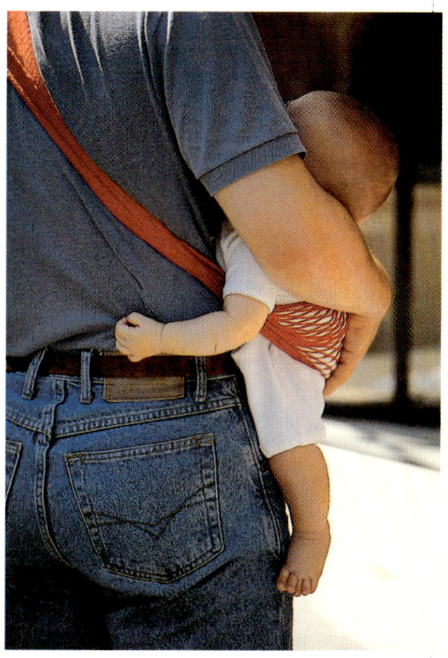

◀ *In pictures of people, the viewer's eye is automatically drawn to the heads – even the backs of them. In this snap, cropping out the adult's head draws attention to the protective grasp, and helps contrast the difference in arm sizes.*

▼ *Cropping extra tightly gives a portrait great impact. Here, the viewer's attention is closely focused on the intense concentration the child is paying to his icecream.*

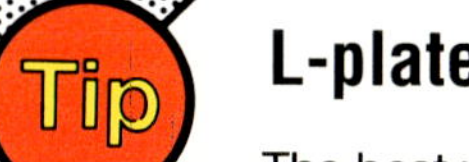

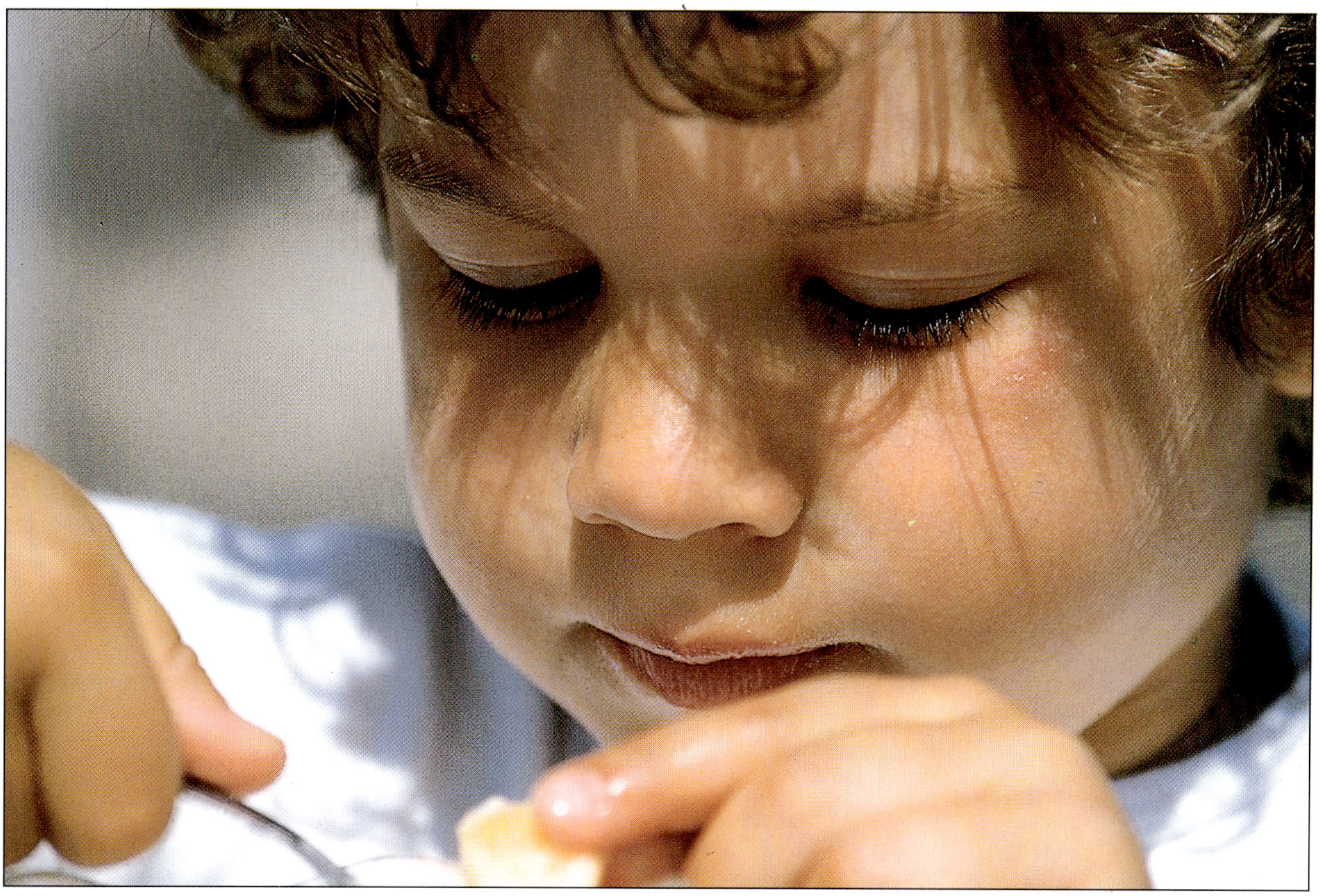

L-plates

The best way to see the variety of effects that you can achieve by cropping your prints is to experiment with a pair of L-shaped pieces (known as 'L's') cut from card. It is essential to cut them square with straight sides.

Place the L's over your own prints and those in books. By moving them to and fro you can change the format, reposition the main subject, change the emphasis or crop out unwanted elements.

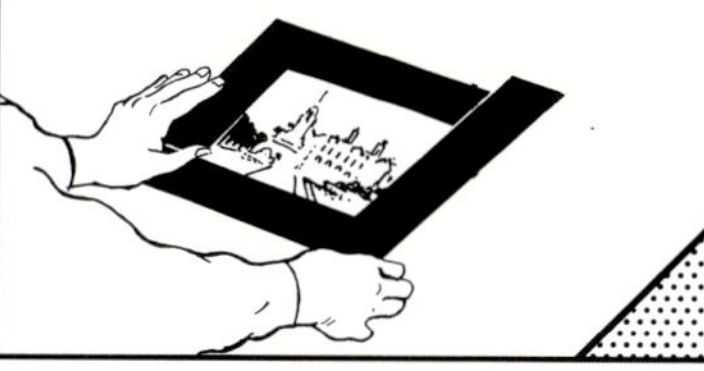

are usually best cropped out. In the same way, you may be able to exclude a background that's too dominant.

Don't be afraid to remove anything that isn't necessary. For example, if you were unable, for various reasons, to get close enough to your subject while shooting, or if, when taking a portrait, there is no way of avoiding an expanse of ceiling, cropping of the print is essential.

Cropping can also be used to intensify the mood of the picture. By eliminating any sense of space around a person or an object you can make it seem to burst from the frame. This is particularly effective if the subject is an emotionally charged one, such as a child crying.

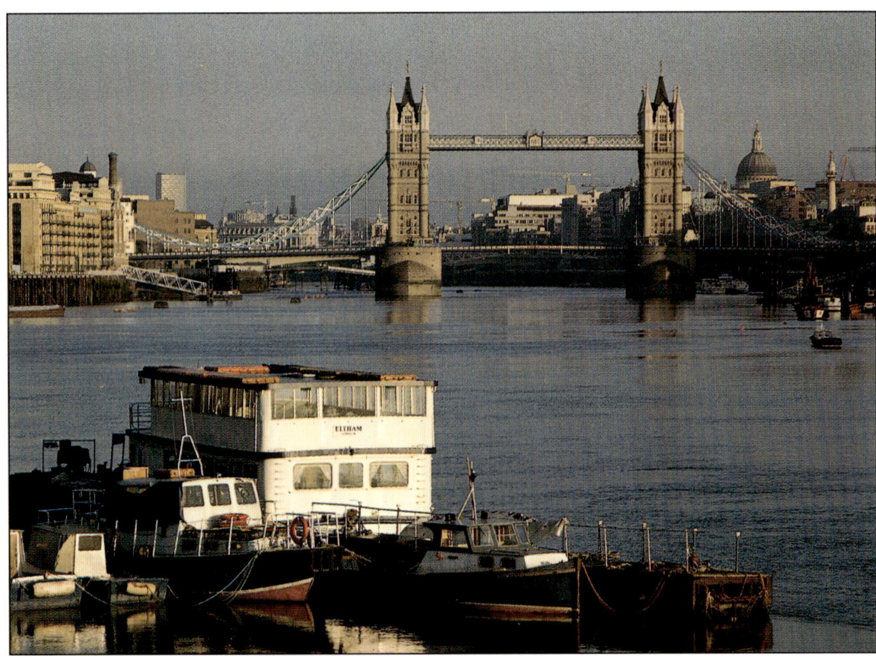

▲ *Sometimes distracting details draw attention away from the main subject. In this shot of Tower Bridge in London, boats were included to add foreground interest. However, in the final print they appear too dominating. The solution (top right): enlarge the whole print – then crop round the bridge.*

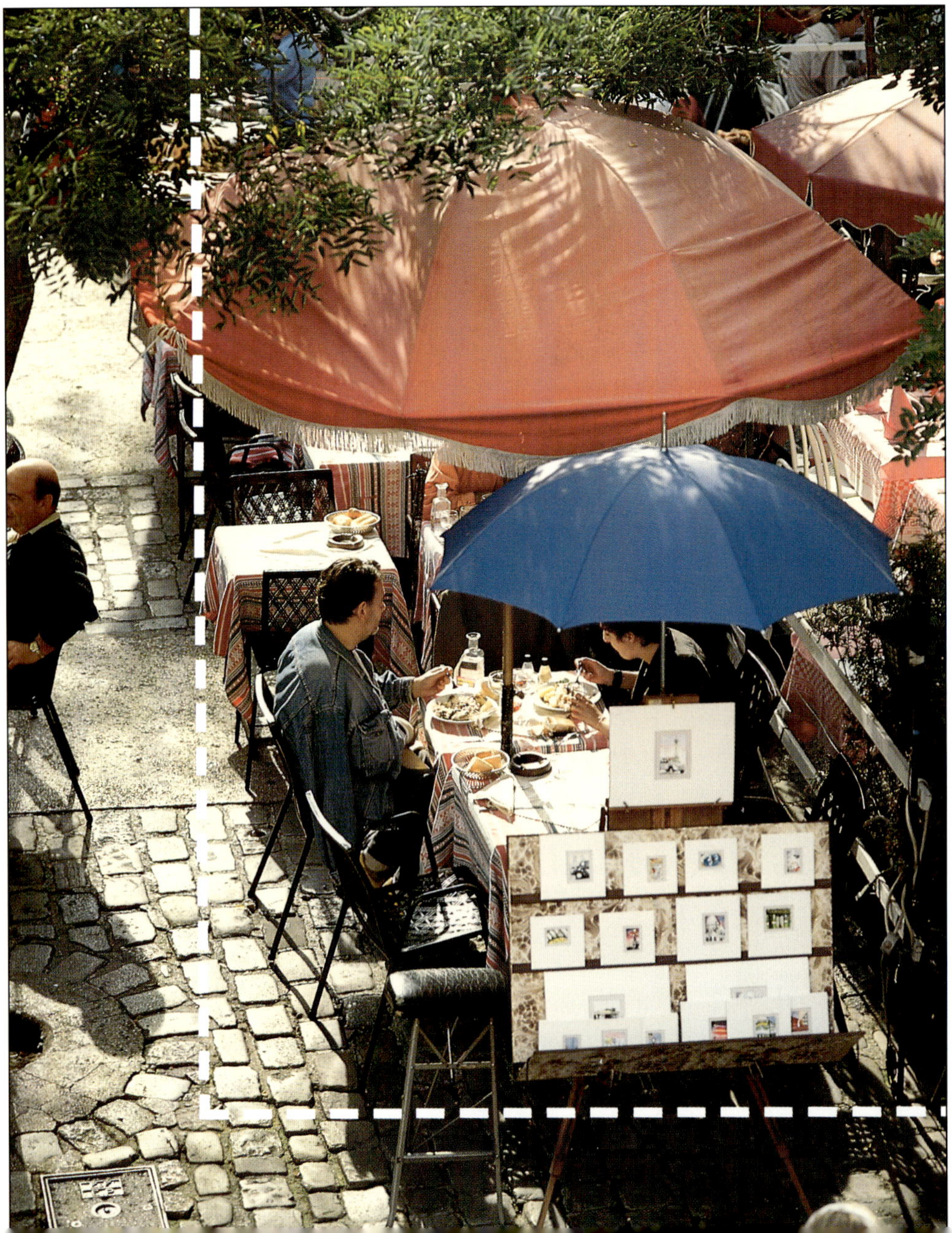

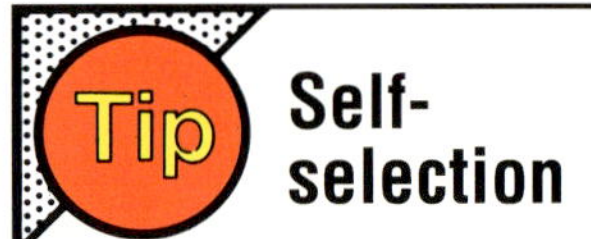

Self-selection

If you want to enlarge part of a print, *don't* ask a lab to make a selective enlargement. You achieve much greater accuracy – and save money – if you get the whole print enlarged, then crop out the unwanted bits yourself.

◄ *The problem of unwanted intrusions at the edges of the picture is extremely common, and is especially annoying in scenes like this, where a person is cut in half. Crop the edges to improve the composition.*

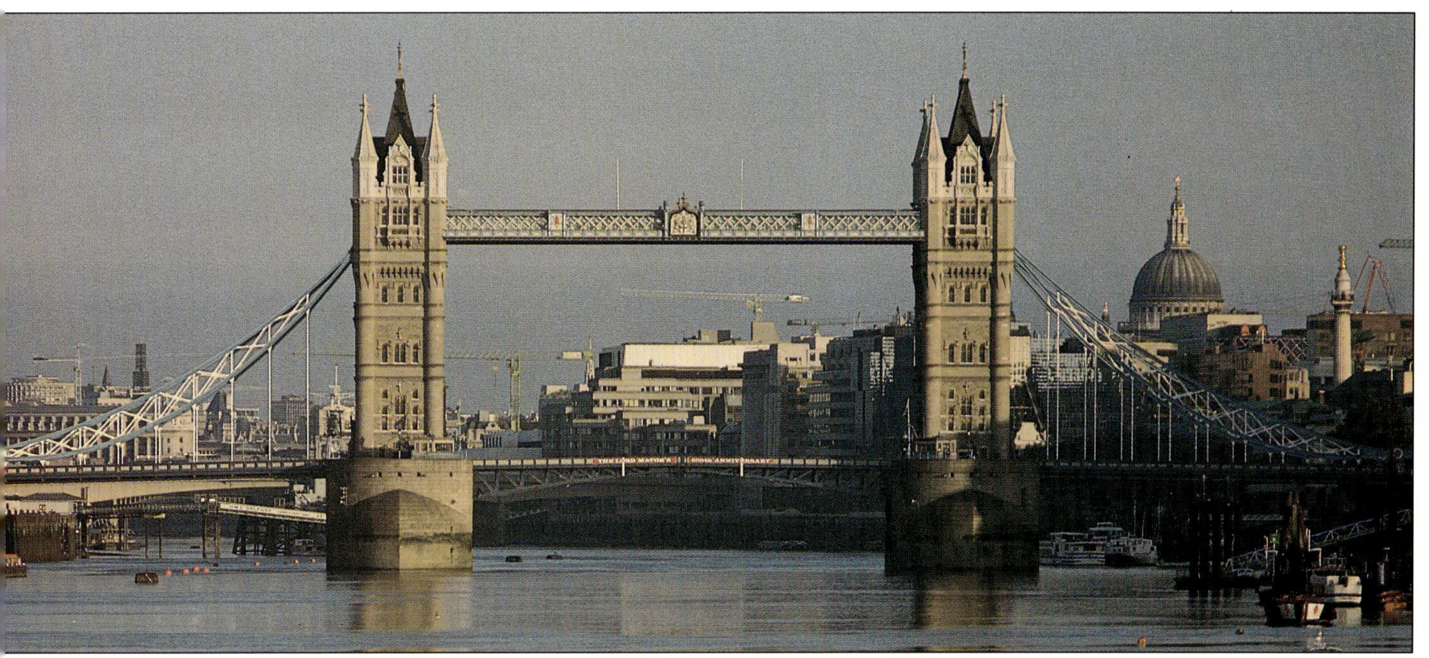

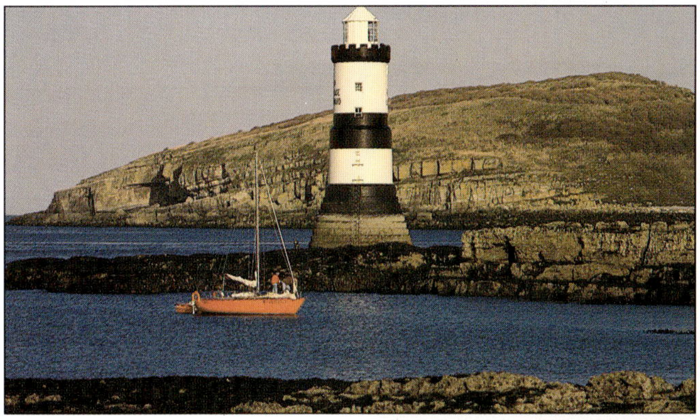

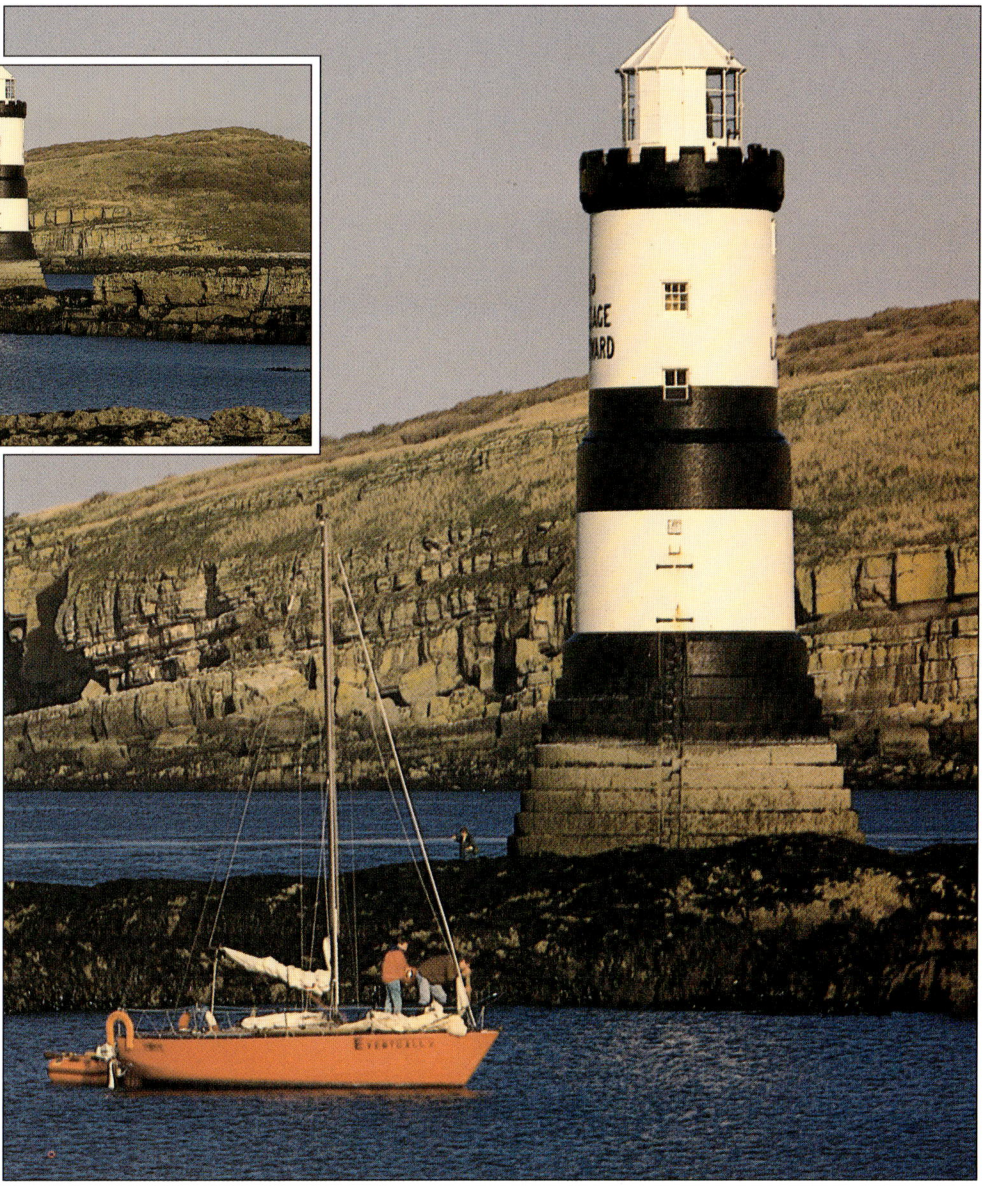

▲ ▶ *You can change the format of a print to a more attractive shape, or one that suits the subject matter better.*

In this example, cropping from landscape to portrait format enhances the composition. It also emphasizes the height of the lighthouse and makes the fact that it touches the top of the frame rather less obvious.

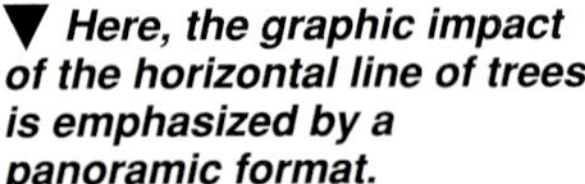 **Some prints lend themselves to several different crops depending on the 'story' you want to tell. This harvest scene could be cropped to become a panoramic study of the pattern of trees in a landscape, a close-up portrait of farm machinery, or a picture of golden evening light and shadows.**

▼ **Here, the graphic impact of the horizontal line of trees is emphasized by a panoramic format.**

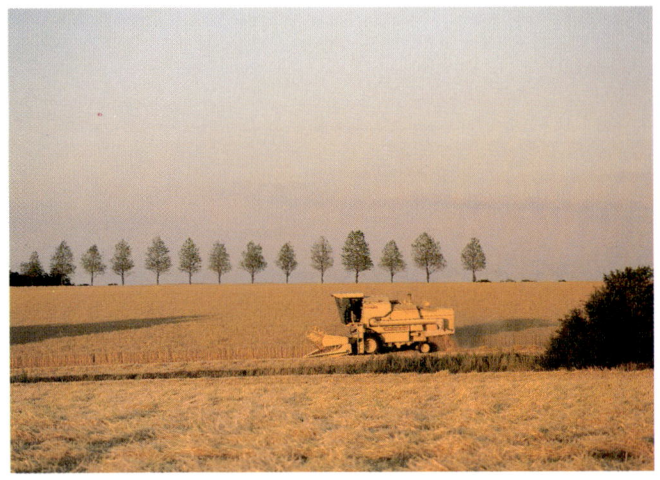

Make contact

If you enlarge your own prints you have the option of cropping images on the contact sheet. Mark each frame you want to crop with a spirit marker or blue wax crayon. Once you've dealt with an entire contact sheet you can begin enlarging.

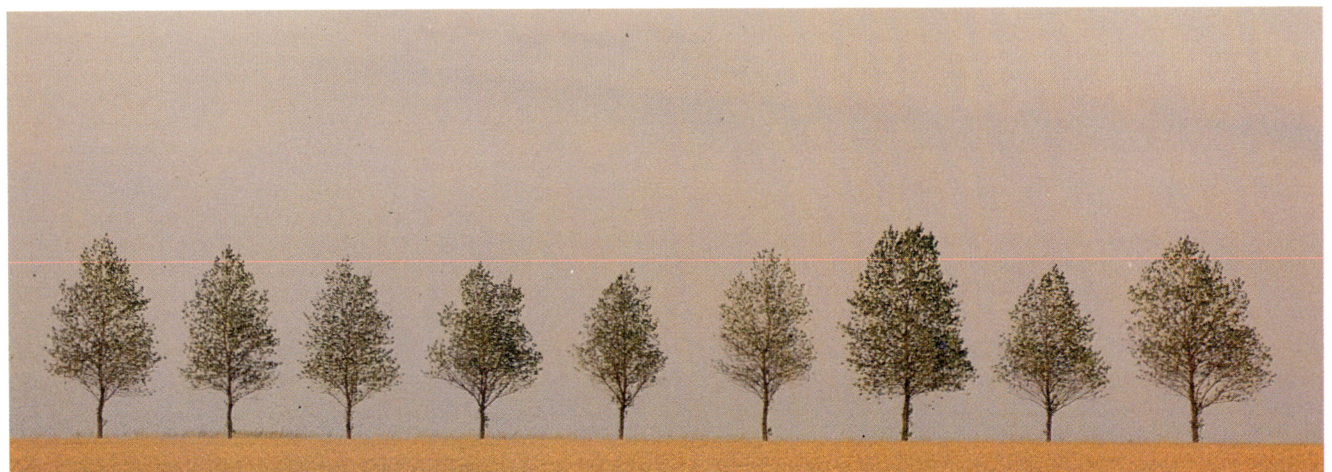

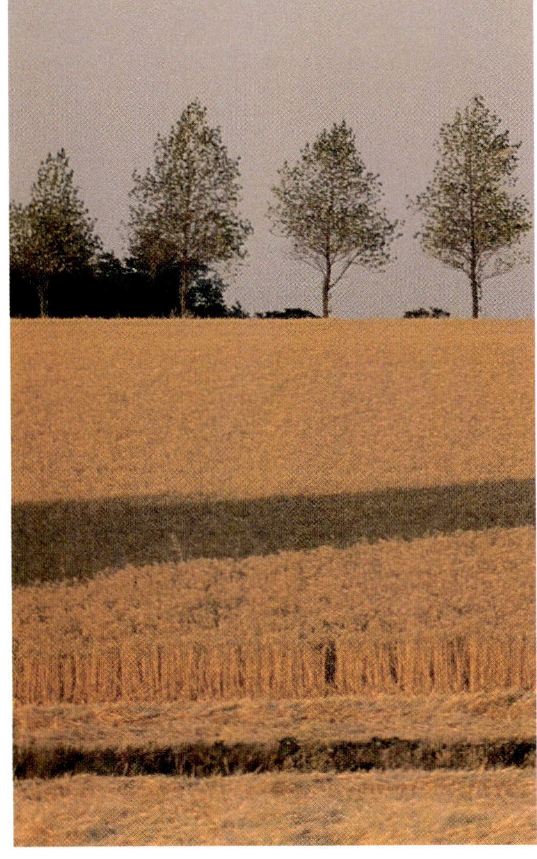

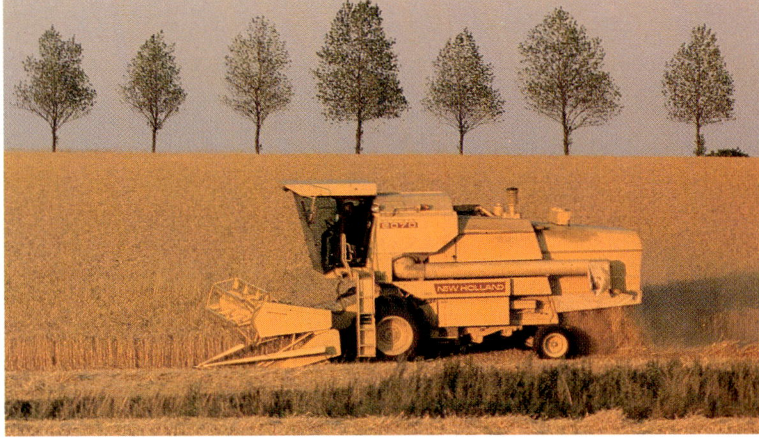

▲ **In this enlargement of the combine harvester, every detail is pin sharp. The evening sun bathes the machine in a warm glow which prevents the shot from looking clinical.**

◄ **When the picture is cropped from horizontal to vertical format, attention is drawn to the long evening shadows forming interesting zigzag patterns across the field.**

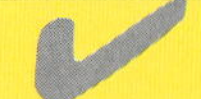

CHECK IT !

Crop your prints when you want to:

❏ remove intrusions.
❏ move in close for extra impact.
❏ focus attention on the main subject.
❏ change the format.
❏ create several 'stories' from one print.

Copying prints and slides

Duplicating slides lets you keep a valuable original in a safe place, while you can give a copy away as a gift or enter it into a competition. Copy a print if the negative's missing but you'd like another one.

It's easy to see why you'd copy pictures in an old family album, but there are other good reasons for copying a picture. If you hold a lot of slide shows, making copies of the slides is a good idea, because the projector lamp can cause fading. If you spend a long time in the darkroom dodging or burning in a print, making a copy negative vastly speeds up the production of copies: you can make more straight prints without bothering with shading.

Cheaper copying

Slide duplication (often known as 'duping') is available through professional laboratories and a few high street processors. You pay less per slide if you want several copies made from one image, but it's still expensive, as is print copying.

If you aim to do a fair amount of copying it's well worth doing it yourself. Take your time and you'll end up with a perfectly acceptable – and cheaper – copy. You can also copy images for creative effect, cropping, using filters and soft-focus screens.

Minus points

For all its benefits, copying does have limitations. When duping slides, for example, you lose definition because the image is passing through a lens for the second time. You may also lose colour saturation because you are photographing the dyes of a flat image rather than the original, three dimensional subject.

There will also be an increase in contrast. As slide film has quite a high contrast anyway, you may lose detail in shadow or highlight areas. If, however, your original was lacking in contrast to start with, this can be an advantage. Low contrast slide duplicating film minimizes the increase in contrast.

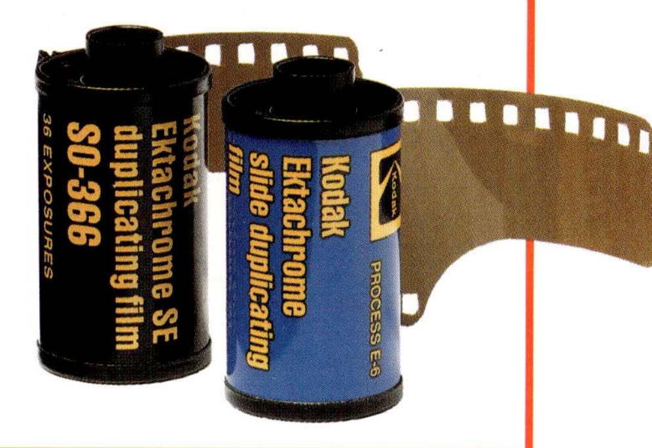

Which film?

Large photographic shops stock low contrast film specially designed for copying. You can also use ordinary slide or print film – these give increased contrast. Choose the right film for the light source you intend to use – daylight balanced film with daylight or flash, and tungsten balanced film for use with tungsten lighting.

Copying film is available in a limited range of speeds, and does not usually have a fixed ISO value. You'll therefore have to set exposure by experiment, as outlined overleaf. For the finest grained dupe with ordinary film, choose the slowest speed you can, such as Kodachrome ISO 25.

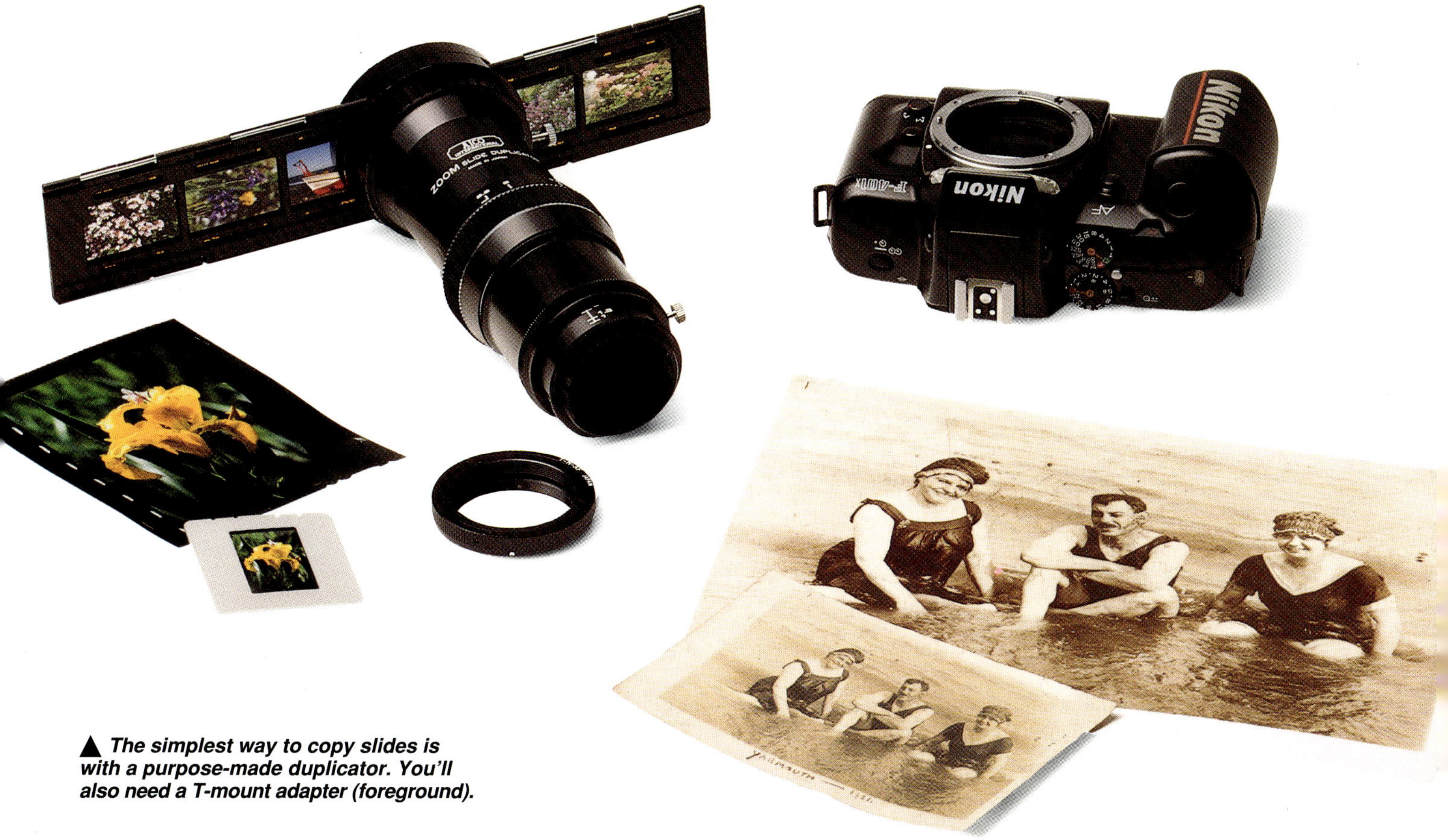

▲ *The simplest way to copy slides is with a purpose-made duplicator. You'll also need a T-mount adapter (foreground).*

Duping slides

There are several methods of copying slide film. If you already have an enlarger, then you may prefer to choose this method to save money. However, it's not as convenient as using a purpose made copier. A makeshift technique is to project the slide on to a white screen or wall and photograph the image. But only try this method if you want to record a long sequence of images in the right order, perhaps for a slide show, and when quality is not an issue.

Enlargers

If you have a camera with a removable lens and an enlarger, you have a ready-made copier. One advantage of this method is that you can use any film format for the copy. This is useful if you're trying to get your work published, because a medium or large format slide is more eyecatching than a 35mm one. Because of the light source, tungsten film must be used in the camera.

For this method, remove the slide from its mount and place it in the enlarger's negative carrier. Take off your camera lens and project the image straight on to the film in the camera. Turn out all room lights before making exposures. For different exposure times, simply cover and uncover the enlarger lens, making a note of the elapsed time. You'll need to take special care in positioning the camera – it's a fiddly process, and it's easy to end up with a crooked horizon on the dupe.

Once the film has been processed, choose the best exposure and repeat this for future copies. You can correct a colour cast by placing the appropriate colour filter in the filter drawer.

Slide duplicating machines

Another method is to use a tabletop slide duplicating machine. These are purpose built and so they provide by far the easiest method of copying slides. However, it is also the most expensive method.

The duplicator consists of a box containing a built-in light source, often with dial-in filtration, rather

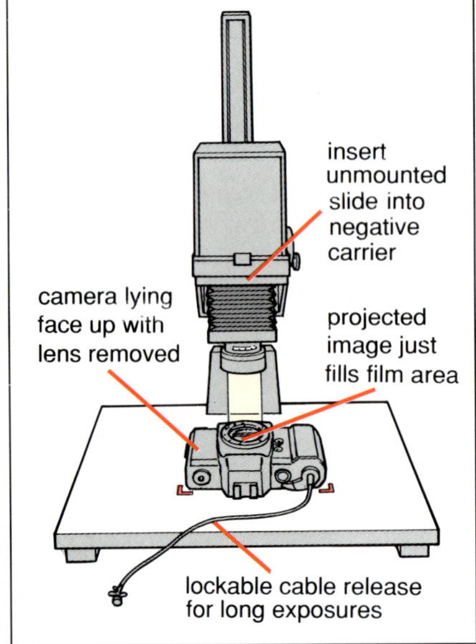

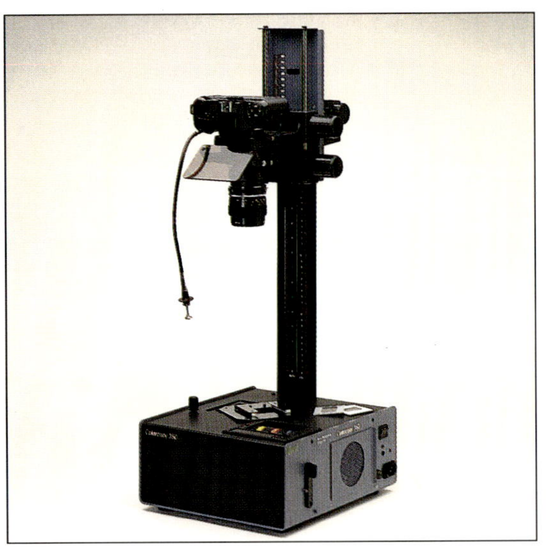

Colour casts

Owing to differences between film brands and even between batch numbers, the copy slide will almost certainly display a different colour cast from the original. If you find that the colour balance on your duplicate is not what you want, there is a solution. You can dupe the original again and place colour filters between the slide and light source, or on the camera lens, to correct this.

◀ *Before you start, you must ensure that the film is correctly lined up under the enlarger's light beam. You'll find that the camera has to be very near the enlarger lens.*

◀ *Professional labs use slide duplicating machines because they produce high quality copies. It's easy to vary the filtration to correct a colour cast – simply dial in the desired filter value.*

like an inverted colour enlarger head.

You fit your camera to a bellows attachment on a column. A lens on the other end forms the image at the correct magnification. The illumination is provided either by built-in flash or a continuous tungsten source.

On a duper with a tungsten light source you must use a tungsten balanced film. Place the slide you want to copy in a holder just above the illuminated platform. Adjust the camera position for the degree of enlargement you want, line it up properly, and focus on the image using the continuous light provided on the machine.

On a duper with a flash light source you use daylight balanced film. Swinging a photocell across and above the slide measures the overall density and, after calibration, the duper automatically determines the exposure from this. Because the flash has a set duration, you can deliberately under or overexpose the image by altering the height of the flash platform. This is useful if the slide is a little too pale or dark to begin with.

It is also possible for you to correct colour casts by means of colour correction filters – cyan, magenta and yellow. These are introduced by turning a dial on the front of the machine, or alternatively by dropping a filter into a drawer below the slide.

Slide copying attachments

A convenient and relatively cheap method of duping slides is to use a copying attachment. This tube-like device replaces your camera lens.

Most kinds consist of a holder (which aligns the slide so that it is parallel with the film plane) plus a screen to diffuse the light source. A simple lens in the tube forms the image on film.

For maximum compatibility, these simple copiers have a T-mount: you must buy an inexpensive adapter to fit the copier to your particular make of camera. More expensive copiers have a handy zoom facility so you can enlarge and crop the slide as you wish.

Other types of simple copier must be used with bellows or extension tubes, which are fitted between the camera body and the lens to give a larger image than your lens can produce on its own. The slide copying attachment then fits on to the end of your lens.

You can also use a macro lens, but to obtain a 1:1 (life-size) image you'll probably also need an extension tube. Bellows, although much more expensive, let you vary the amount of extension, so it's easier to crop the slide.

Extension tubes are in fixed lengths, but as they come in sets of three, you can choose which magnification you want, or use them together. With this equipment, you can use exposure and test procedures similar to those outlined on the right.

The light source

When you use a slide copying attachment, the light source can be either tungsten, daylight or flash. Because daylight fluctuates in both brightness and colour quality, it's a good idea to use artificial light so that your results are uniform.

Tungsten lights are hot and there's a risk that the slide will buckle if it's near the light for too long. So flash, used with an extension lead to position it close to the diffuser screen, is most practical.

Using a slide copier

Note that focusing is preset when using a copier, and the viewfinder image will be very dark, because the simple optics have a small, fixed aperture.

1 FIT COPIER TO CAMERA
Screw the T-mount adapter to the copier, and then attach the other end to your camera body.

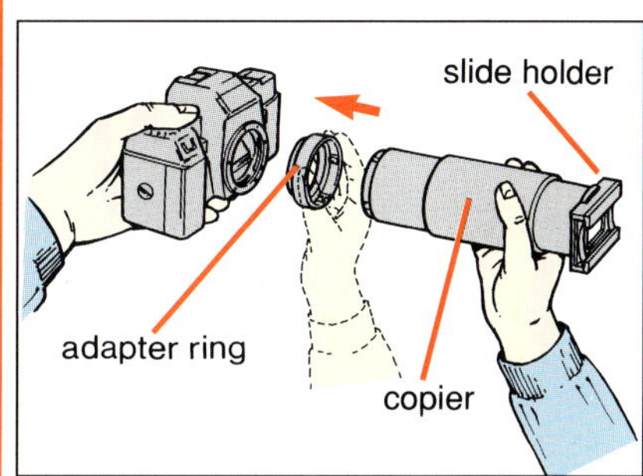

2 INSERT ORIGINAL SLIDE
Position the slide in front of the diffusing screen – you may need to fit it into a holder. Look through the camera's viewfinder and check the framing.

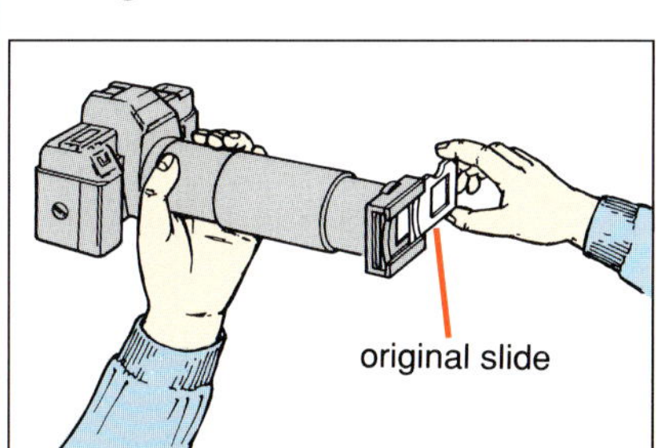

3 SET UP FLASH
Position the flashgun 2cm from the diffusing screen – rest it upside down on a tabletop, with a ruler as a guide. Set the flash to manual, and link it to the camera's synch socket with an extension lead. Load the film, set the camera's shutter to the flash synch speed, and take a picture.

What you need

❑ Original slide – mounted or unmounted: it depends on the copier
❑ Slide copier
❑ SLR camera
❑ Film – daylight balanced for flash
❑ Flashgun – capable of manual operation
❑ Extension lead – to link flash with camera: depending on your equipment, you may need an adapter
❑ Ruler

4 MOVE THE FLASH BACK
Reposition the flash to 2.8cm, and take another picture of the same test slide. Repeat, moving the flash back each time to match the distances on a standard camera aperture scale: 4, 5.6, 8, 11, 16, 22 and 32cm.

5 ASSESS THE RESULTS
The series of exposures will be bracketed at one stop intervals. Look for the slide with the best exposure. If the exposure's perfect, repeat this distance for future copies. If it's a $\frac{1}{2}$ stop out, you'll need to position the flash halfway between the previous distances.

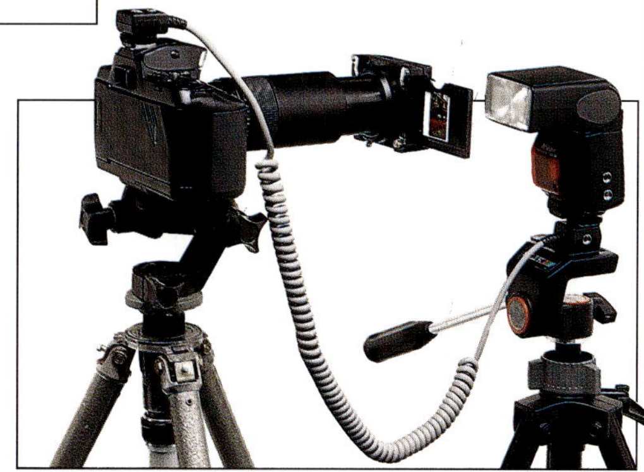

▲ *Once you have found the correct distance between the flash and the diffuser, make a note and keep to this all the time.*

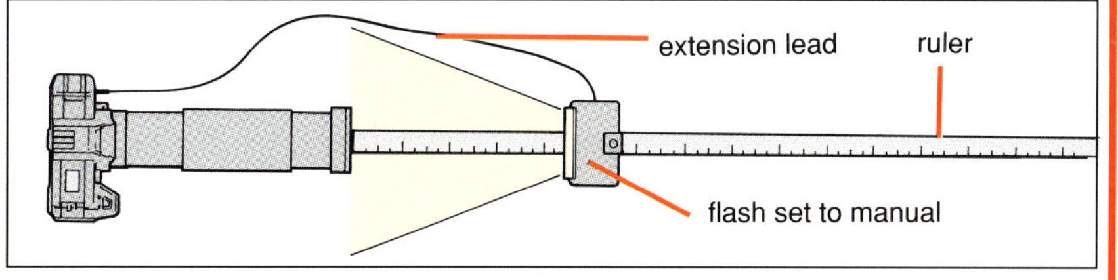

Copying prints

Sooner or later you'll probably want to copy a print or document. You'll need to make slides from prints if you want to publish your work, or for a slide show. You might have lost the negative of a favourite print and you'd like an enlargement. Old or damaged photographs can also be given a new lease of life by producing a copy which you can then re-touch and copy again.

How to do it

The best method of copying a print is to use a copying stand. This is a column with a moveable clamp fixed to a baseboard, to which you attach your camera and two or four lamps. Some enlargers can be adapted for copying – or make your own stand, using clamps fixed to a sheet of heavy board. Use tungsten balanced film.

Position the camera with the aid of the clamp and focus on the print. If the print is small, you may need a close-up lens or extension tubes to fill the viewfinder. Because the viewfinder of most cameras does not show the whole picture area, set up the camera so there's no space visible round the print edges, to avoid excessive borders.

Make sure that your camera is placed square on. Use a spirit level to check that the baseboard is level, then rest it on the camera back to make sure it's parallel to the base – adjust it if required. The exposure is measured as usual, through the lens or with a hand held meter. Remember that when you're using a hand held meter you'll need to allow extra exposure if you're using bellows or extension tubes.

Reduce reflections and flare

Cut down on reflections by switching off all other lights before making your exposure: prints are best copied in a darkened room. To minimize flare, mask off any white areas around the print, use a lens hood and make sure that your camera doesn't pick up any reflections from the lights.

Always cock the shutter before focusing, otherwise you may move the camera out of alignment. Tape the print on to the baseboard to keep it flat. Otherwise the lamps' heat might make the edges of the paper curl up, causing out of focus pictures.

Colour and contrast

Don't expect an exact reproduction as there will always be some visible difference in contrast and colour saturation.

A faded black and white print can be improved by copying in black and white, using filters. If the original is stained, use a filter of the same colour when making the copy. If you want to increase contrast, perhaps to pep up a sepia print, use a complementary filter – in this case, blue.

You can also use development to increase or decrease the contrast of black and white original prints. If you want to decrease it, for instance, you can overexpose and then give the negative less development time. This process is reversed for increasing contrast levels.

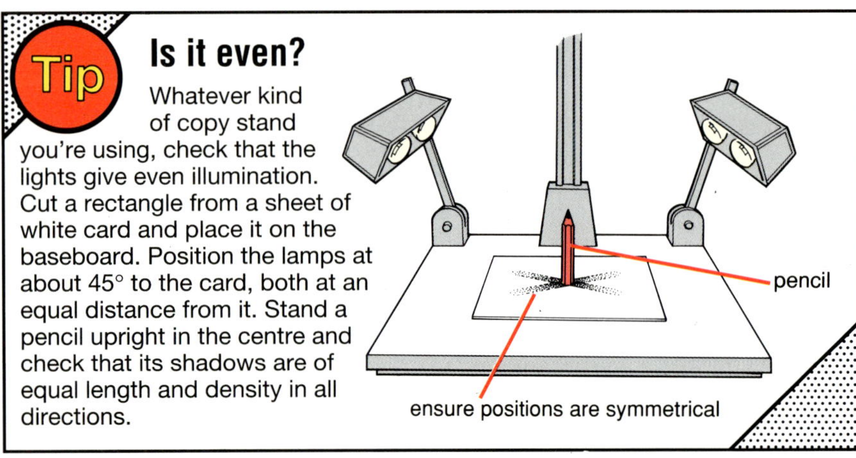

▲ *A specially designed copy stand allows you to fill the frame by adjusting the height of the camera according to the size of the original print.*

Tip — Is it even?

Whatever kind of copy stand you're using, check that the lights give even illumination. Cut a rectangle from a sheet of white card and place it on the baseboard. Position the lamps at about 45° to the card, both at an equal distance from it. Stand a pencil upright in the centre and check that its shadows are of equal length and density in all directions.

Peter Stone – Back to the future

We can learn a lot by looking at the work of past photographers. Peter Stone took his inspiration from early black and white and colour pictures, but you could choose any period: the 1920s, say, or the 1960s.

'For me', says Peter Stone, 'what happens in the darkroom is at least as important as taking the picture, if not more so. You can take an ordinary black and white image and either accentuate or completely transform its mood and feel through printing, hand toning and tinting. Obviously it can't be just any old picture though – you still need a strong, graphic monochrome image to begin with.'

Cropping in camera

'Composition is very important to me', he explains, 'because I tend to do all my cropping in camera and then print the whole image. I'm not that interested in the technicalities of photography though. I shoot mainly on 35mm and use aperture priority most of the time. As long as I have enough depth of field I don't waste time with manual exposure – the shot itself is the most important thing.' Peter occasionally uses a Mamiya

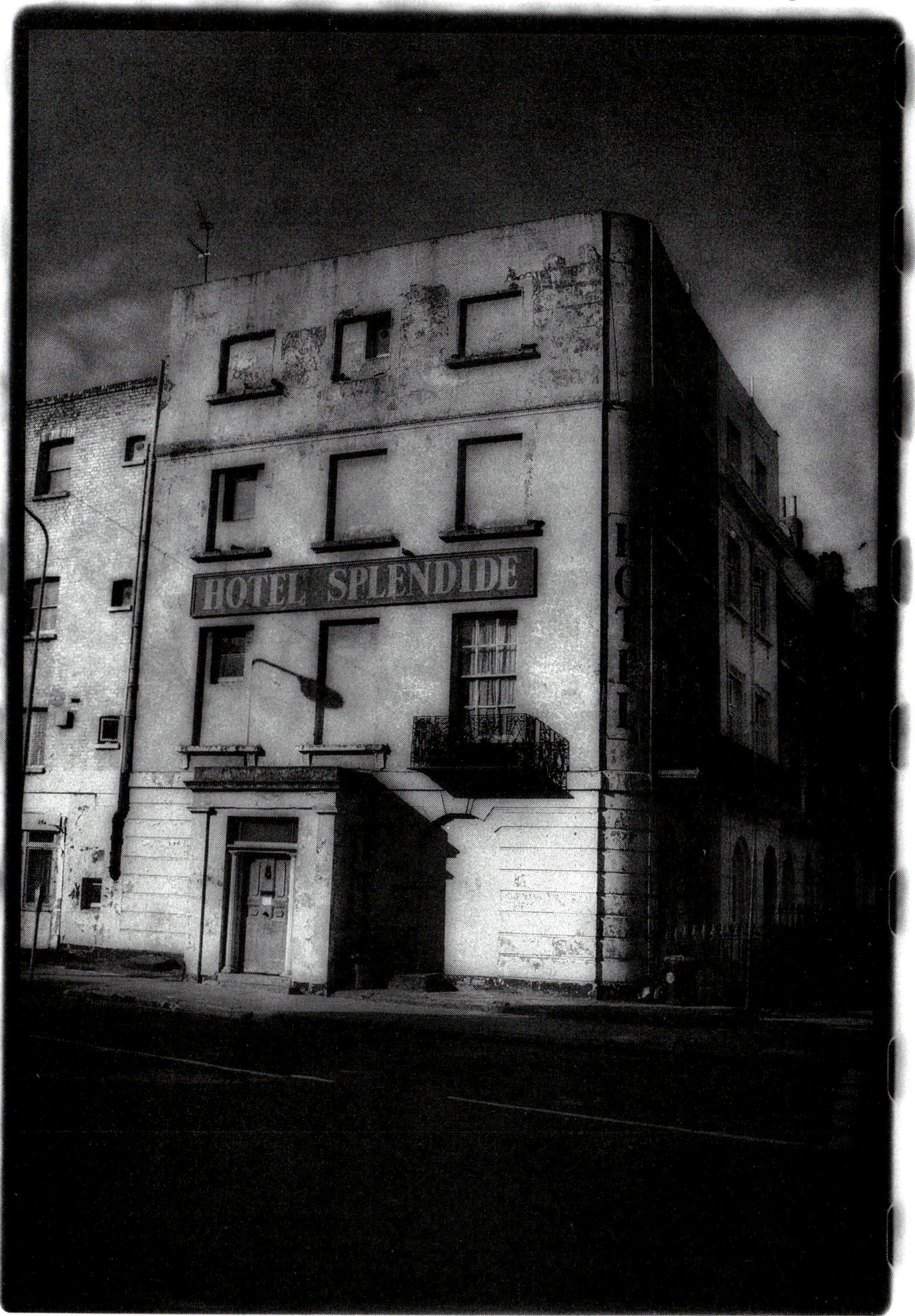

"I used to walk past this hotel every day, and I always thought it would make a great picture. But every time I tried it was in too deep a shadow. Eventually I went back at the end of a day and found it perfectly lit by the setting sun. I used a red filter to accentuate the sunlit building and heighten the contrast by darkening the sky."
Taken on a Nikon F301 with a 24mm lens on Fuji Neopan ISO 400 print film at f5.6 on aperture priority.

Technical details

'All of these views of London were printed in the same way. First I worked out the correct exposure by doing test strips. As I was going to expose the print several times I knocked a few seconds off the first exposure, blocking off any areas that might go too dark. Then I gave it another exposure of the same length, but held back the middle of the image so the edges would go darker. Finally, I opened up the aperture, placed a piece of thin white card over the print and gave it a long exposure. This created the faint outline of a larger image in the print and softened it slightly.'

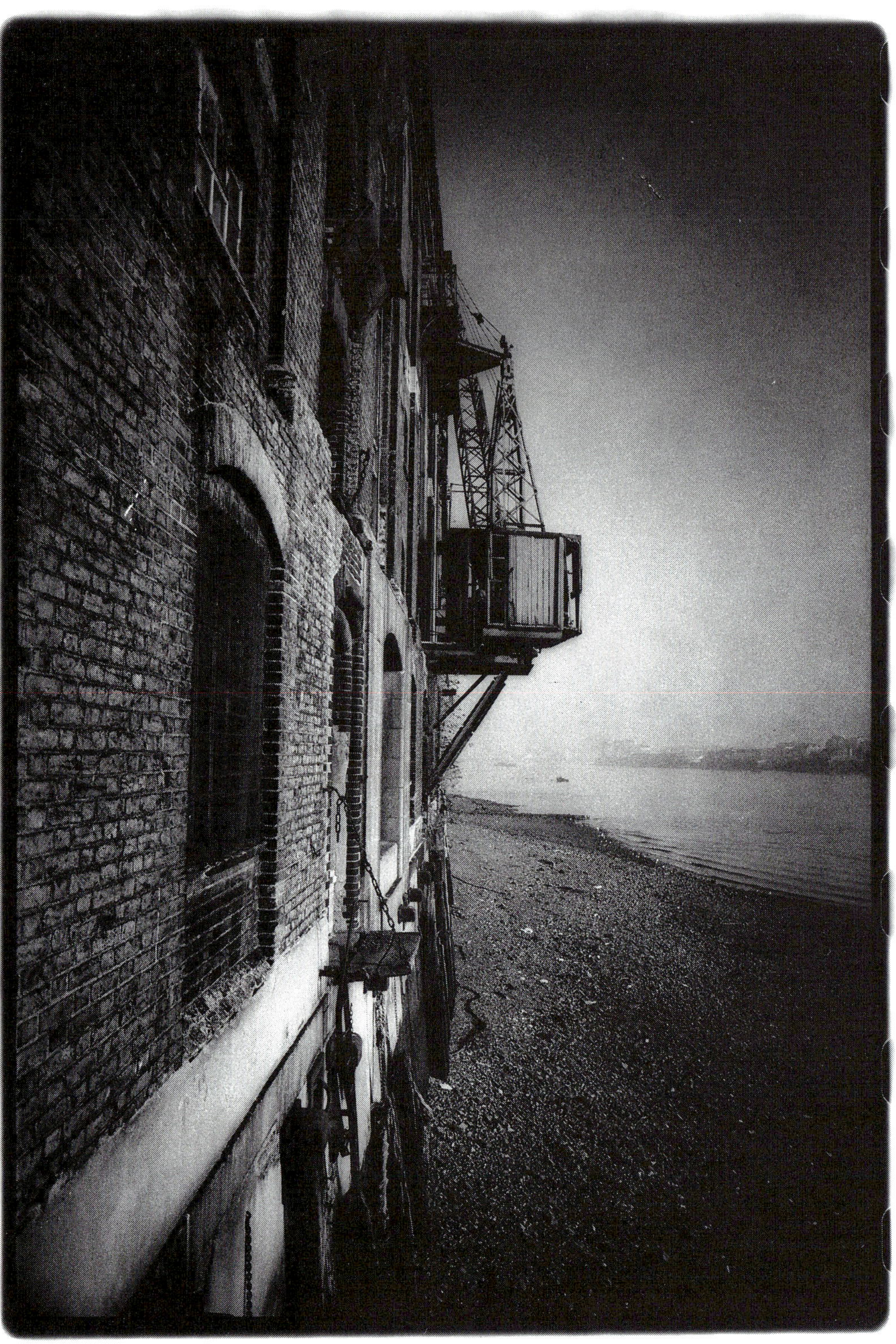

RB67 medium format camera when doing studio photography.

A Victorian influence

When he finished college Peter spent a year working in the archives of the Royal Photographic Society in Bath. It was there that he became interested in the printing techniques and the style of Victorian photographs. 'Printing and presentation was all important at that time,' he explains, 'and seeing those lovingly tinted and hand-toned pictures encouraged me to experiment further in the darkroom.' While at the RPS he also learnt about gum bichromate printing. This is a subtle but basically simple process which allows you to print black and white photographs on ordinary writing paper in any colour you choose.

He does most of his work in black and white, and has recently completed a series of distinctive cityscapes taken in and around the older areas of London. 'I've tried to capture that timeless Victorian look, both in the choice of subject and in the printing and toning. It takes a long time to get each print looking exactly how I want it but it's very satisfying work,' Peter comments.

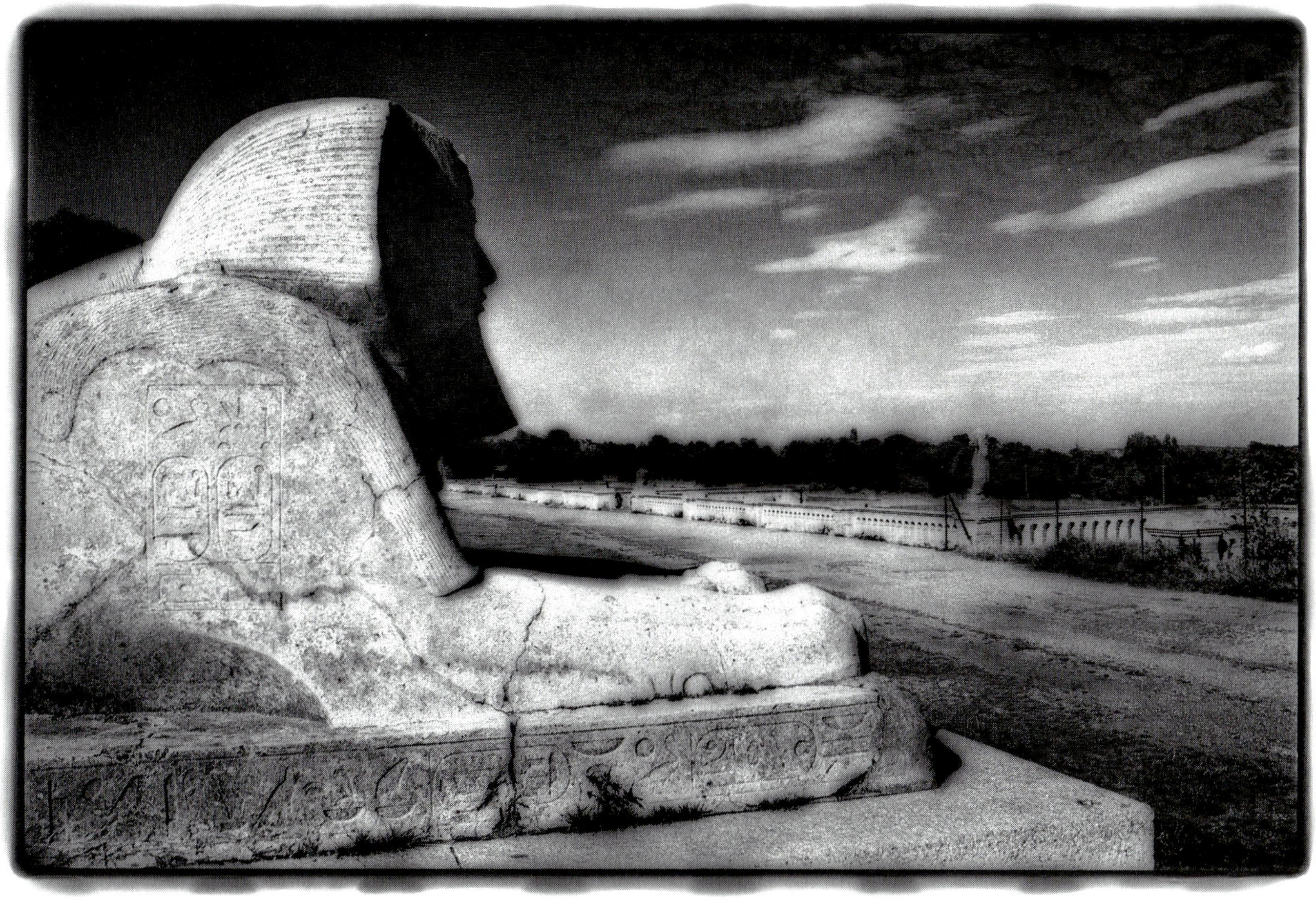

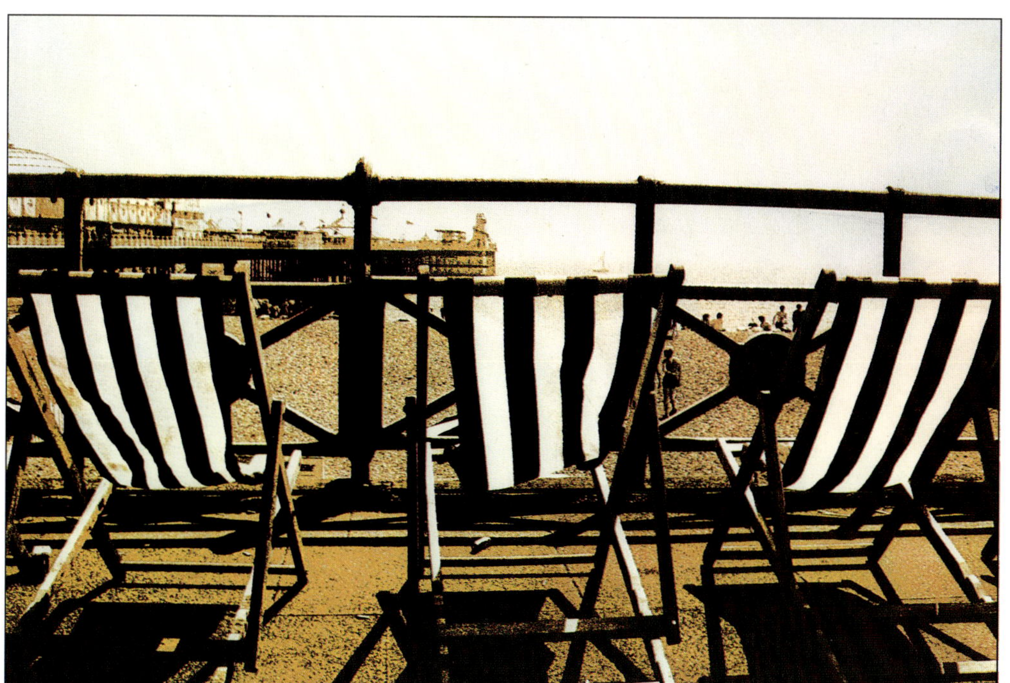

"I found this Egyptian statue down in Crystal Palace and thought it would make a great centrepiece for a landscape. I shot it on ISO 1600 film, which gives very contrasty results in strong sunlight, so I had to hold back the darker areas like the face when printing to make sure they came out. A red filter helped darken the sky."
Taken on a Nikon F301 with a 24mm lens on Fuji Neopan ISO 1600 print film at f22 on aperture priority.

"I took this shot one sunny morning on Brighton pier. I printed it on hard paper and then tinted it chemically using a dye called Colorvir. Most people overdo it when they use Colorvir, but if you're careful and sparing with it you can get quite a subtle effect. It takes time to get the balance right though."
Taken on a Minolta X700 with a 35-70mm lens on Ilford HP5 ISO 400 film at f16 on aperture priority.

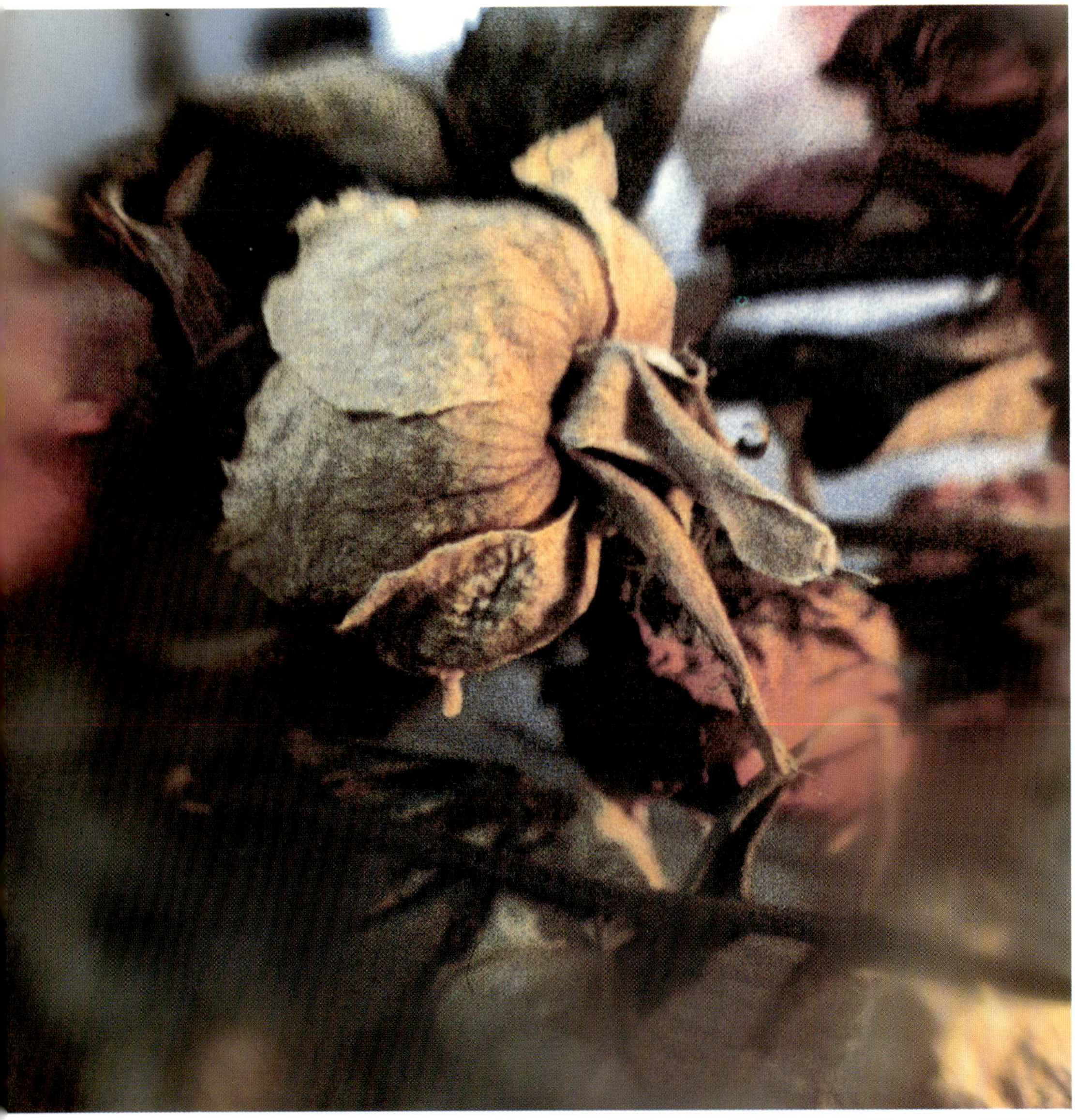

"I used Scotch 1000 to photograph this rose – it's a very grainy film that gives soft colours – and lit it with an anglepoise lamp and flash. The lamp gave the shot a warm wash of colour, while the flash provided the main light. Then I took the original image and put it through a colour photocopier. I copied the resulting laser print on to a 5 x 4 slide using a piece of petroleum jelly covered glass to get that fall off around the edges."

Original shot taken on a Nikon F301 with a 35-70mm zoom lens on Scotch ISO 1000 at 1/4 sec and f8. Copied on a Sinar 5 x 4 camera with a 250mm lens at f16 with Bowens flash.

"The Thames was covered in thick mist the day I took this shot of Metropolitan Wharf. The sun was quite bright, but not strong enough to burn off the haze, which gave the picture lots of atmosphere. I accentuated this by burning the print in heavily around the edges, and softened the shot still further by exposing the print under a thin white card."

Taken on a Nikon F301 with a 24mm lens on Fuji Neopan ISO 400 print film at f8 on aperture priority.

You can do it

If you enjoy experimenting with colour, try reproducing your slides on a colour photocopier as Peter has done here. 'Putting a picture through a copier can really liven it up sometimes', he explains. 'The laser process tends to split the colours up nicely and make the shot look more dramatic. Play around with it until you've got the print you want. If you need a more stable final image you can copy the picture back on to slide film afterwards.'

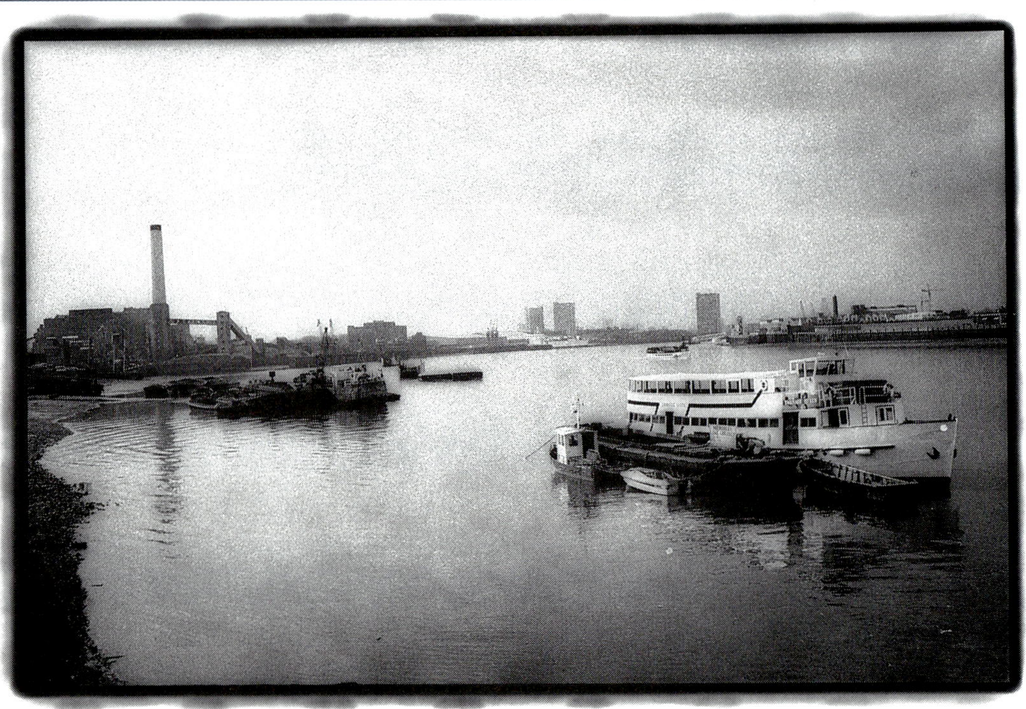

Mounting and storing slides

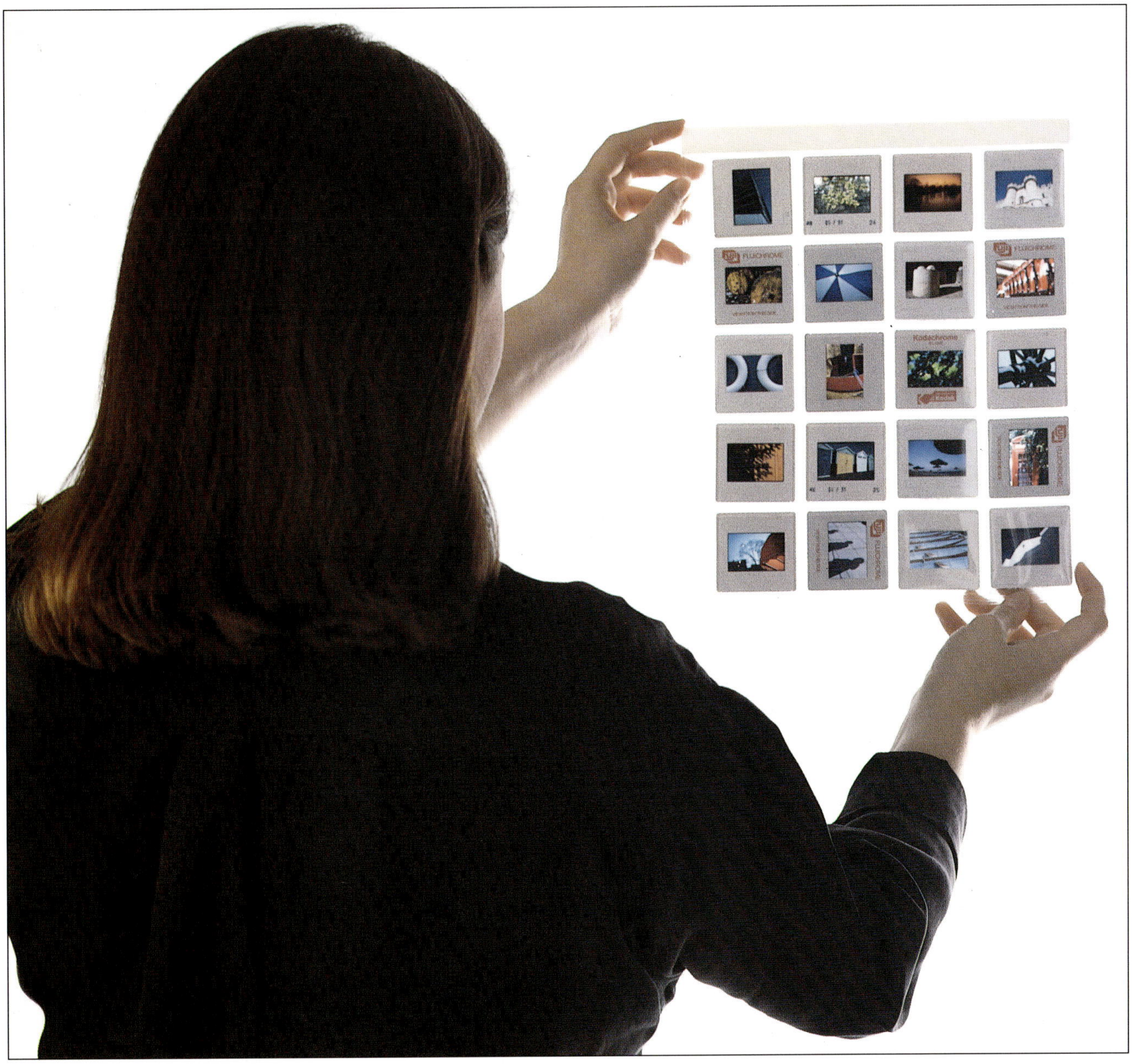

▲ *A slide page lets you look at a group of images together, as well as giving extra protection to your valuable pictures.*

If you prefer to work with slides rather than prints, the first stage is mounting and filing them so that you can find them easily, handle them safely and project them conveniently.

Mounts protect the fragile slide from damage and make it easy for you to add a caption to the photo. This stops you forgetting important details or dates relating to the image, for later reference.

Some makes of slide film are available as process paid. In this case the lab automatically mounts all the frames, saving you the trouble (unless you ask for the film to be returned uncut). However, you have no choice of mounts, and the lab charges for every frame – even the failures, which you end up throwing away.

For these reasons you may prefer to do your own slide mounting. You can buy mounts quite cheaply in boxes of 100 from photographic shops. Buy in bulk and you'll save money. However, if you hand mount every frame, it's usually cheaper to have the film mounted by a lab.

Archival storage

❏ The image on your slide is not permanent – after a few years it will start to fade. If you want to preserve your slides for as long as possible, buy products marked 'archival' which contain no harmful types of plastic that can damage slides in the long term. Polyester is ideal. You'll find these are usually more expensive.

❏ However they are stored, keep your slides cool and in the dark when you're not viewing them, to maximize the life of the image.

Card or plastic?

Many professionals prefer card mounts because you don't need special ink to write on them. With plastic mounts, you need waterproof ink or self-adhesive labels. However, they are stronger and so best for projection. (A damaged card mount can make an automatic machine jam.) Plastic mounts stay locked shut, while the heat of a projector bulb can make card mounts open. Plastic mounts are also re-usable, unlike card ones.

The glass option

Some slide mounts have glass 'windows'. While these protect the image from fingerprints and hold the film flat for projection, many photographers prefer not to use them for the following reasons:

❏ **Damage** If you want to send slides by post, do *not* use glass mounts – the glass is easily broken, and can damage the slide and cut the person opening the parcel. Most publishers insist that glass mounted slides must not be sent to them.

❏ **Dust** Film has two surfaces to keep clean – a glass mount introduces another four. Even if you clean the slide and the glass scrupulously before mounting, it's hard to eliminate every last particle of dust. And however tightly sealed the mount appears to be, somehow dust seems to creep in over time.

❏ **Newton's rings** These are concentric circles which appear where the film presses tightly

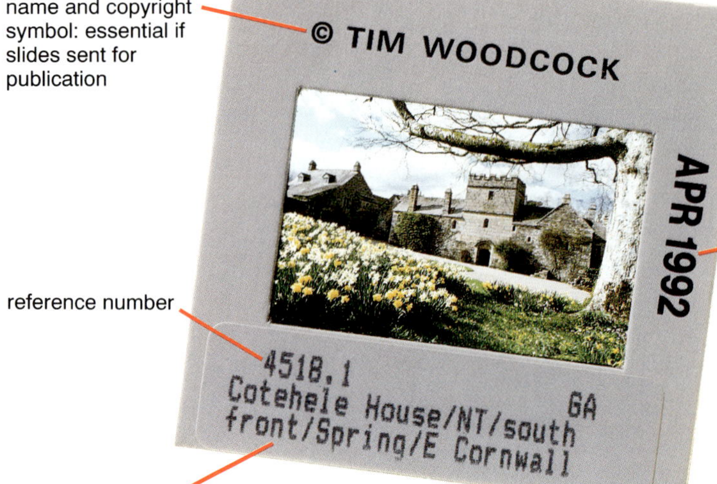

photographer's name and copyright symbol: essential if slides sent for publication

date: may be printed by processor

reference number

caption: subject, location, other information

▲ *A typical captioned slide taken by a professional photographer. A specially printed label was used here, but you can handwrite in pen instead.*

against the glass. As the slide warms up, alternate bands of dark and light circles which are very distracting move across the screen. To prevent this, you need to use mounts with anti-Newton glass.

How to mount slides

You can buy machines to cut your slides automatically into singles and then mount them, but it's just as easy to do it yourself. The mounted slide can be further protected from fingermarks and scratches by encasing it in a transparent protective sleeve. These are available in various sizes.

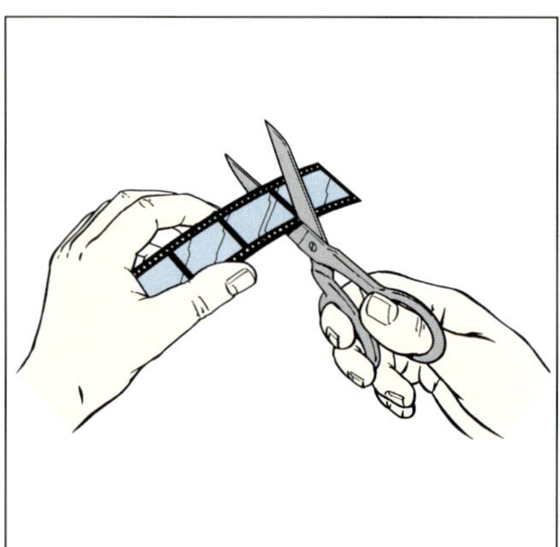

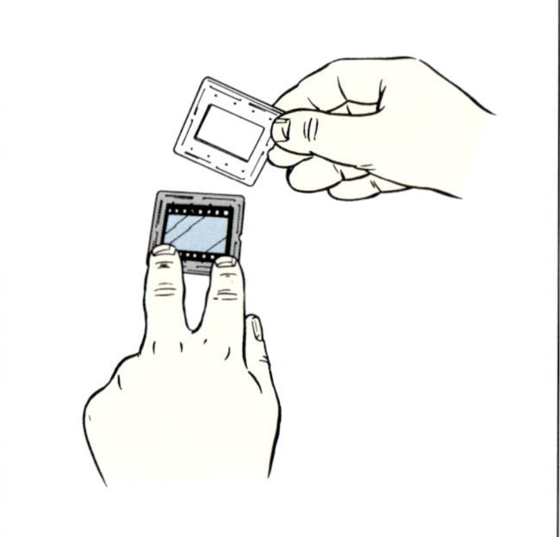

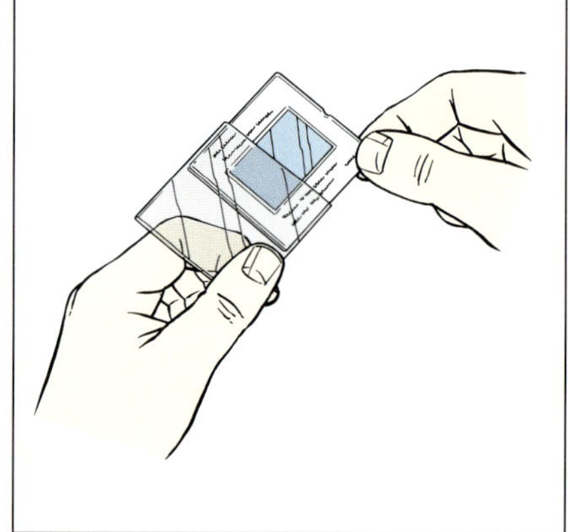

1 TRIM STRIP INTO SINGLES At all times avoid touching the image with your fingers. Work where you can shine a bright light under the film – a lightbox is ideal. Use a sharp pair of scissors and carefully cut down the centre of the black area between images.

2 PLACE FILM IN MOUNT Position the film over the mount's back half, so the frame numbers read correctly. Ensure it's centred over the window. If the mount is plastic, make sure the film rests between the ridges and is held in place by the glue spots, if these are present.

3 CLOSE MOUNT Place the top half of the mount over the film and push down. If you're using a plastic mount, the halves will snap into place. Check the film is lying flat in the mount and not bulging out. Caption the mount and add a protective sleeve if you wish.

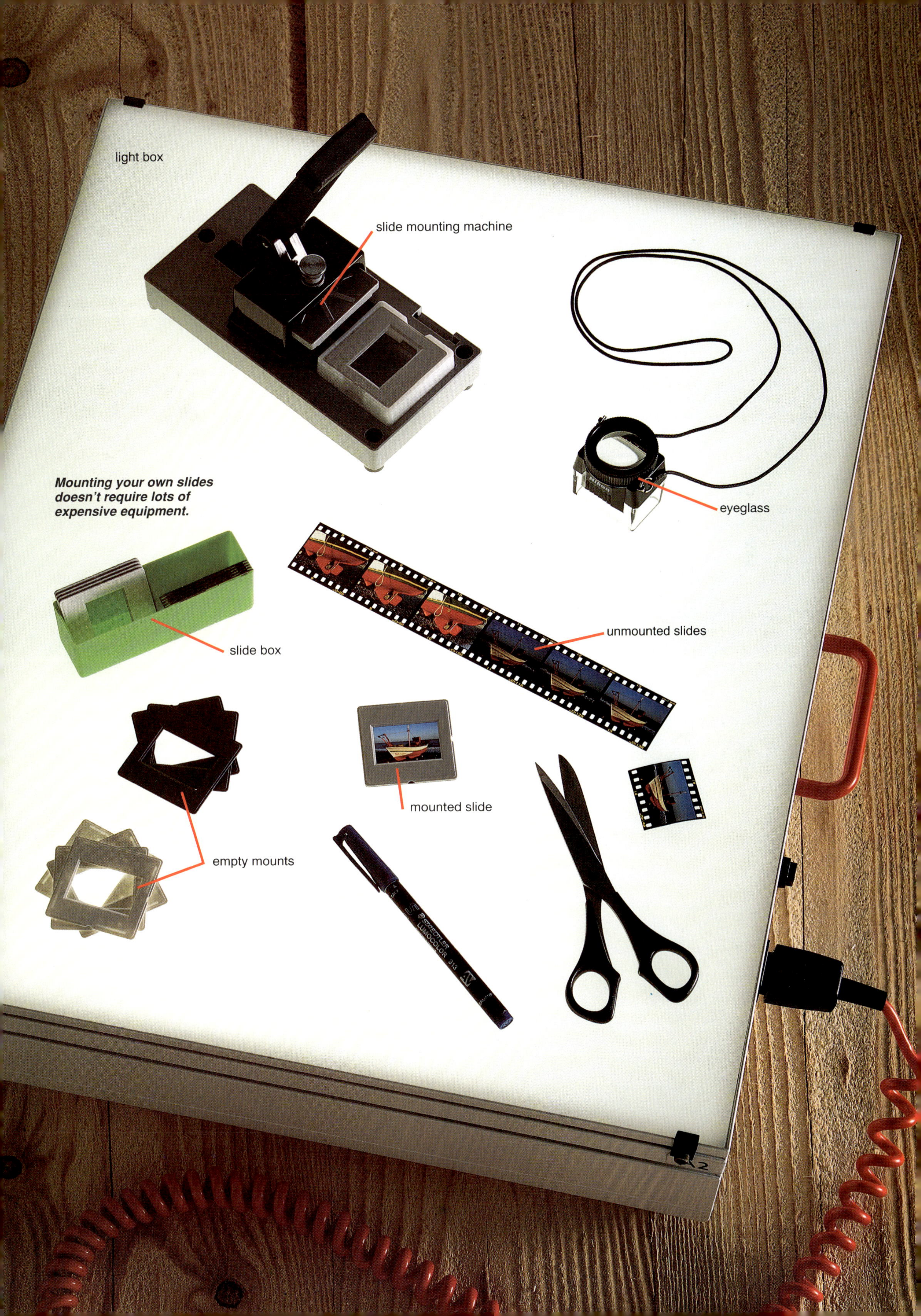

light box
slide mounting machine
eyeglass
Mounting your own slides doesn't require lots of expensive equipment.
slide box
unmounted slides
empty mounts
mounted slide

Storing slides

Storage isn't really a problem if you only shoot a few rolls a year, but any more than this and you'll need an efficient filing system so you can find any image you choose quickly and easily.

There is a range of options, all available for 35mm and other formats:

❑ **Slide boxes** The boxes returned by the processor with your slides are convenient and don't cost anything extra. Label the top of the box with the contents. Finding a particular image is very slow because you cannot see the slides' contents clearly without pulling them out individually.

❑ **Ring binders** These hold see-through slide pages; with 35mm, normally each page contains 20 slides. It's easy to hold a page up to the light and scan the images. Sheets have clear or frosted backs. The latter make it easier to view slides if you don't have a lightbox.

❑ **Wallets** Made of plastic, they contain a fold-out sheet that can hold anything from 35 to 160 35mm slides. They are very useful for protecting slides if you carry them around, and there's usually an index card for recording slide details.

❑ **Projection magazines** These are ideal if you mainly shoot slides for projection, as they can be stored in their correct sequence. They are relatively expensive.

❑ **Card presentation sheets** If you want to show groups of slides to people, these look attractive. With some designs, you tape the unmounted slide edges to the black card – others let you insert mounted slides. The card is then encased in a plastic sleeve. It's fiddly to change slides around later on.

Other methods are more expensive than the above and used mainly by professionals or amateurs who have a vast number of slides:

❑ **Hanging files** With 35mm, these allow you to see (usually) 24 images at a time. They are also available for other film formats. A title strip sticking up above the hanging bar allows you to label each sheet. You need a purpose built cabinet to house them in.

❑ **Drawer files** These hold slides in divided up drawers – they are not as convenient as hanging files.

Keeping track of your slides

It's easy to remember all the images in a few rolls of film – but once you start building up a larger collection, you need a system that lets you find the slide you want quickly and easily. Caption individual mounts as soon as your slides are processed so that you don't miss any details.

How you arrange your slides is up to you; you could put them in date order, or arranged by subject alphabetically or thematically, or use a numbering system if you have a very large number of images. Some photographers store slide details on a computer – specially designed software is available for this purpose.

Whatever system you choose, don't make it too ambitious. It's better to organize all of your slides using a rough and ready method, rather than introducing a complicated system that takes a long time to establish.

▼ *A range of popular slide storage systems. Each method has different advantages and disadvantages.*

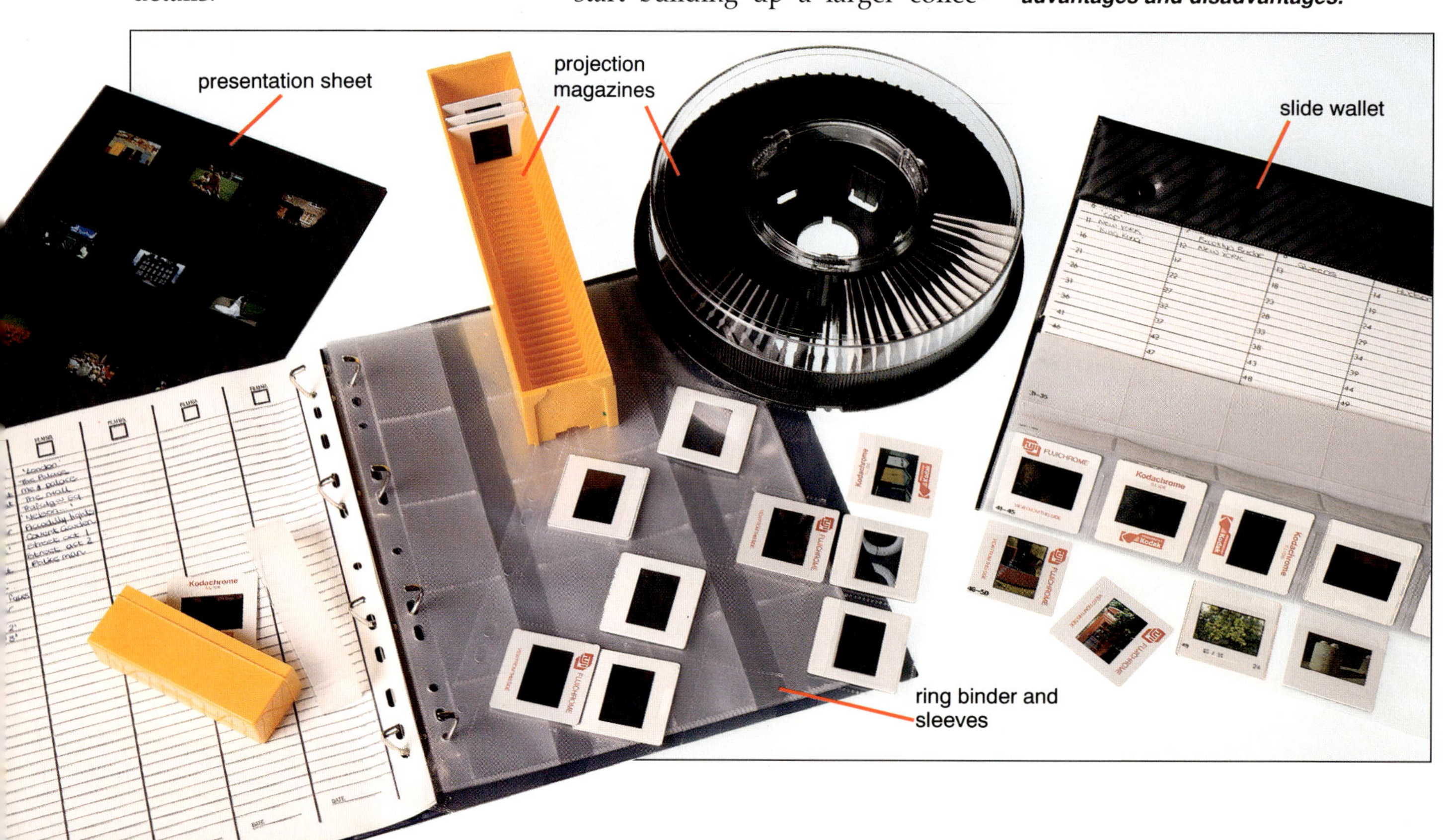

Projecting slides

The best way to bring a slide to life is by projecting it. And with good quality projection, slides give bigger, brighter and more arresting images than prints, that really do justice to your shots.

Often, when slides return from the processor, they are glanced through and then stored away in some dusty drawer. Projecting slides can seem too much trouble to set up and get right. However, a well edited and well projected slide show is almost always worth the effort.

The first thing to consider is the slide mount. This may seem to be one of the most straightforward aspects of photography and have very little to do with quality slide projection.

However, think how often you have seen a slide go out of focus while it is being projected. This happens when a slide becomes overheated in the projector and, as a result, the film warps. This warping – known as 'popping' – throws parts of the slide out of focus. It often occurs in cheap, flimsy mounts.

Often a processor will supply your slides in mounts made of cardboard or thin plastic. If this is the case, it is probably best to order your transparencies unmounted – as strips of film – and mount them yourself. Choose a stiff plastic mount that has positioning lugs to hold the film square and closes so that the film is held flat.

If you want the film to be completely flat, you should use glass mounts (see page 80). Slides cannot pop when they're mounted properly between glass. Glass mounts also make manual focus adjustments and autofocus projectors virtually redundant because, as every slide is held exactly in the same position by the glass, they will all be in focus.

Some projectors have curved field (CF) lenses so that they can project 'popped' slides without problems: warm air pre-heats the slides so that they are uniformly popped before they are projected. Obviously, you should not use glass mounts with CF lenses.

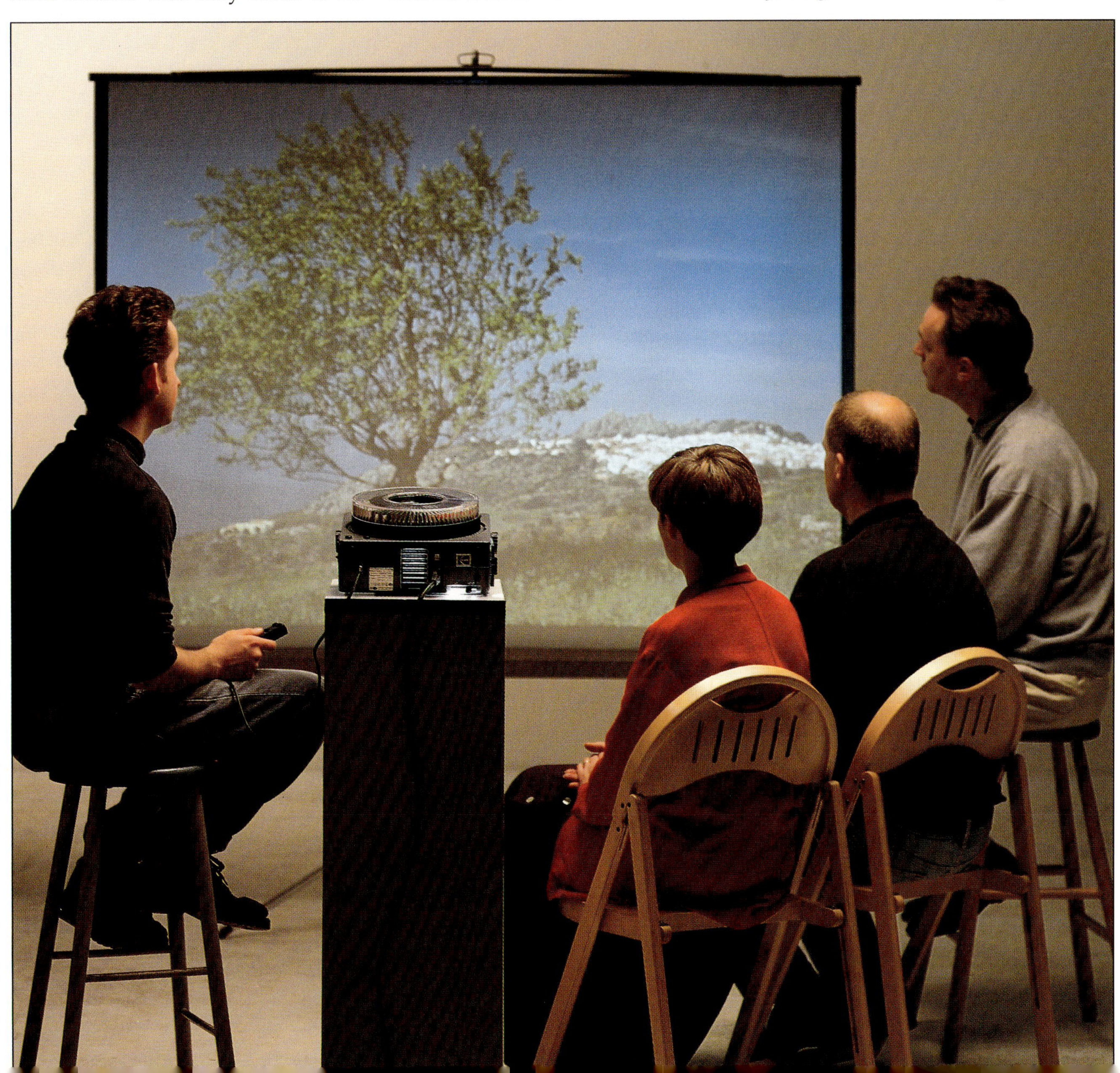
▼ Putting on a slide show is a great way to bring your friends or relatives together and show off your best photographs. If it's done well, it can give you a great sense of accomplishment.

Selection and projection

After you've mounted your slides, you should edit them and arrange them into a coherent sequence. This is best done before you go to the trouble of loading them into the projector. Ideally you should use a lightbox and a magnifying glass or viewing loupe. You could hold the slides up to the light or use a small illuminated screen, but you're not always going to be sure if the image on film is sharp.

When preparing your show, try not to choose badly exposed slides. Overexposed slides are beyond rescue, but you may be able to salvage a slightly underexposed image by making a duplicate, and adjusting the copying exposure so that the dupe is lighter than the original.

Projectors

Projectors have come a long way since the times when you had to manually insert each slide individually. Today, most projectors have magazines which hold at least 36 slides. While most projectors with straight magazines generally hold between 36 and 50 slides, most rotary magazines hold between 80 and 120 slides.

If you want to show, say, 100 slides but your projector's magazine only holds 36 slides, there's no need to buy a new projector. However, it is worthwhile buying more magazines – you don't want to have to keep breaking up your slide show, turning on the lights and reloading your single magazine.

The most important part of the projector is the lens. Like camera lenses, projector lenses come in a variety of focal lengths. And like cameras, projectors use different lenses for different film formats. The standard projector lens for 35mm slides has a focal length of either 85mm or 90mm.

However, if you regularly project slides in a small space, you may need a wide angle lens. With a 35mm film and a wide angle 35mm lens, you need only project from a distance of 2m to obtain an image 2m wide. With a standard 85mm lens, you will need to project from

1▲ SLIDE SELECTION
It's much more convenient to select the slides you want to show and put them into a coherent sequence before you load them into the projector. Using a lightbox and viewing loupe is the best way to do this as you can be sure that each slide is sharp.

2▲ LOADING UP
Slides must be loaded back to front and upside down. To prevent mistakes, hold your slides the correct way and attach a sticky dot on to the bottom left corner. Then turn them upside down and put them in the magazine with the dots facing the back of the projector.

3▶ LINING UP
With a straight magazine, you can draw a line diagonally across the top of the slides from opposite corners of the magazine. Whenever you show this set of slides again, you'll be able to tell at a glance whether you have the complete set loaded and whether they are in order.

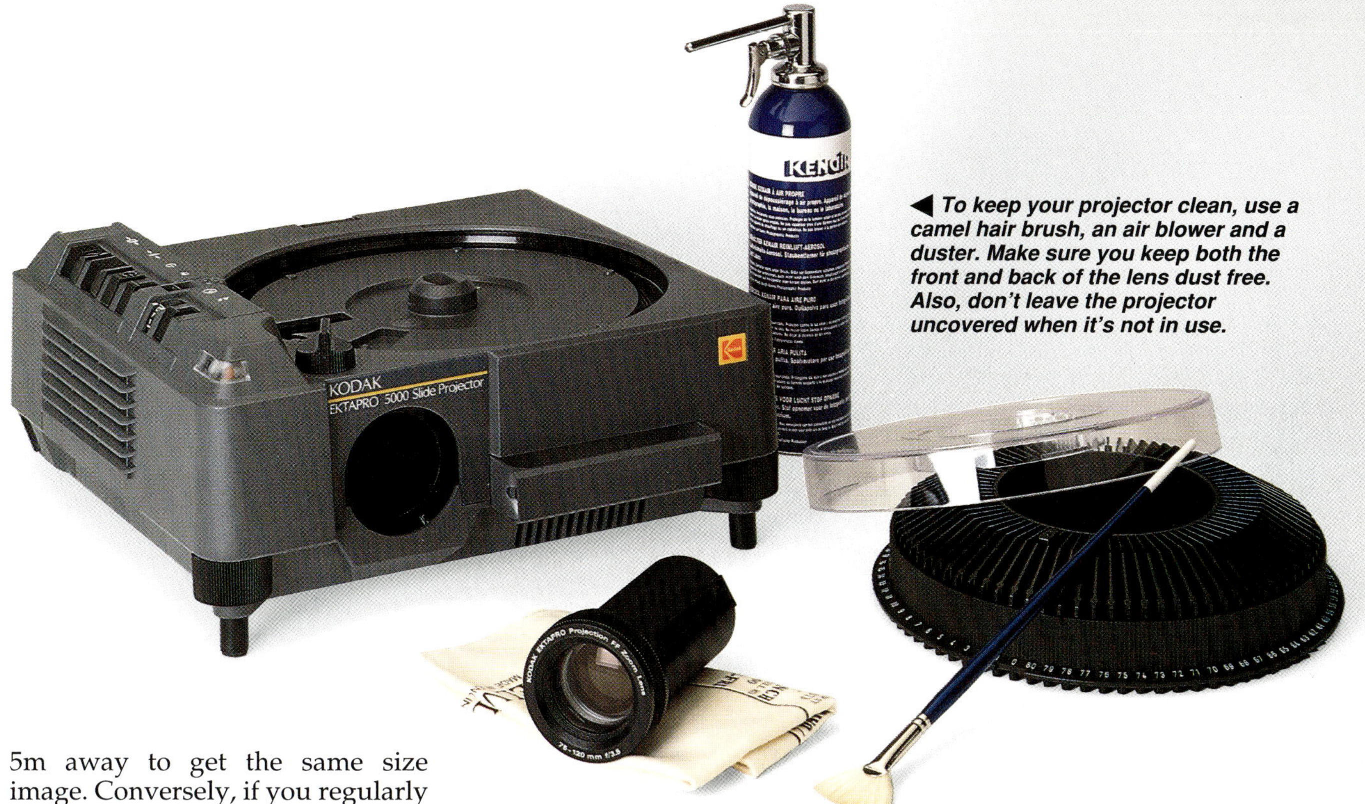

5m away to get the same size image. Conversely, if you regularly project slides in a hall or large room, you may want to invest in a telephoto lens – these are better for longer throws.

You can also buy zoom projector lenses. Typical zooms come in ranges of 70-120mm and 110-200mm. Zoom lenses are useful if you project slides in a variety of rooms. However, zooms generally don't have as large an aperture as fixed focal length lenses, and therefore they don't give as bright an image as fixed length lenses. A typical zoom lens has an aperture of f3.5 whereas a good quality standard fixed focal lens is more likely to have an aperture of f2.5.

Keep it clean

For the brightest projection, it is important to keep the projector clean. With many models, it's possible to take the projector apart and clean the internal components.

As well as the lens, there are many internal surfaces on which dust can accumulate and so dim the image. These include the lamp and the reflective mirror behind the lamp, as well as the parts of the projector through which the light is shone – the condenser lenses, the heat resistant filter and the main lens. Clean these components by dusting with a soft brush. Take care that you don't touch the lamp, as this will shorten its life; you can remove fingerprints using a cloth dipped in methylated spirit. When the projector is not in use, keep it well covered.

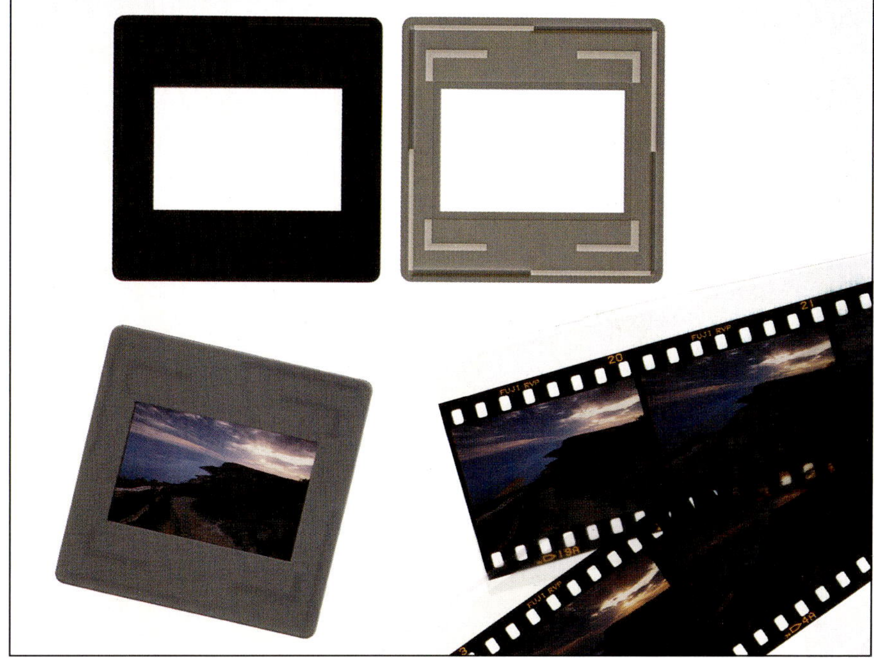

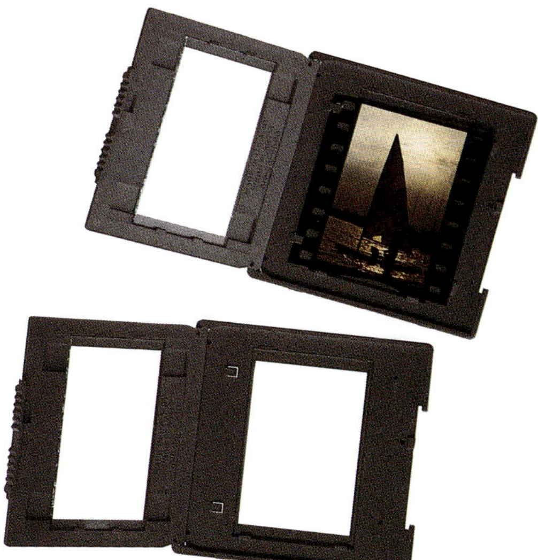

Screens

Buying a screen is not absolutely essential if you already have a flat, matt white wall to project your slides on to. But remember, if the wall is painted any colour – even if it is only cream – this will alter the colours of your photograph.

Also, if the wall is textured in any way, this is likely to be intrusive and mean that the image will not be precisely focused. And, of course, unlike a screen, you won't be able to carry a wall round with you.

Portable screens are available in three different surfaces:

Matt Many of the most expensive screens are made with a matt finish. As the surface of a matt screen is absolutely flat, these screens will give the sharpest possible image. However, a matt screen doesn't reflect light very far and, therefore, is not suitable for projectors with a weak light source.

Glass beaded This will give a long reflection which is especially useful for long halls. However, the glass beads on the surface of this type of screen diffuse the image slightly. Also, if you damage the glass beads, you'll get dark patches on the projected image.

Lenticular This screen often comes with a silver surface, which is a good compromise. It provides a sharper image than a glass beaded screen and a more intense reflection than a matt screen.

When actually projecting slides, make sure your screen is taut. There is not much point in mounting your slides in glass to prevent popping, or investing in a projector which directs warm air to pre-pop slides, if your screen is not completely flat. Some of the best screens come with a glass fibre backing to ensure that the screen hangs straight down.

Keystoning

In addition, you must have the screen square on and level with the projector – otherwise you will see what is called 'keystoning' distortion.

This often happens when the projector is positioned below the level of the screen so that people sitting behind the projector can see. This causes the bottom of the projected image to be narrower than the top, and, as a result, not all of the image is in focus.

Some screens have stands which can be adjusted to compensate for keystoning. If yours doesn't, try to arrange seating so that people are not peering over the projector.

Rope trick

If you project slides at different locations with a fixed focal length lens, you don't want to have to waste time on each occasion getting the distance between your projector and screen right. Once you have established the distance that the projector must be from the screen to obtain an image that fills the screen – either by calculation or testing – cut a piece of thin rope to this distance. Carry this piece of rope with your projector whenever you are going to show slides. All you have to do is erect the screen, lay down the rope, and then set up the projector at the end of the rope. This is particularly useful because you shouldn't move the projector unnecessarily with the light on as this is a sure way to shorten the life of the lamp.

▲ *Three surfaces of screen are generally available – matt (top), lenticular (centre) and beaded (bottom). The beaded screen gives you the longest throw followed by the lenticular and then the matt. If you're after sharply focused images, the matt is best, followed by the lenticular and the beaded. The beaded screen, however, is best when a room cannot be adequately blacked out.*

Different reflections

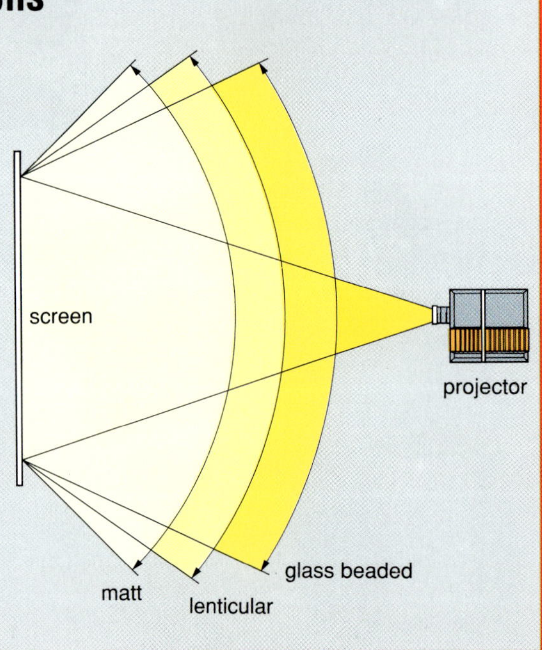

This diagram shows the difference in the extent of reflection given by beaded, lenticular and matt screens.

The beaded screen is highly reflective and will give you a long, brilliant throw. However, the reflection is relatively narrow so that viewers need to sit near to the projection beam.

The lenticular screen gives a wider reflection than the beaded, but the image is not as bright.

The matt screen gives a low intensity reflection – but over a broad angle, making it the best choice for wide rooms.

Structuring a slide show

A badly-presented slide show is a nightmare, but if you do it properly, you can leave your audience eager for more instead of itching to escape.

Like any form of entertainment, a slide show needs careful planning and total confidence to be a success. Everyone's been to a show in which each slide seems to have been chosen randomly, and the commentary, just like the slides, wanders aimlessly from subject to subject.

Rigorous editing is the basis of a successful slide show. Try to have a good reason for showing the slides – even if it's only to show your friends what a wonderful holiday you had. Edit out any images – no matter how stunning – that don't relate to this reason

There are basically two ways of linking up your slides – using a story or using a theme. Weddings, village cricket matches and day trips to the sea lend themselves well to a story based show. Remember, though, that you generally have to work out your story before you start shooting.

A theme

If you're using a theme based show, you can simply look back through your old slides rather than shooting specially. You'll probably find that at least one theme keeps recurring. It might be certain subject matter like portraits, landscapes or architecture. Or you might find that you tend to shoot in one specific locality, and by bringing together many of your images you have a good documentary record of that area.

To achieve a slide show that really hangs together well, be prepared to search through a lot of old slides. To make this search easier, there's nothing to beat a lightbox. Raising each slide to the light can be very tedious – and tiresome! On a light box, you can also organize your slides into a logical order.

If you can't afford a lightbox, support a sheet of glass between two chairs, and put white paper on the floor below. Then train a desk lamp on the paper, and sort your slides on the glass above. The white paper provides a diffuse light source just like a lightbox.

A handy alternative – even if you use a lightbox – is to store slides in transparent pages. These hold 20 or 24 slides, and have a frosted back layer. Holding the sheet up to a window, you can view a couple of dozen images at once, and the plastic sheets protect the fragile film.

▼ *A first class slide show demands several skills of the photographer – from the editing of the images, through commentary to the titling.*

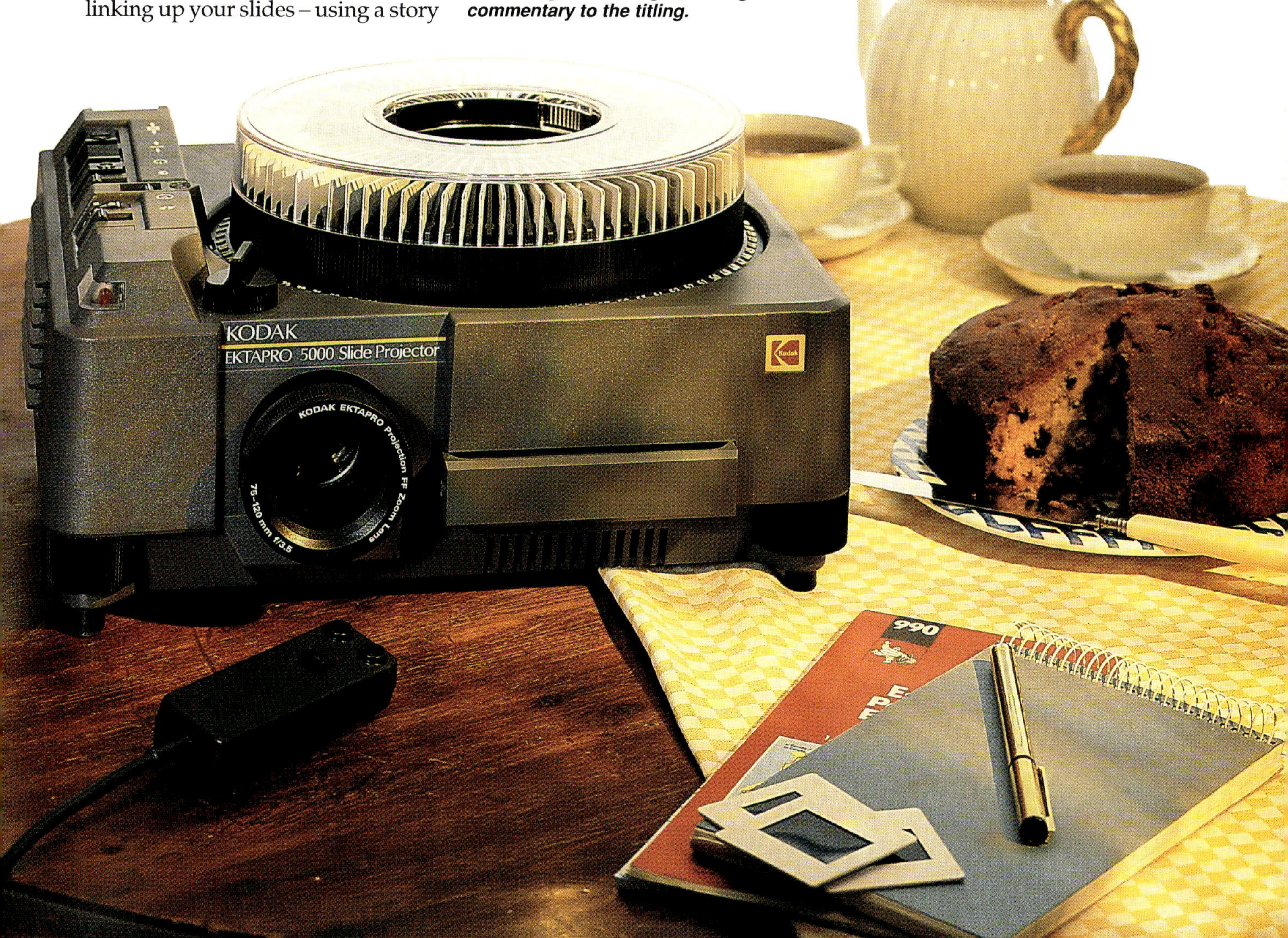

Preparation

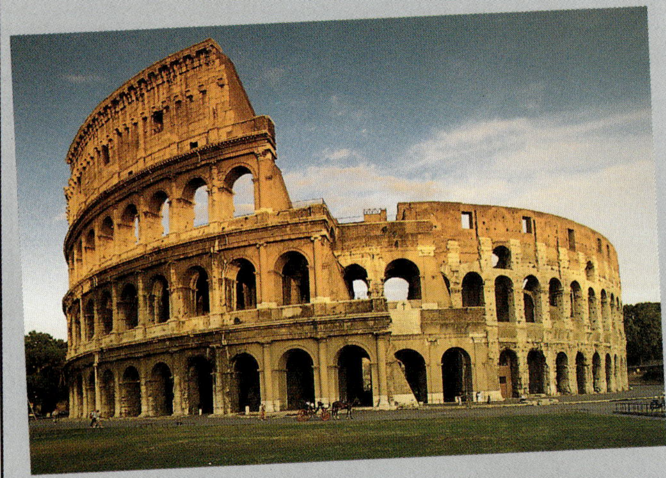

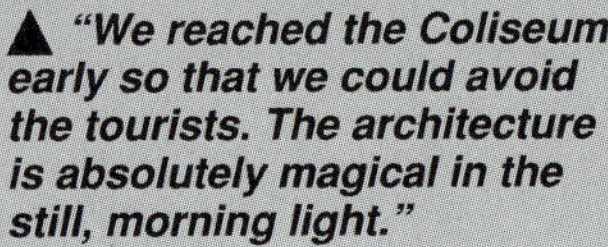
▲ *"We reached the Coliseum early so that we could avoid the tourists. The architecture is absolutely magical in the still, morning light."*

▼ *"Next stop – the Swiss Guards at the Vatican City. They are remarkably picturesque in their colourful uniforms."*

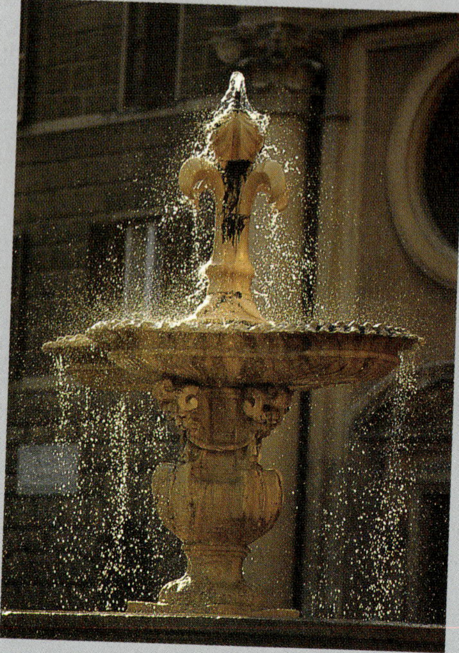

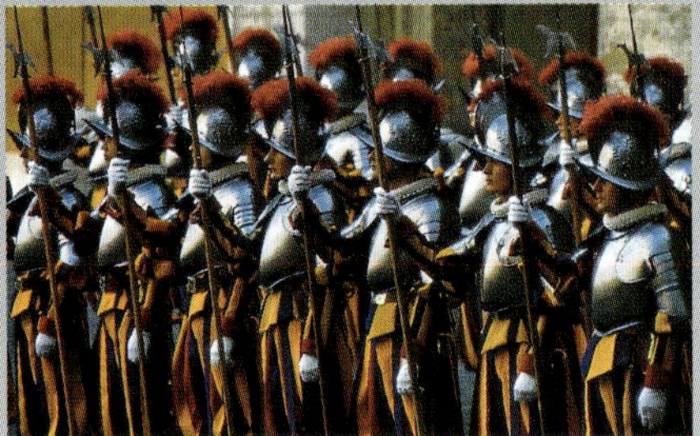
▲ *"We stopped for a rest at this fountain. The water looked so refreshing I nearly jumped in."*

Once you've selected your slides, the first decision you must make is whether or not you want a pre-recorded commentary. A pre-recorded commentary is suitable for more formal presentations. It tends to sound more authoritative and mistakes can be recorded over. This is definitely the option to choose if you become nervous or tongue tied when talking in front of many people.

For gatherings of close friends and family, it's usually better to go without a pre-recorded commentary. This gives your presentation a more personal touch and allows your audience to ask questions. Some slides are bound to provoke more interest than others.

There is no need to write a complete script – short notes on each slide are enough. You may even feel confident enough to ad lib. However, if you are speaking off the cuff, try to avoid introducing every image with the words, 'This is a picture of ...'.

You should be well prepared – expect questions about anything in your slides. If you are showing your holiday slides, consult a guide book so that you know the names of the towns, buildings, monuments and other sites of interest that you've photographed. Some historical knowledge of these sites will also help to liven up the presentation.

Timing

Unless a slide provokes an enormous amount of interest, don't spend more than 30 seconds on each one. But don't run through the slides too rapidly either. Ten seconds for each slide is about the minimum – if an image doesn't deserve ten seconds, it shouldn't really be in the show.

Ideally, the total length of the show should be about 30 minutes. For a longer presentation, it's probably best to have a break. If you're using more than one magazine, the change between magazines is the obvious time for the break.

Always do a trial run of your show. This is not simply to check that the slides are all in the magazine the right way up. You can also see if the show flows and if you deliver your notes well. If possible, do this run with a trusted friend who can give you an outside perspective on your show.

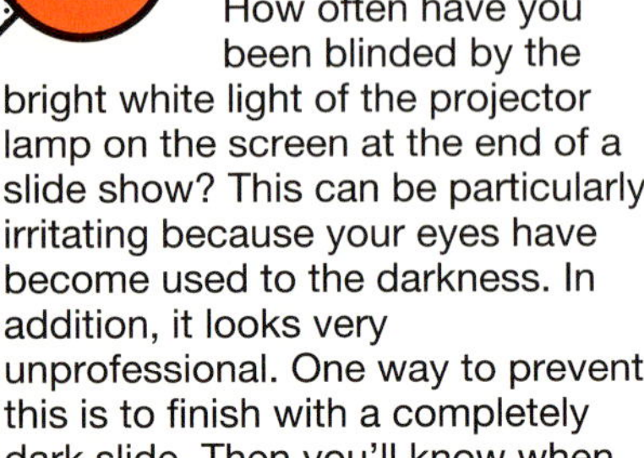

Tip — Blinded by the light

How often have you been blinded by the bright white light of the projector lamp on the screen at the end of a slide show? This can be particularly irritating because your eyes have become used to the darkness. In addition, it looks very unprofessional. One way to prevent this is to finish with a completely dark slide. Then you'll know when you've finished your presentation.

To do this, you can put some black card into a slide mount. (A slide with unexposed film will not be completely black.) When starting the show, it's best to have the first slide lowered into the light path before you turn the projector on so that you don't have a bright white light at the beginning, either.

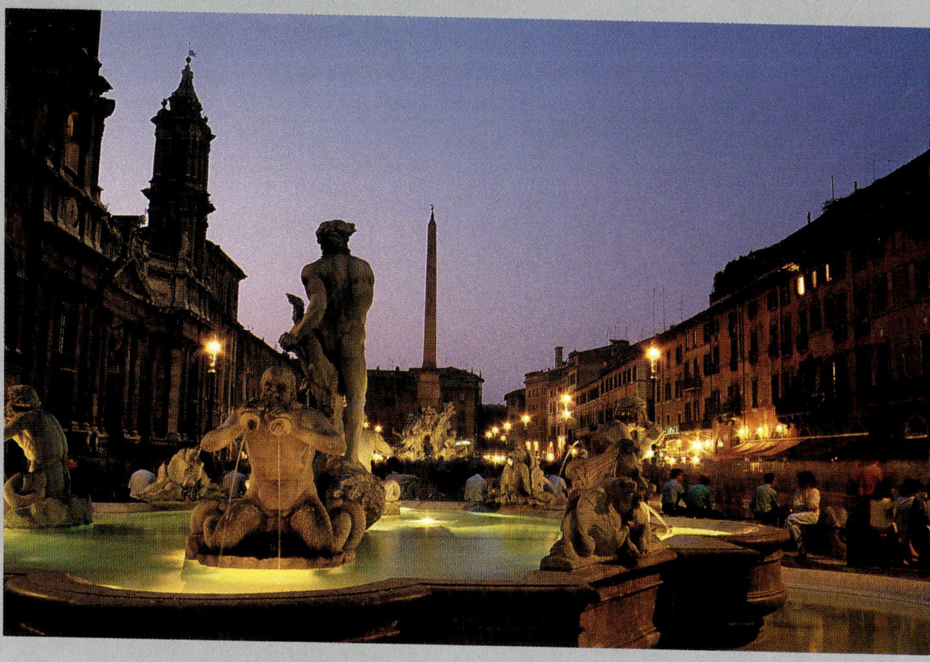

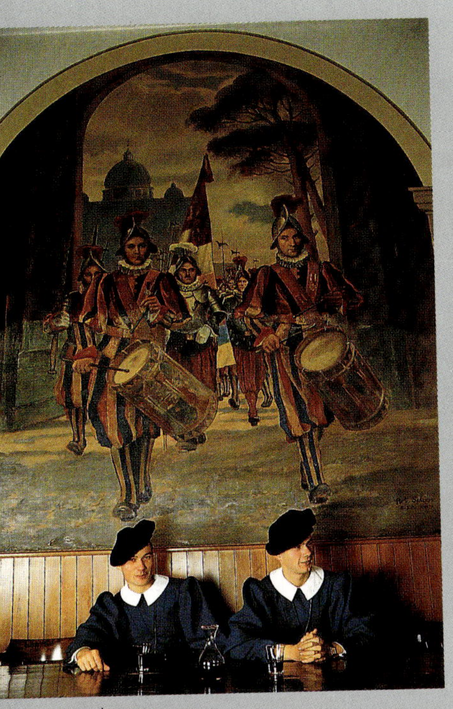

▲ "We stopped at a café and saw these two Swiss Guards."

Titling

For a really professional presentation, try superimposing titles on to one of your shots. This can easily be done by sandwiching.

First, you should make up a title card. You can do this quite simply by using rub-down lettering on white card.

Copy the title card on to slide film, using a tripod. A tripod with a copy arm is convenient as it enables you to get the camera parallel to the title card and the tripod legs out of the picture.

Remember, you need to overexpose the title card by at least one stop compared to your camera's TTL meter or the card will come out as grey. Ideally, you don't want the white of the card to register as a tone at all, just the lettering.

Once the film is processed you can mount it with an appropriate slide. For instance, you might want to sandwich the lettering over the sky of one of your shots. Remember, if the shot with the title card is not overexposed, it'll tend to blacken the sky.

You don't need to sandwich film to do your titles. If you have an artistic flair, why not design an elaborate title card? For instance, for holiday shows, you can montage souvenirs like ticket stubs, maps, beer mats and book matches around the title.

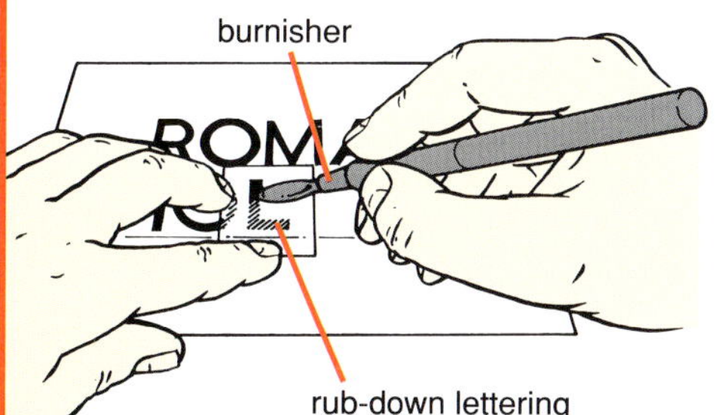

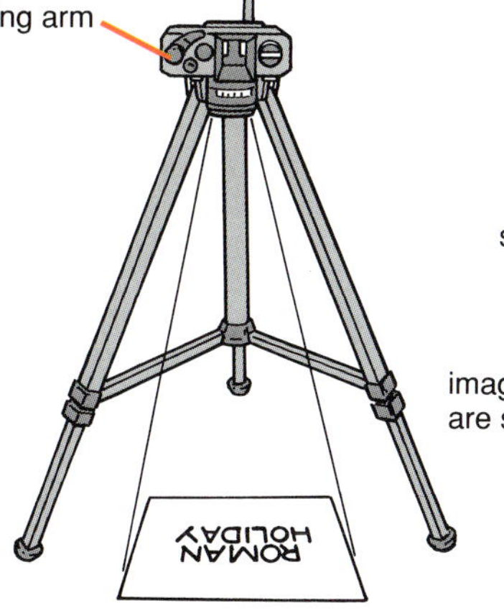

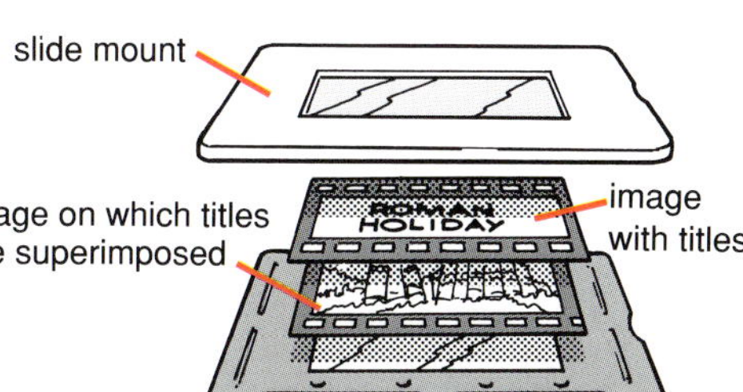

1 MAKE A TITLE CARD
With a burnisher and a set of rub-down lettering, add the title script to a white card.

2 COPY IT ON TO FILM
Copy the title card on to slide film. Use a copy arm on a tripod to keep the camera back parallel.

3 SANDWICH IT IN A MOUNT
In a slide mount, sandwich the title frame with a frame of an appropriate scene.

The dissolve

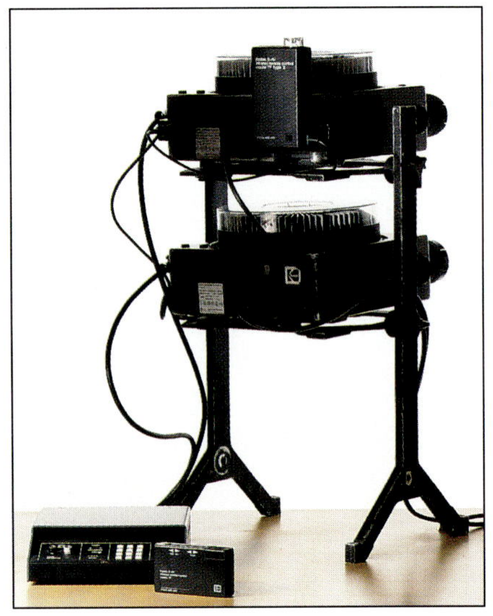

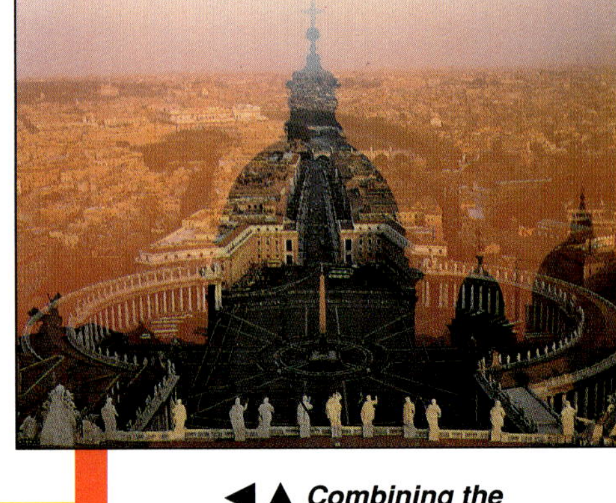

One way to add a creative dimension to your slide show is to use dissolves between slides. To do this, you should have two projectors, both of which have a dimming facility. They must be linked by a dissolve unit.

Many of the sophisticated projectors sold these days have a dimming facility built-in. If yours doesn't, it's sometimes possible to have a dimming device – known as a triac – fitted to your projector. Consult your dealer or the manufacturer of the projector about this.

Remember, even if you manage to convert your projector, you still need another projector with a dimming facility. So it might be just as easy to hire two dimming projectors from a retailer or camera club.

A dissolve unit allows you to control the dimming of the two projector lamps. The most sophisticated dissolve units are operated by pulses on a tape recording so that you can synchronize your show with sound. Simpler units are manually operated and the dissolve is usually controlled by a slider switch that dims one lamp while brightening the other.

Once you have the two projectors hooked up to a dissolve unit, you must set them up so they project your slides on to the same part of the screen. The easiest way of doing this is to put them side by side on the tabletop.

Alternatively, you can stack them on top of each other. This way the lenses are slightly closer together so it is possible to achieve slightly more accurate alignment. Most manufacturers sell stacking trays which are designed for their projectors. Otherwise you might be able to construct shelving yourself.

Striking silhouettes

You can now design a slide show with dissolves in mind. You must find pairs of slides that dissolve effectively with each other. Striking silhouettes, for instance, dissolve well into soft, hazy images.

Pay careful attention to the 'combined' image, created as the images dissolve. If you feel that the combined image works as a picture in itself, then you probably have a good dissolve. When doing the dissolve, you may want to freeze on this combined image for a while.

Try varying the pace of the dissolves according to the subject matter. If you are showing slides of rolling hills and picturesque villages, soft and slow dissolves will look effective. If you then move on to urban subject matter, perhaps market scenes and night shots, you will want to quicken the pace.

Remember that when loading your sequence of slides you have to alternate the slides between the projectors. This means that the first shot in your show goes in projector A, the second in projector B, the third in projector A and so on.

Special effects

Different dissolve units come with different special effects options. Make sure that the one you buy or hire meets your requirements. Here are the main special effects offered:

Fast cut A true fast cut can only be obtained with a unit with push buttons. With a unit which has a slider control, you will always get a dissolve – not a cut. However, you can obtain a relatively fast change by moving the slider very quickly.

Both lamps on With this you can do titles without having to sandwich film in slide mounts. One projector has the slide with the titles on and this can be shown over another slide in the second projector.

Remember, to do this the title slide must have white lettering on black card. Or you can copy the slide on to print film. You may want to do a series of title slides, with the lettering in different positions within the frame so you can match up title slides more easily.

Twinkle This is when both lamps go on and off very rapidly. It can be particularly effective when used with a thunder soundtrack.

Reverse Some dissolve units allow you to go into reverse.

James Elliott – Fine art photography

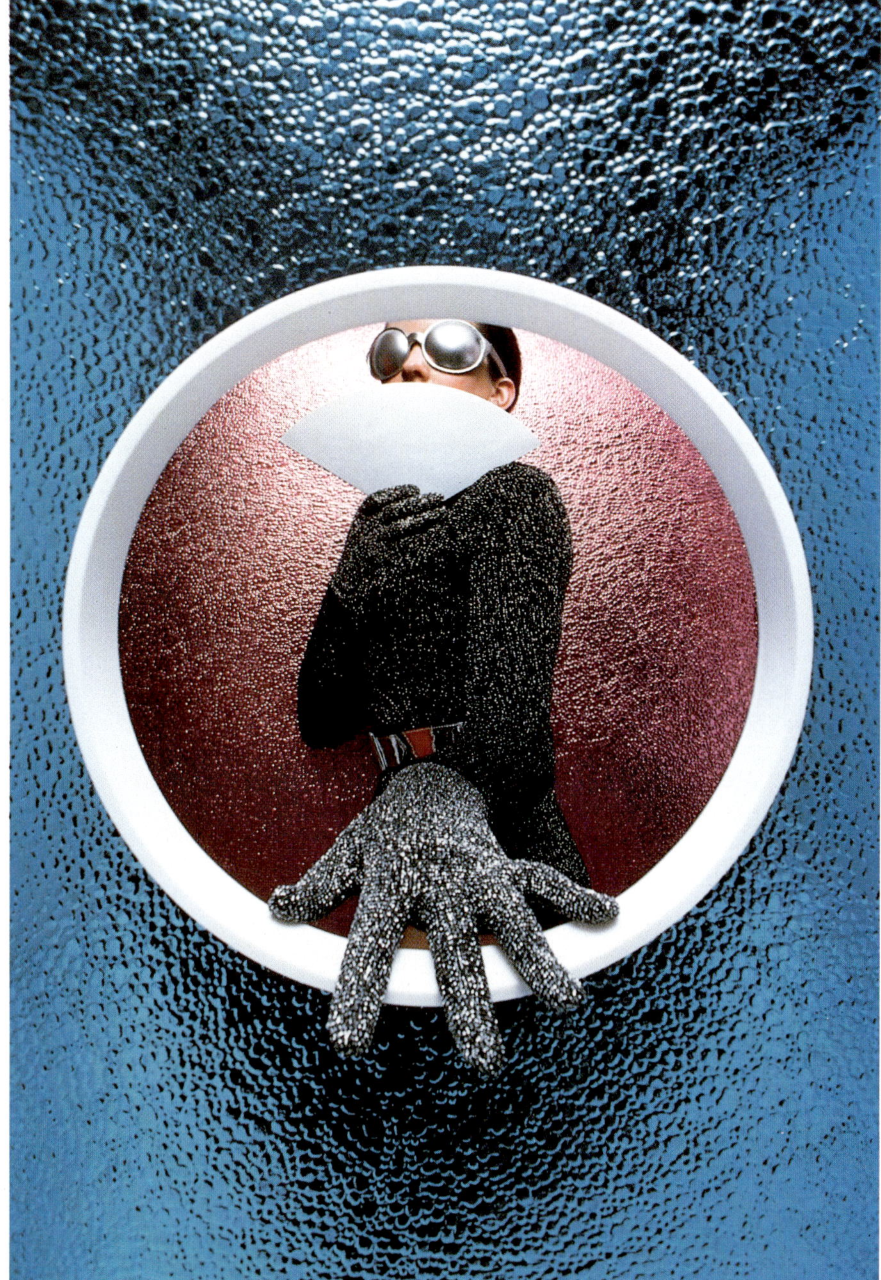

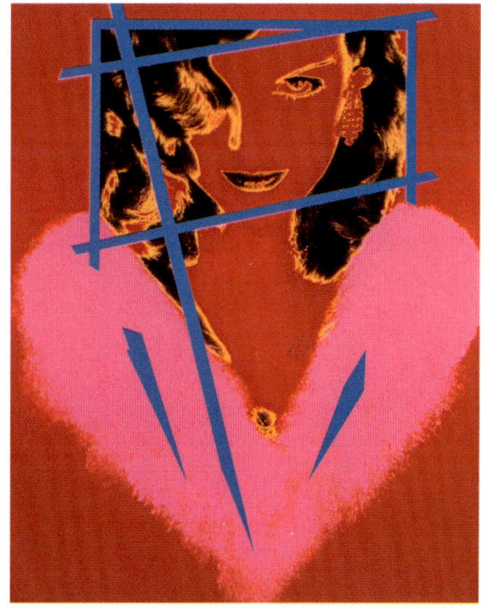

Hanging your pictures on your walls, or projecting your own slides, is one thing. Selling your own personal – and very unusual – vision to galleries is quite another. James Elliott does just that very successfully.

'For me, actually taking the photograph is the easiest and quickest part of a long and painstaking process', says James Elliott. 'I often spend weeks making a model and setting up the shot – only when I'm completely happy with the set up do I start thinking about the camera.

'When I started back in the late '60s, I chose a Nikon 35mm camera because it was all I could afford. I've since switched to medium format but I shot some of my best work on 35mm, which goes to show that equipment isn't everything – good photography is all in the mind.'

Limited editions

James Elliott has always strictly limited the production of his finished work. When he's perfected a small number of prints he destroys the original transparency, so giving the remaining images a higher market value because of their rarity.

But the main reason for this quantity control, he claims, is to prevent other people from printing his work. 'I'm the only one who can properly print my photographs' he says, 'and I don't want people coming along after I'm dead and gone and printing them off in any old way.'

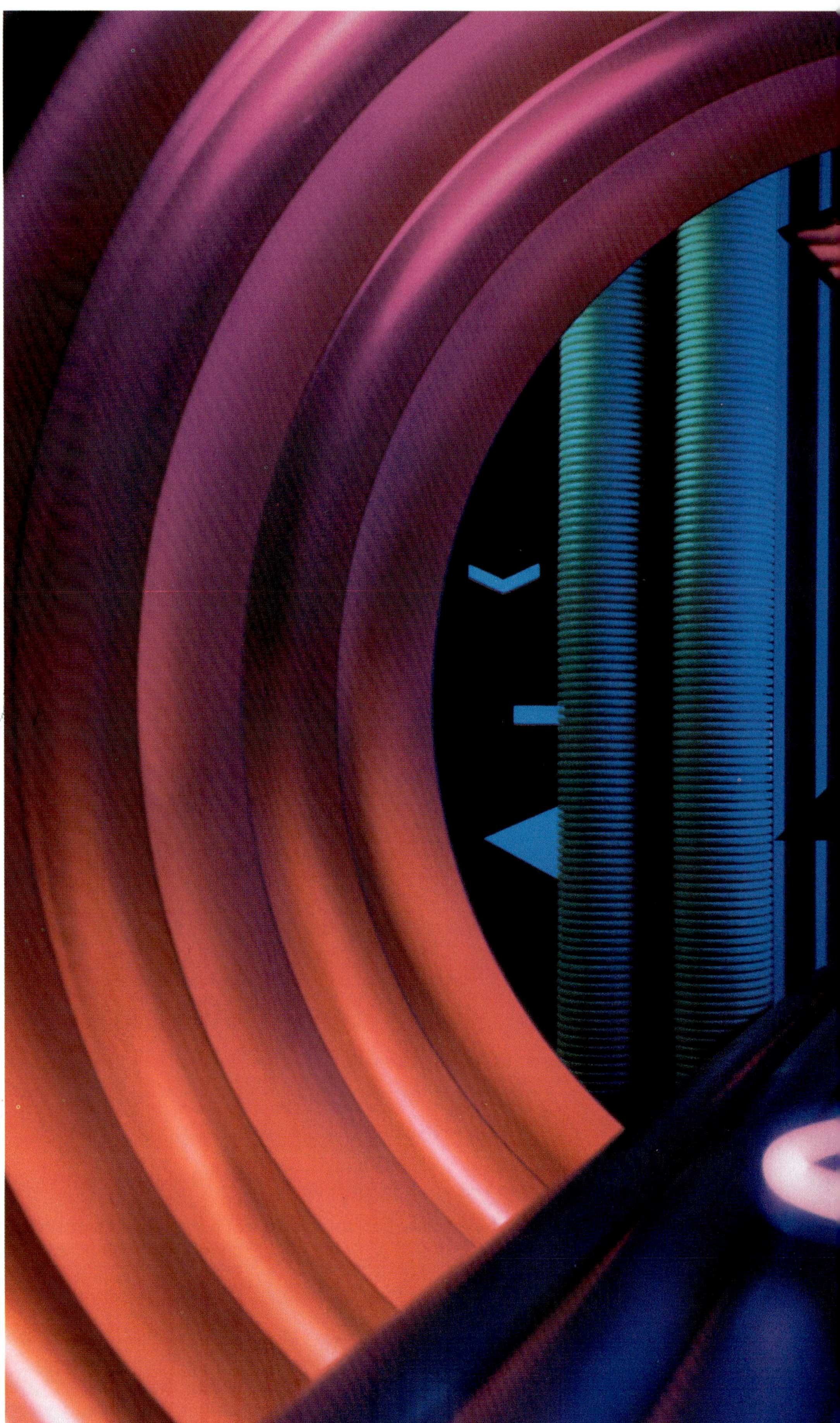

You can do it

James Elliott lit this photograph using a technique known as painting with light. To do it, make sure you're in a totally light tight room and begin experimenting with a simple subject. Open your shutter for a couple of minutes and try moving your flash around to light it from different sides. Once you're a little more sure of the exact effect that you're achieving, you can try longer exposures and more ambitious subjects. Try putting filters in front of the flash face to vary the colours.

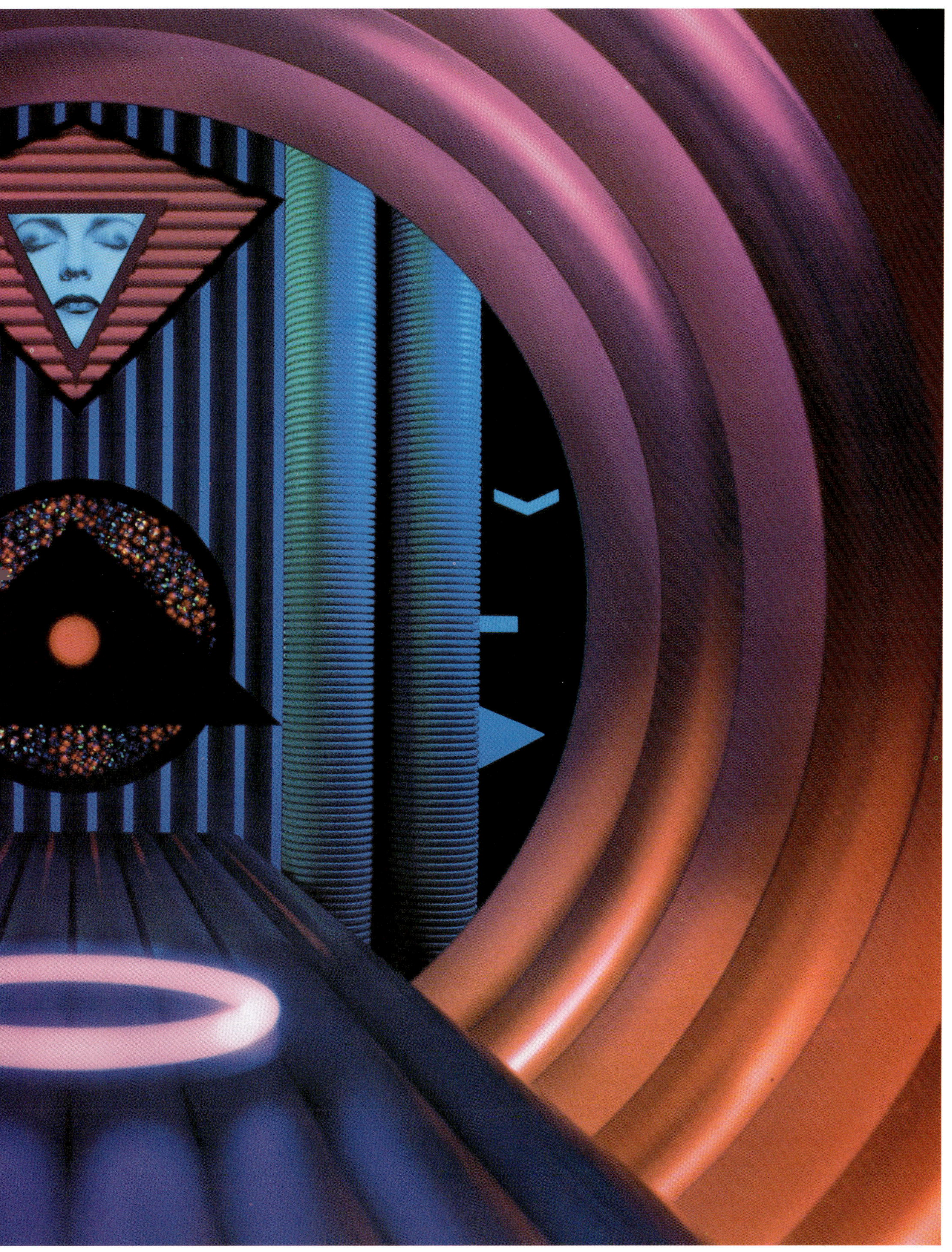

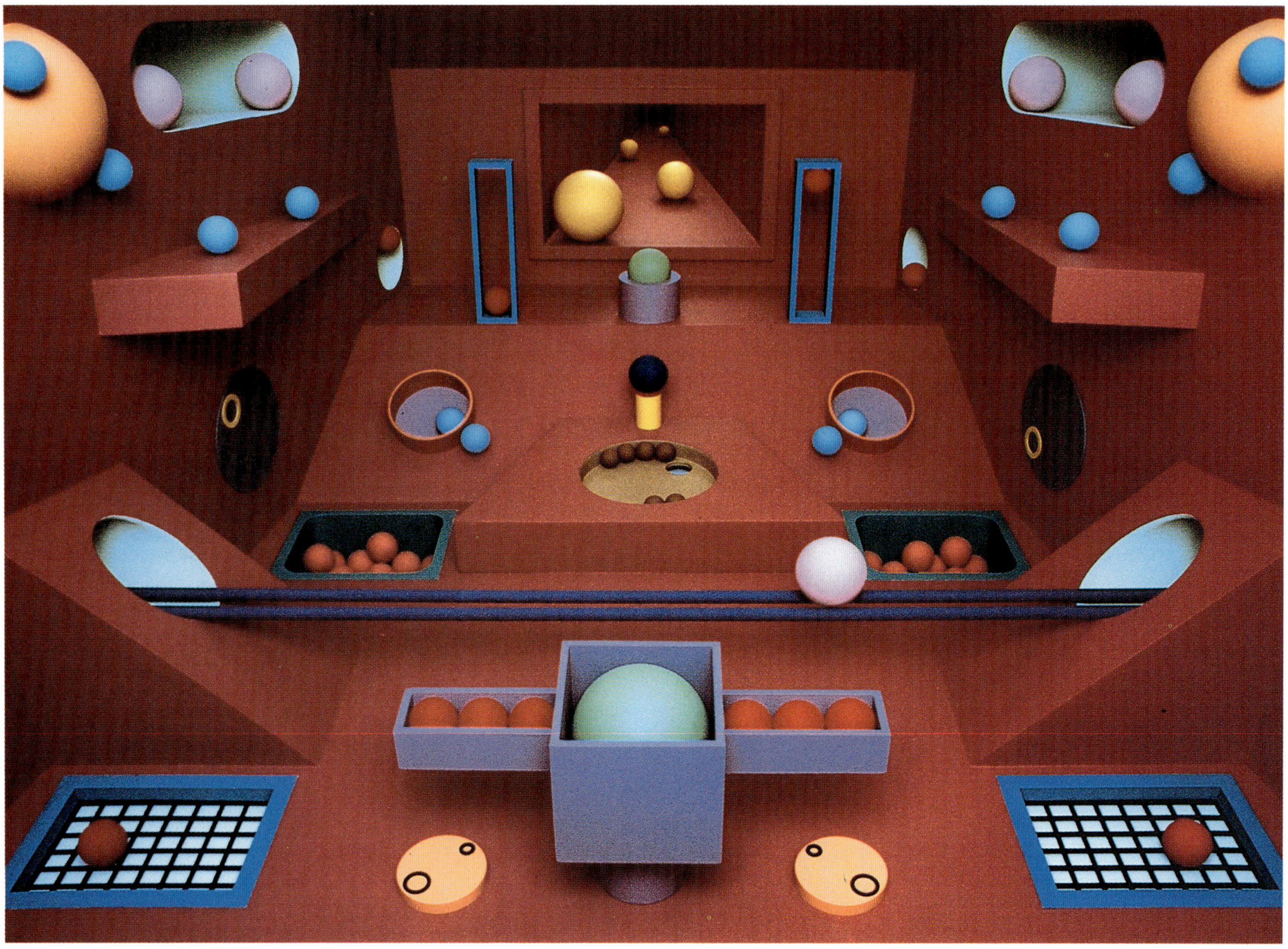

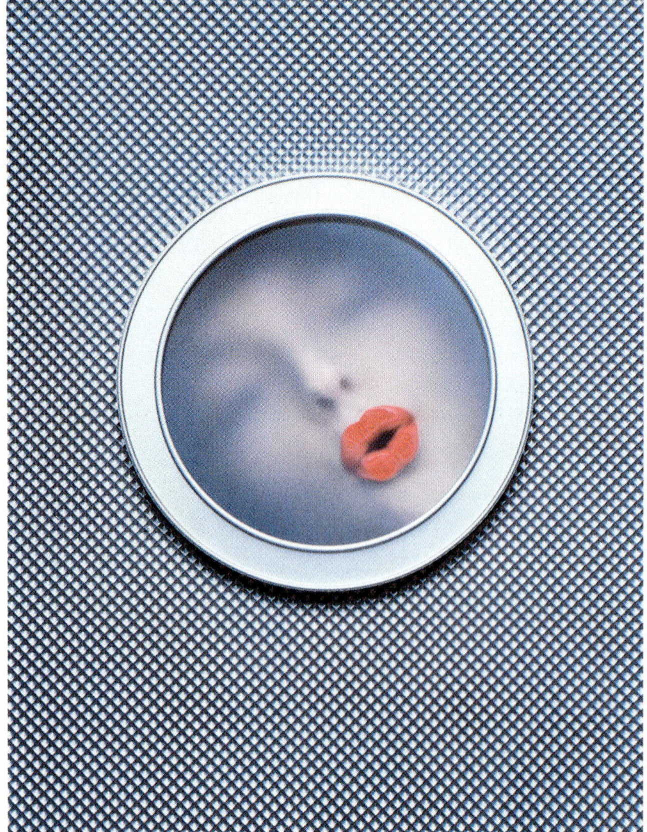

"This was one of the most complicated pictures I've ever photographed. I did the whole thing in a darkened room with the shutter open, and the exposure took 25 minutes. I had to perform a 76 action sequence in order to light the shot properly. I used 21 lights and did 147 test exposures before I was happy. The model itself had no colour – I did all that with filters and reflected light."
Taken on a Bronica ETR 645 with a 150mm lens on Kodachrome 64 with the shutter open at f40.

"I got the inspiration for this shot when I saw someone across the road from my studio picking up mail through a frosted glass front door. So I used an aluminium screen and a piece of frosted glass to create this set up. I shot on Kodak film to give the picture a cold feel."
Taken on a Bronica ETR 645 with a 150mm lens on Kodachrome 64 at 1/60th sec and f22.

Technical details

'I worked in reverse on this shot in the sense that I built the set around the camera. While most people design sculptures to look good in three dimensions, this one only worked from one viewpoint. Because the set was so big I built most of the lighting into it and illuminated the front section with daylight from the studio window. The end result took 332 hours to complete. No double exposure or processing trickery of any kind was involved.'

Sepia toning

Toning can transform a mundane print into a special image, whether you want to re-create a Victorian effect or use it for its own special charms.

Creative photography need not stop when you have processed a black and white print – why not tone your picture to give it even greater impact? Sepia toning can run the entire gamut from dark, brooding landscapes to light, delicate portraits in which the image colour almost reproduces natural flesh tones.

Sepia toning looks particularly attractive in portraits, but it is also well suited to wooded landscapes where it conjures up a more tranquil and peaceful age. Or again, an historic building or a vintage car will often look even better when sepia toned.

A big advantage of toning is that it can be done in normal light, outside the darkroom. What's more, you don't have to tone immediately after you have printed your image – it is often most convenient to process and dry your print one day, and then tone it at another time. However, if you are working with dry prints, always soak them in water again before toning.

How toners work

You can buy toners from photographic shops and specialist mail order firms. There are two sorts of toners available: one-bath and two-bath types. One-bath toners work directly on the silver image of the print, turning it into a new chemical compound of a different colour. One-bath toners are easy to use, but the range of colours is limited.

Two-bath toners involve a bleach bath before the toning bath. The silver image of the print is turned into a silver salt in the bleach. This silver salt then turns to a coloured chemical compound in the toning bath.

Remember, toning effects vary considerably depending on the type of printing paper you use and also on the brand of developer your print has been processed in. To obtain predictable results with toning, standardize your processing practices by using the same sort of paper and developer.

Also note that some toners, such as many two-bath sepia toners, reduce the density of your print. However, other types, like one-bath selenium toners and many colour toners, intensify the image. Always follow the instructions supplied and wear gloves.

Archival toning

Top photographers tone their prints, not only to alter their general colour, but to preserve them. To do this, use a print on fibre based paper and put it into a one-bath selenium toner. Pull the print from the toner as soon as you notice a tone change. Although the print colour will not dramatically alter, the silver in the image will convert to a more stable compound. This process will also make the blacks in the print appear deeper, richer and warmer.

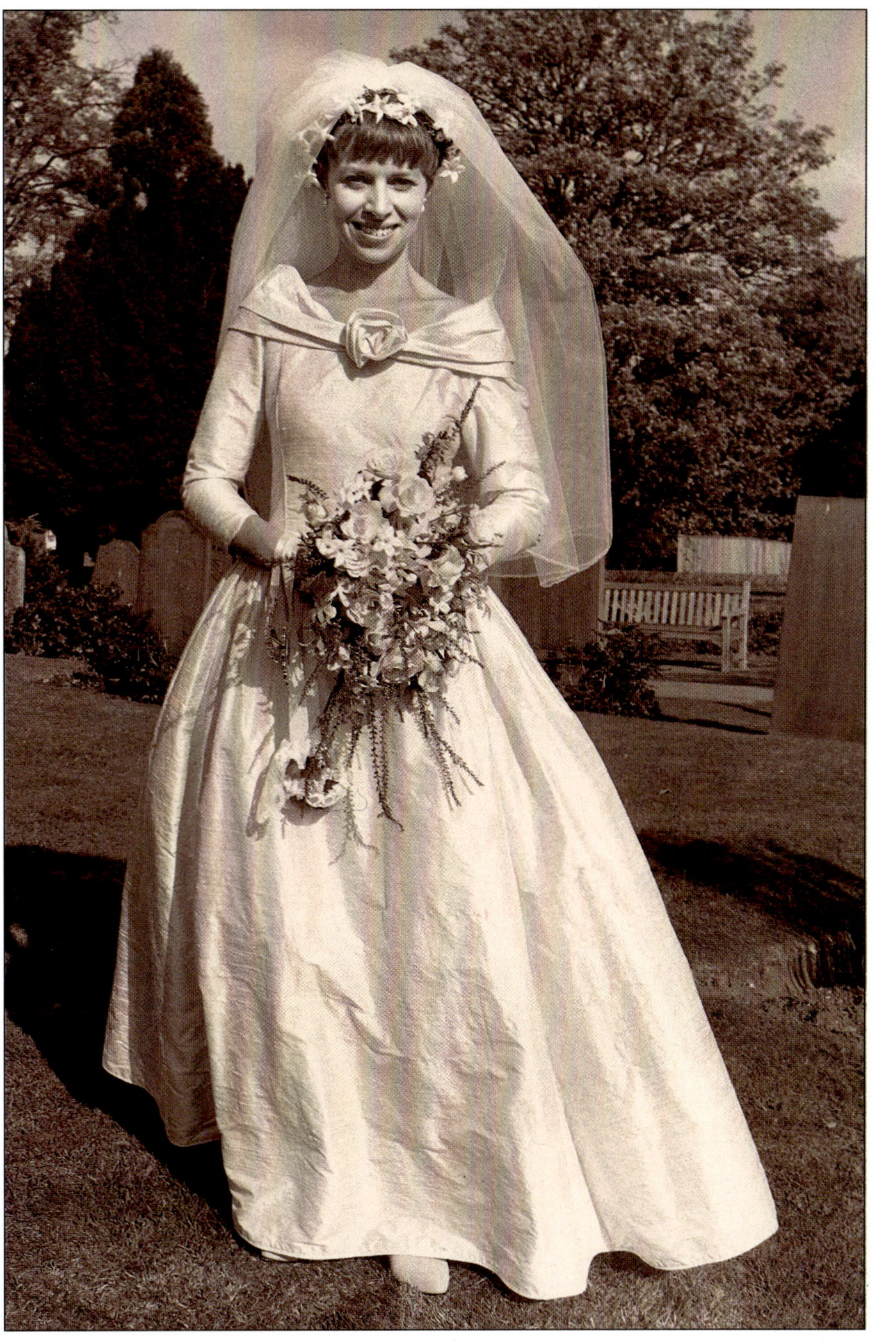

▶ *Sepia toning is the perfect way to emphasize the romantic element of this wedding portrait. It is also particularly effective with historical settings, such as this churchyard.*

Successful toning

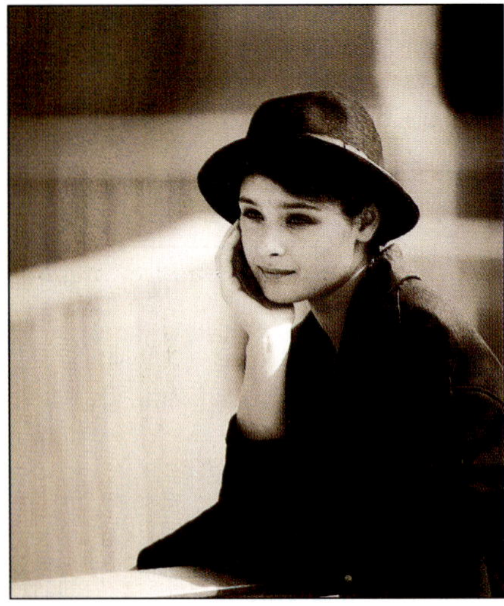

Toning can often leave blotches and uneven marks on the surface of your print. These can be avoided by following some simple rules:

❑ Prints for toning should be freshly made, since old prints tend to tone unevenly. Grease marks and fingerprints may cause blotches.

❑ Make sure that prints used for toning have been properly developed and fully fixed. To be on the safe side, extend the recommended fixing time by about 5-10%.

❑ Prints must be fully washed – you can use hypo-test solution to check. Otherwise any chemical residue will show up as blotches after toning.

❑ Only allow the tongs to touch the borders of the print when using resin coated papers. Tongs can mar the surface of the print.

❑ Make sure that you do not contaminate your toning tray with any other darkroom chemicals.

Other colours

Although sepia is the traditional and often the most effective form of toning, there are other coloured toners including red, yellow, blue and green. These are more difficult to match to suitable subjects, but it can be fun trying. The techniques are identical to those for sepia toning. Try blue for a seascape or snow scene, or bright red or yellow for a car or a very modern building.

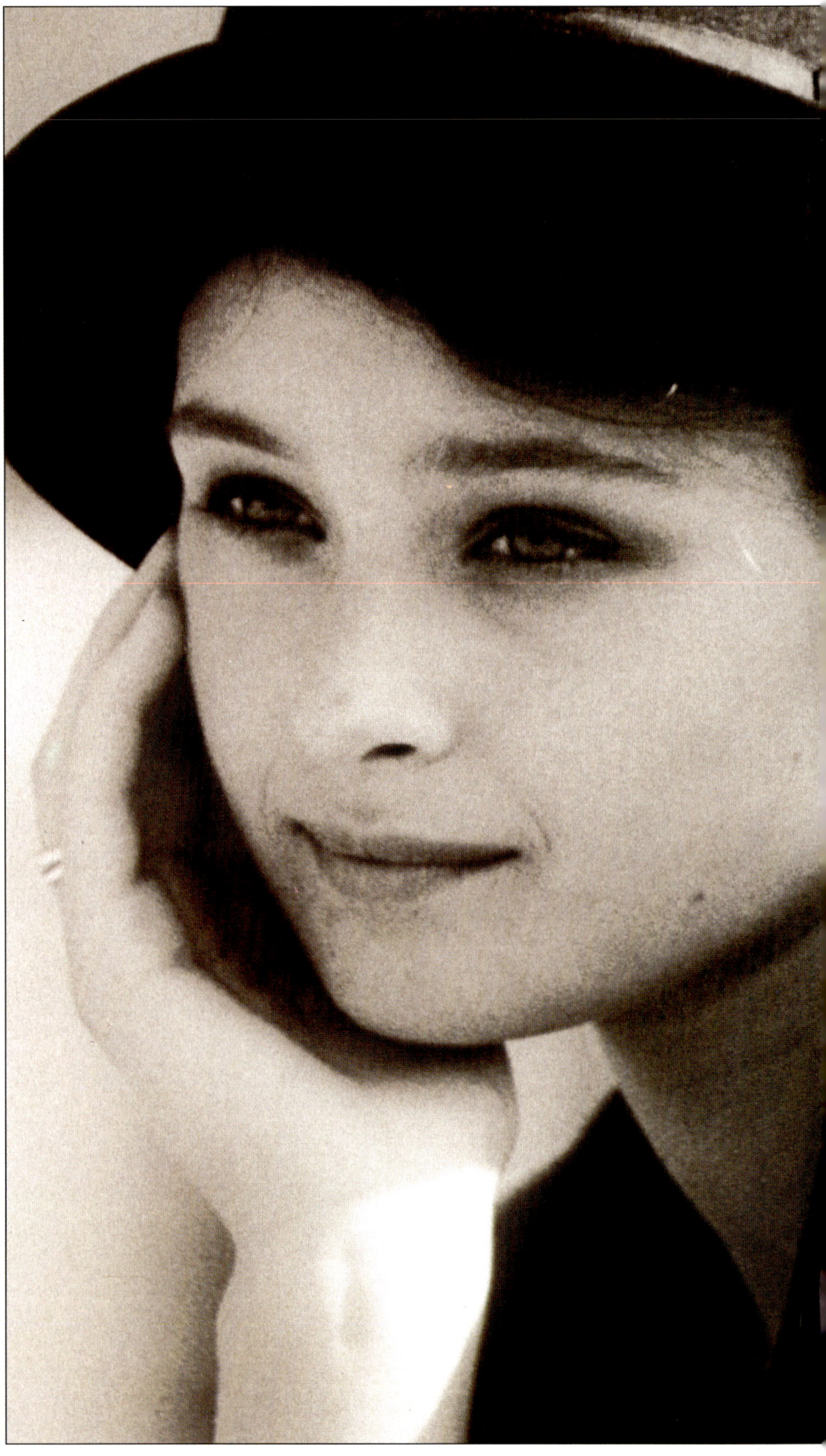

▲ *Making a big blow-up, or blowing up just part of a picture, and then sepia toning it, often emphasizes flaws and* *imperfections (as well as the grain) which can add to the illusion that it is a genuinely old picture.*